MIXED ESSAYS

MIXED ESSAYS

BY

MATTHEW ARNOLD

POPULAR EDITION

LONDON
SMITH, ELDER, & CO., 15 WATERLOO PLACE
1903

PREFACE.

THE FIRST ESSAY in this volume was published nearly twenty years ago, as preface to a work on Continental Schools, which has probably been read by specialists only. The other essays have appeared in well-known reviews.

The present volume touches a variety of subjects, and yet it has a unity of tendency;—a unity which has more interest for an author himself, no doubt, than for other people; but which my friendly readers, whose attention has long been my best encouragement and reward, will not unwillingly suffer me, perhaps, to point out to them.

Whoever seriously occupies himself with literature, will soon perceive its vital connexion with other agencies. Suppose a man to be ever so much convinced that literature is, as indisputably it is, a powerful agency for benefiting the world and for civilising it, such a man cannot but see that there are many obstacles preventing what is salutary in literature from gaining general admission, and from producing due effect. Undoubtedly, literature can of itself do something towards removing those obstacles, and towards making straight its own way. But it cannot do all. In other words, literature is a part of civilisation; it is not the whole. What then is civilisation, which some people seem to conceive of as if it meant railroads and the penny post, and little more, but which is really so complex and vast a matter that a great spiritual power, like literature, is a part of it, and a part only? Civilisation is the humanisation of man in society. Man is civilised, when the whole body of society comes to live with a life worthy to be called *human*, and corresponding to man's true aspirations and powers.

The means by which man is brought towards this goal of his endeavour are various. It is of great importance to us to attain an adequate notion of them, and to keep it present before our minds. They may be conceived quite plainly, and enounced without any parade of hard and abstruse expression.

First and foremost of the necessary means towards man's civilisation we must name *expansion*. The need of expansion is as genuine an instinct in man as the need in plants for the light, or the need in man himself for going upright. All the conveniences of life by which man has enlarged and secured his existence—railroads and the penny post among the number—are due to the working in man of this force or instinct of expansion. But the manifestation of it which we English know best, and prize most, is the love of liberty.

The love of liberty is simply the instinct in man for expansion. Not only to find oneself tyrannised over and outraged is a defeat to this instinct; but in general, to feel oneself over-tutored, over-governed, *sate upon* (as the popular phrase is) by authority, is a defeat to it. Prince Bismarck says: 'After all, a benevolent rational absolutism is the best form of government.' Plenty of arguments may be adduced in support of such a thesis. The one fatal objection to it is that it is against nature, that it contradicts a vital instinct in man—the instinct of expansion. And man is not to be civilised or humanised, call it which you will, by thwarting his vital instincts. In fact, the benevolent rational absolutism always breaks down. It is found that the ruler cannot in the long run be trusted; it is found that the ruled deteriorate. Why? Because the proceeding is against nature.

The other great manifestation of the instinct of expansion is the love of equality. Of the love of equality we English have little; but, undoubtedly, it is no more a false tendency than the love of liberty. Undoubtedly, immense inequality of conditions and property is a defeat to the instinct of expansion; it depresses and degrades the inferior masses. The common people is and must be, as Tocqueville said, more uncivilised in aristocratic countries than in any others. A thousand arguments may be discovered in favour of inequality, just as a thousand arguments may be discovered in favour of absolutism. And the one insuperable objection to inequality is the same as the one insuperable objection to absolutism: namely, that inequality, like absolutism, thwarts a vital instinct, and being thus against nature, is against our humanisation. On the one side, in fact, inequality harms by pampering; on the other, by vulgarising and depressing. A system founded on it is against nature, and in the long run breaks down.

I put first among the elements in human civilisation the instinct of expansion, because it is the basis which man's whole effort to civilise himself presupposes. General civilisation presupposes this instinct, which is inseparable from human nature; presupposes its being satisfied, not defeated. The basis being given, we may rapidly enumerate the powers which, upon this basis, contribute to build up human civilisation. They are the power of conduct, the power of intellect and knowledge, the power of beauty, the power of social life and manners. Expansion, conduct, science, beauty, manners,—here are the conditions of civilisation, the claimants which man must satisfy before he can be humanised.

That the aim for all of us is to make civilisation

pervasive and general; that the requisites for civilisation are substantially what have been here enumerated; that they all of them hang together, that they must all have their development, that the development of one does not compensate for the failure of others; that one nation suffers by failing in this requisite, and another by failing in that: such is the line of thought which the essays in the present volume follow and represent. They represent it in their variety of subject, their so frequent insistence on defects in the present actual life of our nation, their unity of final aim. Undoubtedly, that aim is not given by the life which we now see around us. Undoubtedly, it is given by 'a sentiment of the ideal life.' But then the ideal life is, in sober and practical truth, 'none other than man's normal life, as we shall one day know it.'

CONTENTS.

DEMOCRACY.

In giving an account of education in certain countries of the Continent, I have often spoken of the State and its action in such a way as to offend, I fear, some of my readers, and to surprise others. With many Englishmen, perhaps with the majority, it is a maxim that the State, the executive power, ought to be entrusted with no more means of action than those which it is impossible to withhold from it; that the State neither would nor could make a safe use of any more extended liberty; would not, because it has in itself a natural instinct of despotism, which, if not jealously checked, would become outrageous; could not, because it is, in truth, not at all more enlightened, or fit to assume a lead, than the mass of this enlightened community.

No sensible man will lightly go counter to an opinion firmly held by a great body of his countrymen. He will take for granted, that for any opinion which has struck deep root among a people so powerful, so successful, and so well worthy of respect as the people of this country, there certainly either are, or have been, good and sound reasons. He will venture to impugn such an opinion with real hesitation, and only when he thinks he perceives that the reasons which once supported it exist no longer, or at any rate seem about to disappear very soon. For undoubtedly there arrive periods, when, the circumstances and conditions of government having changed, the guiding maxims of government ought to change also. *J'ai dit souvent*, says Mirabeau,[1] admonishing the Court of France in 1790, *qu'on devait changer de manière de gouverner, lorsque le gouvernement n'est plus le même.* And these decisive changes in the political situation of a people happen gradually as well as violently. 'In the silent lapse of events,' says Burke,[2] writing in England twenty years before the French Revolution, 'as material alterations have been insensibly brought about in the policy and character of governments and nations, as those which have been marked by the tumult of public revolutions.'

I propose to submit to those who have been accustomed to regard all State-action with jealousy, some

[1] *Correspondance entre le Comte de Mirabeau et le Comte de la Marck*, publiée par M. de Bacourt; Paris, 1851; vol. ii, p. 143.

[2] Burke's *Works* (edit. of 1852); vol. iii, p. 115.

reasons for thinking that the circumstances which once made that jealousy prudent and natural have undergone an essential change. I desire to lead them to consider with me, whether, in the present altered conjuncture, that State-action, which was once dangerous, may not become, not only without danger in itself, but the means of helping us against dangers from another quarter. To combine and present the considerations upon which these two propositions are based, is a task of some difficulty and delicacy. My aim is to invite impartial reflexion upon the subject, not to make a hostile attack against old opinions, still less to set on foot and fully equip a new theory. In offering, therefore, the thoughts which have suggested themselves to me, I shall studiously avoid all particular applications of them likely to give offence, and shall use no more illustration and development than may be indispensable to enable the reader to seize and appreciate them.

The dissolution of the old political parties which have governed this country since the Revolution of 1688 has long been remarked. It was repeatedly declared to be happening long before it actually took place, while the vital energy of these parties still subsisted in full vigour, and was threatened only by some temporary obstruction. It has been eagerly deprecated long after it had actually begun to take place, when it was in full progress, and inevitable. These parties, differing in so much else, were yet alike in this, that they were both, in a certain broad sense, *aristocratical* parties. They were combinations of persons considerable, either by great family and estate, or by Court favour, or, lastly, by eminent abilities and popularity; this last body, however, attaining participation in public affairs only through a conjunction with one or other of the former. These connexions, though they contained men of very various degrees of birth and property, were still wholly leavened with the feelings and habits of the upper class of the nation. They had the bond of a common culture; and, however their political opinions and acts might differ, what they said and did had the stamp and style imparted by this culture, and by a common and elevated social condition.

Aristocratical bodies have no taste for a very imposing executive, or for a very active and penetrating domestic administration. They have a sense of equality among themselves, and of constituting in themselves what is greatest and most dignified in the realm, which makes their pride revolt against the overshadowing greatness and dignity of a commanding executive. They have a temper of independence, and a habit of uncontrolled action, which makes them impatient of encountering, in the management of the interior concerns of the country, the machinery and regulations of a superior and peremptory power. The different parties amongst them, as they successively get possession of the government, respect this jealous disposition in their opponents, because they share it themselves. It is a disposition proper to them as great personages, not as ministers; and as they are great personages for their whole life, while they may probably be ministers but for a very short time, the instinct of their social condition avails more with them than the instinct of their official function. To administer as little as possible, to make its weight felt in foreign affairs rather than in domestic, to see in ministerial station rather the means of power and dignity than a means of searching and useful administrative activity, is the natural tendency of an aristocratic executive. It is a tendency which is creditable to the good sense of aristocracies, honourable to their moderation, and at the same time fortunate for their country, of whose internal development they are not fitted to have the full direction.

One strong and beneficial influence, however, the administration of a vigorous and high-minded aristocracy is calculated to exert upon a robust and sound people. I have had occasion, in speaking of Homer, to say very often, and with much emphasis, that he is *in the grand style.* It is the chief virtue of a healthy and uncorrupted aristocracy, that it is, in general, in this grand style. That elevation of character, that noble way of thinking and behaving, which is an eminent gift of nature to some individuals, is also often generated in whole classes of men (at least when these come of a strong and good race) by the possession of power, by the importance and responsibility of high station, by habitual dealing with great things, by being placed above the necessity of constantly struggling for little things. And it is the source of great virtues. It may go along with a not very quick or open intelligence; but it cannot well go along with a conduct vulgar and ignoble. A governing class imbued with it may not be capable of intelligently leading the masses of a people to the highest pitch of welfare for them; but it sets them an invaluable example of qualities without which no really high welfare can exist. This has been done for their nation by the best aristocracies. The Roman aristocracy did it; the English aristocracy has done it. They each fostered in the mass of the peoples they governed,—peoples of sturdy moral constitution and apt to learn such lessons,—a greatness of spirit, the natural growth of the condition of magnates and rulers, but not the natural growth of the condition of the common people. They made, the one of the Roman, the other of the English people, in spite of all the shortcomings of each, great peoples, peoples *in the grand style.* And this they did, while wielding the people according to their own notions, and in the direction which seemed good to them; not as servants and instruments of the people, but as its commanders and heads; solicitous for the good of their country, indeed, but taking for granted that of that good they themselves were the supreme judges, and were to fix the conditions.

The time has arrived, however, when it is becoming impossible for the aristocracy of England to conduct and wield the English nation any longer. It still, indeed, administers public affairs; and it is a great error to suppose, as many persons in England suppose, that it administers but does not govern. He who administers, governs,[1] because he infixes his own mark and stamps his own character on all public affairs as they pass through his hands; and, therefore, so long as the English aristocracy administers the commonwealth, it still governs it. But signs not to be mistaken show that its headship and leadership of the nation, by virtue of the substantial acquiescence of the body of the nation in its

[1] *Administrer, c'est gouverner,* says Mirabeau; ***gouverner, c'est régner**; tout se réduit là.*

predominance and right to lead, is nearly over. That acquiescence was the tenure by which it held its power; and it is fast giving way. The superiority of the upper class over all others is no longer so great; the willingness of the others to recognise that superiority is no longer so ready.

This change has been brought about by natural and inevitable causes, and neither the great nor the multitude are to be blamed for it. The growing demands and audaciousness of the latter, the encroaching spirit of democracy, are, indeed, matters of loud complaint with some persons. But these persons are complaining of human nature itself, when they thus complain of a manifestation of its native and ineradicable impulse. Life itself consists, say the philosophers, in the effort *to affirm one's own essence;* meaning by this, to develop one's own existence fully and freely, to have ample light and air, to be neither cramped nor overshadowed. Democracy is trying *to affirm its own essence;* to live, to enjoy, to possess the world, as aristocracy has tried, and successfully tried, before it. Ever since Europe emerged from barbarism, ever since the condition of the common people began a little to improve, ever since their minds began to stir, this effort of democracy has been gaining strength; and the more their condition improves, the more strength this effort gains. So potent is the charm of life and expansion upon the living; the moment men are aware of them, they begin to desire them, and the more they have of them, the more they crave.

This movement of democracy, like other operations of nature, merits properly neither blame nor praise. Its partisans are apt to give it credit which it does not deserve, while its enemies are apt to upbraid it unjustly. Its friends celebrate it as the author of all freedom. But political freedom may very well be established by aristocratic founders; and, certainly, the political freedom of England owes more to the grasping English barons than to democracy. Social freedom,—equality,—that is rather the field of the conquests of democracy. And here what I must call the injustice of its enemies comes in. For its seeking after equality, democracy is often, in this country above all, vehemently and scornfully blamed; its temper contrasted with that worthier temper which can magnanimously endure social distinctions; its operations all referred, as of course, to the stirrings of a base and malignant envy. No doubt there is a gross and vulgar spirit of envy, prompting the hearts of many of those who cry for equality. No doubt there are ignoble natures which prefer equality to liberty. But what we have to ask is, when the life of democracy is admitted as something natural and inevitable, whether this or that product of democracy is a necessary growth from its parent stock, or merely an excrescence upon it. If it be the latter, certainly it may be due to the meanest and most culpable passions. But if it be the former, then this product, however base and blameworthy the passions which it may sometimes be made to serve, can in itself be no more reprehensible than the vital impulse of democracy is in itself reprehensible; and this impulse is, as has been shown, identical with the ceaseless vital effort of human nature itself.

Now, can it be denied, that a certain approach to equality, at any rate a certain reduction of signal inequalities, is a natural, instinctive demand of that impulse which drives society as a whole,—no longer individuals and limited classes only, but the mass of a community,—to develop itself with the utmost possible fulness and freedom? Can it be denied, that to live in a society of equals tends in general to make a man's spirits expand, and his faculties work easily and actively; while, to live in a society of superiors, although it may occasionally be a very good discipline, yet in general tends to tame the spirits and to make the play of the faculties less secure and active? Can it be denied, that to be heavily overshadowed, to be profoundly insignificant, has, on the whole, a depressing and benumbing effect on the character? I know that some individuals react against the strongest impediments, and owe success and greatness to the efforts which they are thus forced to make. But the question is not about individuals. The question is about the common bulk of mankind, persons without extraordinary gifts or exceptional energy, and who will ever require, in order to make the best of themselves, encouragement and directly favouring circumstances. Can any one deny, that for these the spectacle, when they would rise, of a condition of splendour, grandeur, and culture, which they cannot possibly reach, has the effect of making them flag in spirit, and of disposing them to sink despondingly back into their own condition? Can any one deny, that the knowledge how poor and insignificant the best condition of improvement and culture attainable by them must be esteemed by a class incomparably richer-endowed, tends to cheapen this modest possible amelioration in the account of those classes also for whom it would be relatively a real progress, and to disenchant their imaginations with it?

It seems to me impossible to deny this. And therefore a philosophic observer,[1] with no love for democracy, but rather with a terror of it, has been constrained to remark, that 'the common people is more uncivilised in aristocratic countries than in any others;' because there 'the lowly and the poor feel themselves, as it were, overwhelmed with the weight of their own inferiority.' He has been constrained to remark,[2] that 'there is such a thing as a manly and legitimate passion for equality, prompting men to desire to be, *all* of them, in the enjoyment of power and consideration.' And, in France, that very equality, which is by us so impetuously decried, while it has by no means improved (it is said) the upper classes of French society, has undoubtedly given to the lower classes, to the body of the common people, a self-respect, an enlargement of spirit, a consciousness of counting for something in their country's action, which has raised them in the scale of humanity. The common

[1] M. de Tocqueville. See his *Démocratie en Amérique* (edit. of 1835); vol. i, p. 11. 'Le peuple est plus grossier dans les pays aristocratiques que partout ailleurs. Dans ces lieux, où se rencontrent des hommes si forts et si riches, les faibles et les pauvres se sentent comme accablés de leur bassesse; ne découvrant aucun point par lequel ils puissent regagner l'égalité, ils désespèrent entièrement d'eux-mêmes, et se laissent tomber au-dessous de la dignité humaine.'

[2] *Démocratie en Amérique;* vol. i, p. 60.

people, in France, seems to me the soundest part of the French nation. They seem to me more free from the two opposite degradations of multitudes, brutality and servility, to have a more developed human life, more of what distinguishes elsewhere the cultured classes from the vulgar, than the common people in any other country with which I am acquainted.

I do not say that grandeur and prosperity may not be attained by a nation divided into the most widely distinct classes, and presenting the most signal inequalities of rank and fortune. I do not say that great national virtues may not be developed in it. I do not even say that a popular order, accepting this demarcation of classes as an eternal providential arrangement, not questioning the natural right of a superior order to lead it, content within its own sphere, admiring the grandeur and highmindedness of its ruling class, and catching on its own spirit some reflex of what it thus admires, may not be a happier body, as to the eye of the imagination it is certainly a more beautiful body, than a popular order, pushing, excited, and presumptuous; a popular order, jealous of recognising fixed superiorities, petulantly claiming to be as good as its betters, and tastelessly attiring itself with the fashions and designations which have become unalterably associated with a wealthy and refined class, and which, tricking out those who have neither wealth nor refinement, are ridiculous. But a popular order of that old-fashioned stamp exists now only for the imagination. It is not the force with which modern society has to reckon. Such a body may be a sturdy, honest, and sound-hearted lower class; but it is not a democratic people. It is not that power, which at the present day in all nations is to be found existing; in some, has obtained the mastery; in others, is yet in a state of expectation and preparation.

The power of France in Europe is at this day mainly owing to the completeness with which she has organised democratic institutions. The action of the French State is excessive; but it is too little understood in England that the French people has adopted this action for its own purposes, has in great measure attained those purposes by it, and owes to its having done so the chief part of its influence in Europe. The growing power in Europe is democracy; and France has organised democracy with a certain indisputable grandeur and success. The ideas of 1789 were working everywhere in the eighteenth century; but it was because in France the State adopted them that the French Revolution became an historic epoch for the world, and France the lode-star of Continental democracy. Her airs of superiority and her overweening pretensions come from her sense of the power which she derives from this cause. Every one knows how Frenchmen proclaim France to be at the head of civilisation, the French army to be the soldier of God, Paris to be the brain of Europe, and so on. All this is, no doubt, in a vein of sufficient fatuity and bad taste; but it means, at bottom, that France believes she has so organised herself as to facilitate for all members of her society full and free expansion; that she believes herself to have remodelled her institutions with an eye to reason rather than custom, and to right rather than fact; it means, that she believes the other peoples of Europe to be preparing themselves, more or less rapidly, for a like achievement, and that she is conscious of her power and influence upon them as an initiatress and example. In this belief there is a part of truth and a part of delusion. I think it is more profitable for a Frenchman to consider the part of delusion contained in it; for an Englishman, the part of truth.

It is because aristocracies almost inevitably fail to appreciate justly, or even to take into their mind, the instinct pushing the masses towards expansion and fuller life, that they lose their hold over them. It is the old story of the incapacity of aristocracies for ideas;

the secret of their want of success in modern epochs. The people treats them with flagrant injustice, when it denies all obligation to them. They can, and often do, impart a high spirit, a fine ideal of grandeur, to the people; thus they lay the foundations of a great nation. But they leave the people still the multitude, the crowd; they have small belief in the power of the ideas which are its life. Themselves a power reposing on all which is most solid, material, and visible, they are slow to attach any great importance to influences impalpable, spiritual, and viewless. Although, therefore, a disinterested looker-on might often be disposed, seeing what has actually been achieved by aristocracies, to wish to retain or replace them in their preponderance, rather than commit a nation to the hazards of a new and untried future; yet the masses instinctively feel that they can never consent to this without renouncing the inmost impulse of their being; and that they should make such a renunciation cannot seriously be expected of them. Except on conditions which make its expansion, in the sense understood by itself, fully possible, democracy will never frankly ally itself with aristocracy; and on these conditions perhaps no aristocracy will ever frankly ally itself with it. Even the English aristocracy, so politic, so capable of compromises, has shown no signs of being able so to transform itself as to render such an alliance possible. The reception given by the Peers to the bill for establishing life-peerages was, in this respect, of ill omen. The separation between aristocracy and democracy will probably, therefore, go on still widening.

And it must in fairness be added, that as in one most important part of general human culture,—openness to ideas and ardour for them,—aristocracy is less advanced than democracy, to replace or keep the latter under the tutelage of the former would in some respects be actually unfavourable to the progress of the world. At epochs when new ideas are powerfully fermenting in a society, and profoundly changing its spirit, aristocracies, as they are in general not long suffered to guide it without question, so are they by nature not well fitted to guide it intelligently.

In England, democracy has been slow in developing itself, having met with much to withstand it, not only in the worth of the aristocracy, but also in the fine qualities of the common people. The aristocracy has been more in sympathy with the common people than perhaps any other aristocracy. It has rarely given them great umbrage; it has neither been frivolous, so as to provoke their contempt, nor impertinent, so as to provoke their irritation. Above all, it has in general meant to act with justice, according to its own notions of justice. Therefore the feeling of admiring deference to such a class was more deep-rooted in the people of this country, more cordial, and more persistent, than in any people of the Continent. But, besides this, the vigour and high spirit of the English common people bred in them a self-reliance which disposed each man to act individually and independently; and so long as this disposition prevails through a nation divided into classes, the predominance of an aristocracy, of the class containing the greatest and strongest individuals of the nation, is secure. Democracy is a force in which the concert of a great number of men makes up for the weakness of each man taken by himself; democracy accepts a certain relative rise in their condition, obtainable by this concert for a great number, as something desirable in itself, because though this is undoubtedly far below grandeur, it is yet a good deal above insignificance. A very strong, self-reliant people neither easily learns to act in concert, nor easily brings itself to regard any middling good, any good short of the best, as an object ardently to be coveted and striven for. It keeps its eye on the grand prizes, and these are to be won only by distancing competitors, by getting before one's comrades, by succeeding all by one's self; and so long as a people works thus individually, it does not work democratically. The English people has all the qualities which dispose a people to work individually; may it never lose them! A people without the salt of these qualities, relying wholly on mutual co-operation, and proposing to itself second-rate ideals, would arrive at the pettiness and stationariness of China. But the English people is no longer so entirely ruled by them as not to show visible beginnings of democratic action; it becomes more and more sensible to the irresistible seduction of democratic ideas, promising to each individual of the multitude increased self-respect and expansion with the increased importance and authority of the multitude to which he belongs, with the diminished preponderance of the aristocratic class above him.

While the habit and disposition of deference are thus dying out among the lower classes of the English nation, it seems to me indisputable that the advantages which command deference, that eminent superiority in high feeling, dignity, and culture, tend to diminish among the highest class. I shall not be suspected of any inclination to underrate the aristocracy of this country. I regard it as the worthiest, as it certainly has been the most successful, aristocracy of which history makes record. If it has not been able to develop excellences which do not belong to the nature of an aristocracy, yet it has been able to avoid defects to which the nature of an aristocracy is peculiarly prone. But I cannot read the history of the flowering time of the English aristocracy, the eighteenth century, and then look at this aristocracy in our own century, without feeling that there has been a change. I am not now thinking of private and domestic virtues, of morality, of decorum. Perhaps with respect to these there has in this class, as in society at large, been a change for the better. I am thinking of those public and conspicuous virtues by which the multitude is captivated and led, —lofty spirit, commanding character, exquisite culture. It is true that the advance of all classes in culture and refinement may make the culture of one class, which, isolated, appeared remarkable, appear so no longer; but exquisite culture and great dignity are always something rare and striking, and it is the distinction of the English aristocracy, in the eighteenth century, that not only was their culture something rare by comparison with the rawness of the masses, it was something rare and admirable in itself. It is rather that this rare culture of the highest class has actually somewhat declined,[1] than

[1] This will appear doubtful to no one well acquainted with the literature and memoirs of the last century. To give but two illus-

that it has come to look less by juxtaposition with the augmented culture of other classes.

Probably democracy has something to answer for in this falling off of her rival. To feel itself raised on high, venerated, followed, no doubt stimulates a fine nature to keep itself worthy to be followed, venerated, raised on high; hence that lofty maxim, *noblesse oblige.* To feel its culture something precious and singular, makes such a nature zealous to retain and extend it. The elation and energy thus fostered by the sense of its advantages, certainly enhances the worth, strengthens the behaviour, and quickens all the active powers of the class enjoying it. *Possunt quia posse videntur.* The removal of the stimulus a little relaxes their energy. It is not so much that they sink to be somewhat less than themselves, as that they cease to be somewhat more than themselves. But, however this may be, whencesoever the change may proceed, I cannot doubt that in the aristocratic virtue, in the intrinsic commanding force of the English upper class, there is a diminution. Relics of a great

trations out of a thousand. Let the reader refer to the anecdote told by Robert Wood in his *Essay on the Genius of Homer* (London, 1775), p. vii, and to Lord Chesterfield's *Letters* (edit. of 1845), vol. i, pp. 115, 143, vol. ii, p. 54; and then say, whether the culture there indicated as the culture of a *class* has maintained itself at that level.

generation are still, perhaps, to be seen amongst them, surviving exemplars of noble manners and consummate culture; but they disappear one after the other, and no one of their kind takes their place. At the very moment when democracy becomes less and less disposed to follow and to admire, aristocracy becomes less and less qualified to command and to captivate.

On the one hand, then, the masses of the people in this country are preparing to take a much more active part than formerly in controlling its destinies; on the other hand, the aristocracy (using this word in the widest sense, to include not only the nobility and landed gentry, but also those reinforcements from the classes bordering upon itself, which this class constantly attracts and assimilates), while it is threatened with losing its hold on the rudder of government, its power to give to public affairs its own bias and direction, is losing also that influence on the spirit and character of the people which it long exercised.

I know that this will be warmly denied by some persons. Those who have grown up amidst a certain state of things, those whose habits, and interests, and affections, are closely concerned with its continuance, are slow to believe that it is not a part of the order of nature, or that it can ever come to an end. But I think that what I have here laid down will not appear doubtful either to the most competent and friendly foreign observers of this country, or to those Englishmen who, clear of all influences of class or party, have applied themselves steadily to see the tendencies of their nation as they really are. Assuming it to be true, a great number of considerations are suggested by it; but it is my purpose here to insist upon one only.

That one consideration is: On what action may we rely to replace, for some time at any rate, that action of the aristocracy upon the people of this country, which we have seen exercise an influence in many respects elevating and beneficial, but which is rapidly, and from inevitable causes, ceasing? In other words, and to use a short and significant modern expression which every one understands, what influence may help us to prevent the English people from becoming, with the growth of democracy, *Americanised?* I confess I am disposed to answer: On the action of the State.

I know what a chorus of objectors will be ready. One will say: Rather repair and restore the influence of aristocracy. Another will say: It is not a bad thing, but a good thing, that the English people should be Americanised. But the most formidable and the most widely entertained objection, by far, will be that which founds itself upon the present actual state of things in another country; which says: Look at France! there you have a signal example of the alliance of democracy with a powerful State-action, and see how it works.

This last and principal objection I will notice at once. I have had occasion to touch upon the first already, and upon the second I shall touch presently. It seems to me, then, that one may save one's self from much idle terror at names and shadows if one will be at the pains to remember what different conditions the different character of two nations must necessarily impose on the operation of any principle. That which operates noxiously in one, may operate wholesomely in the other; because the unsound part of the one's character may be yet further inflamed and enlarged by it, the unsound part of the other's may find in it a corrective and an abatement. This is the great use which two unlike characters may find in observing each other. Neither is likely to have the other's faults, so each may safely adopt as much as suits him of the other's qualities. If I were a Frenchman I should never be weary of admiring the independent, individual, local habits of action in England, of directing attention to the evils occasioned in France by the excessive action of the State; for I should be very sure that, say what I might, the part of the State would never be too small in France, nor that of the individual too large. Being an Englishman, I see nothing but good in freely recognising the coherence, rationality, and efficaciousness which characterise the strong State-action of France, of acknowledging the want of method, reason, and result which attend the feeble State-action of England; because I am very sure that, strengthen in England the action of the State as one may, it will always find itself sufficiently controlled. But when either the *Constitutionnel* sneers at the do-little talkativeness of parliamentary government, or when the *Morning Star* inveighs against the despotism of a centralised administration, it seems to me that they lose their labour, because they are hardening themselves against dangers to which they are neither of them liable. Both the one and the other, in plain truth,

> Compound for sins they are inclined to,
> By damning those they have no mind to.

They should rather exchange doctrines one with the other, and each might thus, perhaps, be profited.

So that the exaggeration of the action of the State, in France, furnishes no reason for absolutely refusing to enlarge the action of the State in England; because the genius and temper of the people of this country are such as to render impossible that exaggeration which the genius and temper of the French rendered easy. There is no danger at all that the native independence and individualism of the English character will ever belie itself, and become either weakly prone to lean on others, or blindly confiding in them.

English democracy runs no risk of being overmastered by the State; it is almost certain that it will throw off the tutelage of aristocracy. Its real danger is, that it will have far too much its own way, and be left far too much to itself. 'What harm will there be in that?' say some; 'are we not a self-governing people?' I answer: 'We have never yet been a *self-governing democracy*, or anything like it.' The difficulty for democracy is, how to find and keep high ideals. The individuals who compose it are, the bulk of them, persons who need to follow an ideal, not to set one; and one ideal of greatness, high feeling, and fine culture, which an aristocracy once supplied to them, they lose by the very fact of ceasing to be a lower order and becoming a democracy. Nations are not truly great solely because the individuals composing them are numerous, free, and active; but they are great when these numbers, this freedom, and this activity are employed in the service of an ideal higher than that of an ordinary man, taken by himself. Our society is probably destined to become much more democratic; who or what will give a high tone to the nation then? That is the grave question.

The greatest men of America, her Washingtons, Hamiltons, Madisons, well understanding that aristocratical institutions are not in all times and places possible; well perceiving that in their Republic there was no place for these; comprehending, therefore, that from these that security for national dignity and greatness, an ideal commanding popular reverence, was not to be obtained, but knowing that this ideal was indispensable, would have been rejoiced to found a substitute for it in the dignity and authority of the State. They deplored the weakness and insignificance of the executive power as a calamity. When the inevitable course of events has made our self-government something really like that of America, when it has removed or weakened that security for national dignity, which we possessed in *aristocracy*, will the substitute of the *State* be equally wanting to us? If it is, then the dangers of America will really be ours; the dangers which come from the multitude being in power, with no adequate ideal to elevate or guide the multitude.

It would really be wasting time to contend at length, that to give more prominence to the idea of the State is now possible in this country, without endangering liberty. In other countries the habits and dispositions of the people may be such that the State, if once it acts, may be easily suffered to usurp exorbitantly; here they certainly are not. Here the people will always sufficiently keep in mind that any public authority is a trust delegated by themselves, for certain purposes, and with certain limits; and if that authority pretends to an absolute, independent character, they will soon enough (and very rightly) remind it of its error. Here there can be no question of a paternal government, of an irresponsible executive power, professing to act for the people's good, but without the people's consent, and, if necessary, against the people's wishes; here no one dreams of removing a single constitutional control, of abolishing a single safe-guard for securing a correspondence between the acts of government and the will of the nation. The question is, whether, retaining all its power of control over a government which should abuse its trust, the nation may not now find advantage in voluntarily allowing to it purposes somewhat ampler, and limits somewhat wider within which to execute them, than formerly; whether the nation may not thus acquire in the State an ideal of high reason and right feeling, representing its best self, commanding general respect, and forming a rallying-point for the intelligence and for the worthiest instincts of the community, which will herein find a true bond of union.

I am convinced that if the worst mischiefs of democracy ever happen in England, it will be, not because a new condition of things has come upon us unforeseen, but because, though we all foresaw it, our efforts to deal with it were in the wrong direction. At the present time, almost every one believes in the growth of democracy, almost every one talks of it, almost every one laments it; but the last thing people can be brought to do is to make timely preparation for it. Many of those who, if they would, could do most to forward this work of preparation, are made slack and hesitating by the belief that, after all, in England, things may probably never go very far; that it will be possible to keep much more of the past than speculators say. Others, with a more robust faith, think that all democracy wants is vigorous putting-down; and that, with a good will and strong hand, it is perfectly possible to retain or restore the whole system of the Middle Ages. Others, free from the prejudices of class and position which warp the judgment of these, and who would, I believe, be the first and greatest gainers by strengthening the hands of the State, are averse from doing so by reason of suspicions and fears, once perfectly well-grounded, but, in this age and in the present circumstances, well-grounded no longer.

I speak of the middle classes. I have already shown how it is the natural disposition of an aristocratical class to view with jealousy the development of a considerable State-power. But this disposition has in England found extraordinary favour and support in regions not aristocratical,—from the middle classes; and, above all, from the kernel of these classes, the Protestant Dissenters. And for a very good reason. In times when passions ran high, even an aristocratical executive was easily stimulated into using, for the gratification of its friends and the abasement of its enemies, those administrative engines which, the moment it chose to stretch its hand forth, stood ready for its grasp. Matters of domestic concern, matters of religious profession and religious exercise, offered a peculiar field for an intervention gainful and agreeable to friends, injurious and irritating to enemies. Such an intervention was attempted and practised. Government lent its machinery and authority to the aristocratical and ecclesiastical party, which it regarded as its best support. The party which suffered comprised the flower and strength of that middle class of society, always very flourishing and robust in this country. That powerful class, from this specimen of the administrative activity of government, conceived a strong antipathy against all intervention of the State in certain spheres. An active, stringent administration in those spheres, meant at that time a High Church and Prelatic administration in them, an administration galling to the Puritan party and to the middle class; and this aggrieved class had naturally no proneness to draw nice philosophical distinctions between State-action in these spheres, as a thing for abstract consideration, and State-action in them as they practically felt it and supposed themselves likely long to feel it, guided by their adversaries. In the minds of the English middle class, therefore, State-action in social and domestic concerns became inextricably associated with the idea of a Conventicle Act, a Five-Mile Act, an Act of Uniformity. Their abhorrence of such a State-action as this they extended to State-action in general; and, having never known a beneficent and just State-power, they enlarged their hatred of a cruel and partial State-power, the only one they had ever known, into a maxim that no State-power was to be trusted, that the least action, in certain provinces, was rigorously to be denied to the State, whenever this denial was possible.

Thus that jealousy of an important, sedulous, energetic executive, natural to grandees unwilling to suffer their personal authority to be circumscribed, their individual grandeur to be eclipsed, by the authority and grandeur of the State, became reinforced in this country by a like sentiment among the middle classes, who had no such authority or grandeur to lose, but who, by a hasty reasoning, had theoretically condemned for ever an agency which they had practically found at times oppressive. *Leave us to ourselves!* magnates and middle classes alike cried to the State. Not only from those who were full and abounded went up this prayer, but also from those whose condition admitted of great amelioration. Not only did the whole repudiate the physician, but also those who were sick.

For it is evident, that the action of a diligent, an impartial, and a national government, while it can do little to better the condition, already fortunate enough, of the highest and richest class of its people, can really do much, by institution and regulation, to better that of the middle and lower classes. The State can bestow certain broad collective benefits, which are indeed not much if compared with the advantages already possessed by individual grandeur, but which are rich and valuable if compared with the make-shifts of mediocrity and poverty. A good thing meant for the many cannot well be so exquisite as the good things of the few; but it can easily, if it comes from a donor of great resources and wide power, be incomparably better than what the many could, unaided, provide for themselves.

In all the remarks which I have been making, I have hitherto abstained from any attempt to suggest a positive application of them. I have limited myself to simply pointing out in how changed a world of ideas we are living; I have not sought to go further, and to discuss in what particular manner the world of facts is to adapt itself to this changed world of ideas. This has been my rule so far; but from this rule I shall here venture to depart, in order to dwell for a moment on a matter of practical institution, designed to meet new social exigencies: on the intervention of the State in public education.

The public secondary schools of France, decreed by the Revolution and established under the Consulate, are said by many good judges to be inferior to the old colleges. By means of the old colleges and of private tutors, the French aristocracy could procure for its children (so it is said, and very likely with truth) a better training than that which is now given in the lyceums. Yes; but the boon conferred by the State, when it founded the lyceums, was not for the aristocracy, it was for the vast middle class of Frenchmen. This class, certainly, had not already the means of a better training for its children, before the State interfered. This class, certainly, would not have succeeded in procuring by its own efforts a better training for its children, if the State had not interfered. Through the intervention of the State this class enjoys better schools for its children, not than the great and rich enjoy (that is not the question), but than the same class enjoys in any country where the State has not interfered to found them. The lyceums may not be so good as Eton or Harrow; but they are a great deal better than a *Classical and Commercial Academy*.

The aristocratic classes in England may, perhaps, be well content to rest satisfied with their Eton and Harrow. The State is not likely to do better for them. Nay, the superior confidence, spirit, and style, engendered by a training in the great public schools, constitute for these classes a real privilege, a real engine of command, which they might, if they were selfish, be sorry to lose by the establishment of schools great enough to beget a like spirit in the classes below them. But the middle classes in England have every reason not to rest content with their private schools; the State can do a great deal better for them. By giving to schools for these classes a public character, it can bring the instruction in them under a criticism which the stock of knowledge and judgment in our middle classes is not of itself at present able to supply. By giving to them a national character, it can confer on them a greatness and a noble spirit, which the tone of these classes is not of itself at present adequate to impart. Such schools would soon prove notable competitors with the existing public schools; they would do these a great service by stimulating them, and making them look into their own weak points more closely. Economical, because with charges uniform and under severe revision, they would do a great service to that large body of persons who, at present, seeing that on the whole the best secondary instruction to be found is that of the existing public schools, obtain it for their children from a sense of duty, although they can ill afford it, and although its cost is certainly exorbitant. Thus the middle classes might, by the aid of the State, better their instruction, while still keeping its cost moderate. This in itself would be a gain; but this gain would be slight in comparison with that of acquiring the sense of belonging to great and honourable seats of learning, and of breathing in their youth the air of the best culture of their nation. This sense would be an educational influence for them of the highest value. It would really augment their self-respect and moral force; it would truly fuse them with the class above, and tend to bring about for them the equality which they are entitled to desire.

So it is not State-action in itself which the middle and lower classes of a nation ought to deprecate; it is State-action exercised by a hostile class, and for their oppression. From a State-action reasonably, equitably, and nationally exercised, they may derive great benefit; greater, by the very nature and necessity of things, than can be derived from this source by the class above them. For the middle or lower classes to obstruct such a State-action, to repel its benefits, is to play the game of their enemies, and to prolong for themselves a condition of real inferiority.

This, I know, is rather dangerous ground to tread upon. The great middle classes of this country are conscious of no weakness, no inferiority; they do not want any one to provide anything for them. Such as they are, they believe that the freedom and prosperity of England are their work, and that the future belongs to them. No one esteems them more than I do; but those who esteem them most, and who most believe in their capabilities, can render them no better service than by pointing out in what they underrate their deficiencies, and how their deficiencies, if unremedied, may impair their future. They want culture and dignity; they want ideas. Aristocracy has culture and dignity; democracy has readiness for new ideas, and ardour for what ideas it possesses. Of these, our middle class has the last only: ardour for the ideas it already possesses. It believes ardently in liberty, it believes ardently in industry; and, by its zealous belief in these two ideas, it has accomplished great things. What it has accomplished by its belief in industry is patent to all the world. The liberties of England are less its exclusive work than it supposes; for these, aristocracy has achieved nearly as much. S.ill, of one inestimable part of liberty, liberty of thought, the middle class has been (without precisely intending it) the principal champion. The intellectual action of the Church of England upon the nation has been insignificant; its social action has been great. The social action of Protestant Dissent, that genuine product of the English middle class, has not been civilising; its positive intellectual action has been insignificant; its negative intellectual action,—in so far as by strenuously maintaining for itself, against persecution, liberty of conscience and the right of free opinion, it at the same time maintained and established this right as a universal principle,—has been invaluable. But the actual results of this negative intellectual service rendered by Protestant Dissent,—by the middle class,—to the whole community, great as they undoubtedly are, must not be taken for something which they are not. It is a very great thing to be able to think as you like; but, after all, an important question remains: *what* you think. It is a fine thing to secure a free stage and no favour; but, after all, the part which you play on that stage will have to be criticised. Now, all the liberty and industry in the world will not ensure these two things: a high reason and a fine culture. They may favour them, but they will not of themselves produce them; they may exist without them. But it is by the appearance of these two things, in some shape or other, in the life of a nation, that it becomes something more than an independent, an energetic, a successful nation,—that it becomes a *great* nation.

In modern epochs the part of a high reason, of ideas, acquires constantly increasing importance in the conduct of the world's affairs. A fine culture is the complement of a high reason, and it is in the conjunction of both with character, with energy, that the ideal for men and nations is to be placed. It is common to hear remarks on the frequent divorce between culture and character, and to infer from this that culture is a mere varnish, and that character only deserves any serious attention. No error can be more fatal. Culture without character is, no doubt, something frivolous, vain, and weak ; but character without culture is, on the other hand, something raw, blind, and dangerous. The most interesting, the most truly glorious peoples, are those in which the alliance of the two has been effected most successfully, and its result spread most widely. This is why the spectacle of ancient Athens has such profound interest for a rational man ; that it is the spectacle of the culture of a *people*. It is not an aristocracy, leavening with its own high spirit the multitude which it wields, but leaving it the unformed multitude still ; it is not a democracy, acute and energetic, but tasteless, narrow-minded, and ignoble ; it is the middle and lower classes in the highest development of their humanity that these classes have yet reached. It was the *many* who relished those arts, who were not satisfied with less than those monuments. In the conversations recorded by Plato, or even by the matter-of-fact Xenophon, which for the free yet refined discussion of ideas have set the tone for the whole cultivated world, shopkeepers and tradesmen of Athens mingle as speakers. For any one but a pedant, this is why a handful of Athenians of two thousand years ago are more interesting than the millions of most nations our contemporaries. Surely, if they knew this, those friends of progress, who have confidently pronounced the remains of the ancient world to be so much lumber, and a classical education an aristocratic impertinence, might be inclined to reconsider their sentence.

The course taken in the next fifty years by the middle classes of this nation will probably give a decisive turn to its history. If they will not seek the alliance of the State for their own elevation, if they go on exaggerating their spirit of individualism, if they persist in their jealousy of all governmental action, if they cannot learn that the antipathies and the Shibboleths of a past age are now an anachronism for them,—that will not prevent them, probably, from getting the rule of their country for a season, but they will certainly *Americanise* it. They will rule it by their energy, but they will deteriorate it by their low ideals and want of culture. In the decline of the aristocratical element, which in some sort supplied an ideal to ennoble the spirit of the nation and to keep it together, there will be no other element present to perform this service. It is of itself a serious calamity for a nation that its tone of feeling and grandeur of spirit should be lowered or dulled. But the calamity appears far more serious still, when we consider that the middle classes, remaining as they are now, with their narrow, harsh, unintelligent, and unattractive spirit and culture, will almost certainly fail to mould or assimilate the masses below them, whose sympathies are at the present moment actually wider and more liberal than theirs. They arrive, these masses, eager to enter into possession of the world, to gain a more vivid sense of their own life and activity. In this their irrepressible development, their natural educators and initiators are those immediately above them, the middle classes. If these classes cannot win their sympathy or give them their direction, society is in danger of falling into anarchy.

Therefore, with all the force I can, I wish to urge upon the middle classes of this country, both that they might be very greatly profited by the action of the State, and also that they are continuing their opposition to such action out of an unfounded fear. But at the same time I say that the middle classes have the right, in admitting the action of government, to make the condition that this government shall be one of their own adoption, one that they can trust. To ensure this is now in their own power. If they do not as yet ensure this, they ought to do so, they have the means of doing so. Two centuries ago they had not; now they have. Having this security, let them now show themselves jealous to keep the action of the State equitable and rational, rather than to exclude the action of the State altogether. If the State acts amiss, let them check it; but let them no longer take it for granted that the State cannot possibly act usefully.

The State,—but what is *the State?* cry many. Speculations on the idea of a State abound, but these do not satisfy them; of that which is to have practical effect and power they require a plain account. The full force of the term, *the State*, as the full force of any other important term, no one will master without going a little deeply, without resolutely entering the world of ideas; but it is possible to give in very plain language an account of it sufficient for all practical purposes. The State is properly just what Burke called it: *the nation in its collective and corporate character*. The State is the representative acting-power of the nation; the action of the State is the representative action of the nation. Nominally emanating from the Crown, as the ideal unity in which the nation concentrates itself, this action, by the constitution of our country, really emanates from the Ministers of the Crown. It is common to hear the depreciators of State-action run through a string of Ministers' names, and then say: 'Here is really your *State*; would you accept the action of these men as your own representative action? in what respect is their judgment on national affairs likely to be any better than that of the rest of the world?' In the first place I answer: Even supposing them to be originally no better or wiser than the rest of the world, they have two great advantages from their position: access to almost boundless means of information, and the enlargement of mind which the habit of dealing with great affairs tends to produce. Their position itself, therefore, if they are men of only average honesty and capacity, tends to give them a fitness for acting on behalf of the nation superior to that of other men of equal honesty and capacity who are not in the same position. This fitness may be yet further increased by treating them as persons on whom, indeed, a very grave responsibility has fallen, and from whom very much will be expected;—nothing less than the representing, each of them in his own department, under the control of Parliament, and aided by the suggestions of public opinion, the collective energy and intelligence of his nation. By treating them as men on whom all this devolves to do, to their honour if they do it well, to their shame if they do it ill, one probably augments their faculty of well-doing; as it is excellently said: 'To treat men as if they were better than they are, is the surest way to *make* them better than they are.' But to treat them as if they had been shuffled into their places by a lucky accident, were most likely soon to be shuffled out of them again, and meanwhile ought to magnify themselves and their office as little as possible; to treat them as if they and their functions could without much inconvenience be quite dispensed with, and they ought perpetually to be admiring their own inconceivable good fortune in being permitted to discharge them;—this is the way to paralyse all high effort in the executive government, to extinguish all lofty sense of responsibility; to make its members either merely solicitous for the gross advantages, the emolument and self-importance, which they derive from their offices, or else timid, apologetic, and self-mistrustful in filling them; in either case, formal and inefficient.

But in the second place I answer: If the executive government is really in the hands of men no wiser than the bulk of mankind, of men whose action an intelligent man would be unwilling to accept as representative of his own action, whose fault is that? It is the fault of the nation itself, which, not being in the hands of a despot or an oligarchy, being free to control the choice of those who are to sum up and concentrate its action, controls it in such a manner that it allows to be chosen agents so little in its confidence, or so mediocre, or so incompetent, that it thinks the best thing to be done with them is to reduce their action as near as possible to a nullity. Hesitating, blundering, unintelligent, inefficacious, the action of the State may be ; but, such as it is, it is the collective action of the nation itself, and the nation is responsible for it. It is our own action which we suffer to be thus unsatisfactory. Nothing can free us from this responsibility. The conduct of our affairs is in our own power. To carry on into its executive proceedings the indecision, conflict, and discordance of its parliamentary debates, may be a natural defect of a free nation, but it is certainly a defect ; it is a dangerous error to call it, as some do, a perfection. The want of concert, reason, and organisation in the State, is the want of concert, reason, and organisation in the collective nation.

Inasmuch, therefore, as collective action is more efficacious than isolated individual efforts, a nation having great and complicated matters to deal with must greatly gain by employing the action of the State. Only, the State-power which it employs should be a power which really represents its best self, and whose action its intelligence and justice can heartily avow and adopt ; not a power which reflects its inferior self, and of whose action, as of its own second-rate action, it has perpetually to be ashamed. To offer a worthy initiative, and to set a standard of rational and equitable action,—this is what the nation should expect of the State; and the more the State fulfils this expectation, the more will it be accepted in practice for what in idea it must always be. People will not then ask the State, what title it has to commend or reward genius and merit, since commendation and reward imply an attitude of superiority, for it will then be felt that the State truly acts for the English nation; and the genius of the English nation is greater than the genius of any individual, greater even than Shakspeare's genius, for it includes the genius of Newton also.

I will not deny that to give a more prominent part to the State would be a considerable change in this country; that maxims once very sound, and habits once very salutary, may be appealed to against it. The sole question is, whether those maxims and habits are sound and salutary at this moment. A yet graver and more difficult change,—to reduce the all-effacing prominence of the State, to give a more prominent part to the individual,—is imperiously presenting itself to other countries. Both are the suggestions of one irresistible force, which is gradually making its way everywhere, removing old conditions and imposing new, altering long-fixed habits, undermining venerable institutions, even modifying national character: *the modern spirit.*

Undoubtedly we are drawing on towards great changes; and for every nation the thing most needful is to discern clearly its own condition, in order to know in what particular way it may best meet them. Openness and flexibility of mind are at such a time the first of virtues. *Be ye perfect*, said the Founder of Christianity; *I count not myself to have apprehended*, said its greatest Apostle. Perfection will never be reached; but to recognise a period of transformation when it comes, and to adapt themselves honestly and rationally to its laws, is perhaps the nearest approach to perfection of which men and nations are capable. No habits or attachments should prevent their trying to do this; nor indeed, in the long run, can they. Human thought, which made all institutions, inevitably saps them, resting only in that which is absolute and eternal.

EQUALITY.[1]

THERE is a maxim which we all know, which occurs in our copy-books, which occurs in that solemn and beautiful formulary against which the Nonconformist genius is just now so angrily chafing,—the Burial Service. The maxim is this: 'Evil communications corrupt good manners.' It is taken from a chapter of the First Epistle to the Corinthians; but originally it is a line of poetry, of Greek poetry. *Quid Athenis et Hierosolymis?* asks a Father; what have Athens and Jerusalem to do with one another? Well, at any rate, the Jerusalemite Paul, exhorting his converts, enforces what he is saying by a verse of Athenian comedy,—a verse, probably, from the great master of that comedy, a man unsurpassed for fine and just observation of human life, Menander. *Φθείρουσιν ἤθη χρήσθ' ὁμιλίαι κακαί*—'Evil communications corrupt good manners.'

In that collection of single, sententious lines, printed at the end of Menander's fragments, where we now find

[1] Address delivered at the Royal Institution.

the maxim quoted by St. Paul, there is another striking maxim, not alien certainly to the language of the Christian religion, but which has not passed into our copy-books: 'Choose equality and flee greed.' The same profound observer, who laid down the maxim so universally accepted by us that it has become commonplace, the maxim that evil communications corrupt good manners, laid down also, as a no less sure result of the accurate study of human life, this other maxim as well: 'Choose equality and flee greed'—Ἰσότητα δ' αἱροῦ καὶ πλεονεξίαν φύγε.

Pleonexia, or greed, the wishing and trying for the bigger share, we know under the name of covetousness. We understand by covetousness something different from what *pleonexia* really means: we understand by it the longing for other people's goods: and covetousness, so understood, it is a commonplace of morals and of religion with us that we should shun. As to the duty of pursuing equality, there is no such consent amongst us. Indeed, the consent is the other way, the consent is against equality. Equality before the law we all take as a matter of course; that is not the equality which we mean when we talk of equality. When we talk of equality, we understand social equality; and for equality in this Frenchified sense of the term almost everybody in England has a hard word. About four years ago Lord Beaconsfield held it up to reprobation in a speech to the students at Glasgow;—a speech so interesting, that being asked soon afterwards to hold a discourse at Glasgow, I said that if one spoke there at all at that time it would be impossible to speak on any other subject but equality. However, it is a great way to Glasgow, and I never yet have been able to go and speak there.

But the testimonies against equality have been steadily accumulating from the date of Lord Beaconsfield's Glasgow speech down to the present hour. Sir Erskine May winds up his new and important *History of Democracy* by saying: 'France has aimed at social equality. The fearful troubles through which she has passed have checked her prosperity, demoralised her society, and arrested the intellectual growth of her people.' Mr. Froude, again, who is more his own master than I am, has been able to go to Edinburgh and to speak there upon equality. Mr. Froude told his hearers that equality splits a nation into 'a multitude of disconnected units,' that 'the masses require leaders whom they can trust,' and that 'the natural leaders in a healthy country are the gentry.' And only just before the *History of Democracy* came out, we had that exciting passage of arms between Mr. Lowe and Mr. Gladstone, where equality, poor thing, received blows from them both. Mr. Lowe declared that 'no concession should be made to the cry for equality, unless it appears that the State is menaced with more danger by its refusal than by its admission. No such case exists now or ever has existed in this country.' And Mr. Gladstone replied that equality was so utterly unattractive to the people of this country, inequality was so dear to their hearts, that to talk of concessions being made to the cry for equality was absurd. 'There is no broad political idea,' says Mr. Gladstone quite truly, 'which has entered less into the formation of the political system of this country than the love of equality.' And he adds: 'It is not the love of equality which has carried into every corner of the country the distinct undeniable popular preference, wherever other things are equal, for a man who is a lord over a man who is not. The love of freedom itself is hardly stronger in England than the love of aristocracy.' Mr. Gladstone goes on to quote a saying of Sir William Molesworth, that with our people the love of aristocracy 'is a religion.' And he concludes in his copious and eloquent way: 'Call this love of inequality by what name you please,—the complement of the love of freedom, or its negative pole, or the shadow which the love of freedom casts, or the reverberation of its voice in the halls of the constitution,—it is an active, living, and life-giving power, which forms an inseparable essential element in our political habits of mind, and asserts itself at every step in the processes of our system.'

And yet, on the other side, we have a consummate critic of life like Menander, delivering, as if there were no doubt at all about the matter, the maxim: 'Choose equality!' An Englishman with any curiosity must surely be inclined to ask himself how such a maxim can ever have got established, and taken rank along with 'Evil communications corrupt good manners.' Moreover, we see that among the French, who have suffered so grievously, as we hear, from choosing equality, the most gifted spirits continue to believe passionately in it nevertheless. 'The human ideal, as well as the social ideal, is,' says George Sand, 'to achieve equality.' She calls equality 'the goal of man and the law of the future.' She asserts that France is the most civilised of nations, and that its pre-eminence in civilisation it owes to equality.

But Menander lived a long while ago, and George Sand was an enthusiast. Perhaps their differing from us about equality need not trouble us much. France, too, counts for but one nation, as England counts for one also. Equality may be a religion with the people of France, as inequality, we are told, is a religion with the people of England. But what do other nations seem to think about the matter?

Now, my discourse to-night is most certainly not meant to be a disquisition on law, and on the rules of bequest. But it is evident that in the societies of Europe, with a constitution of property such as that which the feudal Middle Age left them with,—a constitution of property full of inequality,—the state of the law of bequest shows us how far each society wishes the inequality to continue. The families in possession of great estates will not break them up if they can help it. Such owners will do all they can, by entail and settlement, to prevent their successors from breaking them up. They will preserve inequality. Freedom of bequest, then, the power of making entails and settlements, is sure, in an old European country like ours, to maintain inequality. And with us, who have the religion of inequality, the power of entailing and settling, and of willing property as one likes, exists, as is well known, in singular fulness,—greater fulness than in any country of the Continent. The proposal of a measure such as the Real Estates Intestacy Bill is, in a country like ours, perfectly puerile. A European country like ours, wishing not to preserve inequality but to abate it, can only do so by interfering with the freedom of bequest. This is what Turgot, the wisest of French statesmen, pronounced before the Revolution to be necessary, and what was done in France at the great Revolution. The *Code Napoléon*, the actual law of France, forbids entails altogether, and leaves a man free to dispose of but one-fourth of his property, of whatever kind, if he have three children or more, of one-third if he have two children, of one-half if he have but one child. Only in the rare case, therefore, of a man's having but one child, can that child take the whole of his father's property. If there are two children, two-thirds of the property must be equally divided between them; if there are more than two, three-fourths. In this way has France, desiring equality, sought to bring equality about.

Now the interesting point for us is, I say, to know how far other European communities, left in the same situation with us and with France, having immense inequalities of class and property created for them by the Middle Age, have dealt with these inequalities by means of the law of bequest. Do they leave bequest free, as we do? then, like us, they are for inequality. Do they interfere with the freedom of bequest, as France does? then, like France, they are for equality. And we shall be most interested, surely, by what the most civilised European communities do in this matter,--communities such as those of Germany, Italy, Belgium, Holland, Switzerland. And among those communities we are most concerned, I think, with such as, in the conditions of freedom and of self-government which they demand for their life, are most like ourselves. Germany, for instance, we shall less regard, because the conditions which the Germans seem to accept for their life are so unlike what we demand for ours; there is so much personal government there, so much *junkerism*, militarism, officialism; the community is so much more trained to submission than we could bear, so much more used to be, as the popular phrase is, sat upon. Countries where the community has more a will of its own, or can more show it, are the most important for our present purpose,—such countries as Belgium, Holland, Italy, Switzerland. Well, Belgium adopts purely and simply, as to bequest and inheritance, the provisions of the *Code Napoléon*. Holland adopts them purely and simply. Italy has adopted them substantially. Switzerland is a republic, where the general feeling against inequality is strong, and where it might seem less necessary, therefore, to guard against inequality by interfering with the power of bequest. Each Swiss canton has its own law of bequest. In Geneva, Vaud, and Zurich,—perhaps the three most distinguished cantons,—the law is identical with that of France. In Berne, one-third is the fixed proportion which a man is free to dispose of by will; the rest of his property must go among his children equally. In all the other cantons there are regulations of a like kind. Germany, I was saying, will interest us less than these freer countries. In Germany,—though there is not the English freedom of bequest, but the rule of the Roman law prevails, the rule obliging the parent to assign a certain portion to each child,—in Germany entails and settlements in favour of an eldest son are generally permitted. But there is a remarkable exception. The Rhine countries, which in the early part of this century were under French rule, and which then received the *Code Napoléon*, these countries refused to part with it when they were restored to Germany; and to this day Rhenish Prussia, Rhenish Hesse, and Baden, have the French law of bequest, forbidding entails, and dividing property in the way we have seen.

The United States of America have the English liberty of bequest. But the United States are, like Switzerland, a republic, with the republican sentiment for equality. Theirs is, besides, a new society; it did not inherit the system of classes and of property which feudalism established in Europe. The class by which the United States were settled was not a class with feudal habits and ideas. It is notorious that to acquire great landed estates and to entail them upon an eldest son, is neither the practice nor the desire of any class in America. I remember hearing it said to an American in England: 'But, after all, you have the same freedom of bequest and inheritance as we have, and if a man to-morrow chose in your country to entail a great landed estate rigorously, what could you do?' The American answered: 'Set aside the will on the ground of insanity.'

You see we are in a manner taking the votes for and against equality. We ought not to leave out our own colonies. In general they are, of course, like the United States of America, new societies. They have the English liberty of bequest. But they have no feudal past, and were not settled by a class with feudal habits and ideas. Nevertheless it happens that there have arisen, in Australia, exceedingly large estates, and that the proprietors seek to keep them together. And what have we seen happen lately? An Act has been passed which in effect inflicts a fine upon every proprietor who holds a landed estate of more than a certain value. The measure has been severely blamed in England; to Mr. Lowe such a 'concession to the cry for equality' appears, as we might expect, pregnant with warnings. At present I neither praise it nor blame it; I simply count it as one of the votes for equality. And is it not a singular thing, I ask you, that while we have the religion of inequality, and can hardly bear to hear equality spoken of, there should be, among the nations of Europe which have politically most in common with us, and in the United States of America, and in our own colonies, this diseased appetite, as we must think it, for equality? Perhaps Lord Beaconsfield may not have turned your minds to this subject as he turned mine, and what Menander or George Sand happen to have said may not interest you much; yet surely, when you think of it, when you see what a practical revolt against inequality there is amongst so many people not so very unlike to ourselves, you must feel some curiosity to sift the matter a little further, and may be not ill-disposed to follow me while I try to do so.

I have received a letter from Clerkenwell, in which the writer reproaches me for lecturing about equality at this which he calls 'the most aristocratic and exclusive place out.' I am here because your secretary invited me. But I am glad to treat the subject of equality before such an audience as this. Some of you may remember that I have roughly divided our English society into Barbarians, Philistines, Populace, each of them with their prepossessions, and loving to hear what gratifies them. But I remarked at the same time, that scattered throughout all these three classes were a certain number of generous and humane souls, lovers of man's perfection, detached from the prepossessions of the class to which they might naturally belong, and desirous that he who speaks to them should, as Plato says, not try to please his fellow-servants, but his true and legitimate masters, the heavenly Gods. I feel sure that among the members and frequenters of an institution like this, such humane souls are apt to congregate in numbers. Even from the reproach which my Clerkenwell friend brings against you of being too aristocratic, I derive some comfort. Only I give to the term *aristocratic* a rather wide extension. An accomplished American, much known and much esteemed in this country, the late Mr. Charles Sumner, says that what particularly struck him in England was the large class of gentlemen as distinct from the nobility, and the abundance amongst them of serious knowledge, high accomplishment, and refined taste,—taste fastidious perhaps, says Mr. Sumner, to excess, but erring on virtue's side. And he goes on: 'I do not know that there is much difference between the manners and social observances of the highest classes of England and those of the corresponding classes of

France and Germany; but in the rank immediately below the highest,—as among the professions, or military men, or literary men,—there you will find that the Englishmen have the advantage. They are better educated and better bred, more careful in their personal habits and in social conventions, more refined.' Mr. Sumner's remark is just and important; this large class of gentlemen in the professions, the services, literature, politics,—and a good contingent is now added from business also,—this large class, not of the nobility, but with the accomplishments and taste of an upper class, is something peculiar to England. Of this class I may probably assume that my present audience is in large measure composed. It is aristocratic in this sense, that it has the tastes of a cultivated class, a certain high standard of civilisation. Well, it is in its effects upon *civilisation* that equality interests me. And I speak to an audience with a high standard of civilisation. If I say that certain things in certain classes do not come up to a high standard of civilisation, I need not prove how and why they do not; you will feel instinctively whether they do or no. If they do not, I need not prove that this is a bad thing, that a high standard of civilisation is desirable; you will instinctively feel that it is. Instead of calling this 'the most aristocratic and exclusive place out,' I conceive of it as a *civilised* place; and in speaking about civilisation half one's labour is saved when one speaks about it among those who are civilised.

Politics are forbidden here; but equality is not a question of English politics. The abstract right to equality may, indeed, be a question of speculative politics. French equality appeals to this abstract natural right as its support. It goes back to a state of nature where all were equal, and supposes that 'the poor consented,' as Rousseau says, 'to the existence of rich people,' reserving always a natural right to return to the state of nature. It supposes that a child has a natural right to his equal share in his father's goods. The principle of abstract right, says Mr. Lowe, has never been admitted in England, and is false. I so entirely agree with him, that I run no risk of offending by discussing equality upon the basis of this principle. So far as I can sound human consciousness, I cannot, as I have often said, perceive that man is really conscious of any abstract natural rights at all. The natural right to have work found for one to do, the natural right to have food found for one to eat, rights sometimes so confidently and so indignantly asserted, seem to me quite baseless. It cannot be too often repeated: peasants and workmen have no natural rights, not one. Only we ought instantly to add, that kings and nobles have none either. If it is the sound English doctrine that all rights are created by law and are based on expediency, and are alterable as the public advantage may require, certainly that orthodox doctrine is mine. Property is created and maintained by law. It would disappear in that state of private war and scramble which legal society supersedes. Legal society creates, for the common good, the right of property, and for the common good that right is by legal society limitable. That property should exist, and that it should be held with a sense of security and with a power of disposal, may be taken, by us here at any rate, as a settled matter of expediency. With these conditions a good deal of inequality is inevitable. But that the power of disposal should be practically *unlimited*, that the inequality should be *enormous*, or that the degree of inequality admitted at one time should be admitted *always*,—this is by no means so certain. The right of bequest was in early times, as Sir Henry Maine and Mr. Mill have pointed out, seldom recognised. In later times it has been limited in many countries in the way that we have seen; even in England itself it is not formally quite unlimited. The question is one of expediency. It is assumed, I grant, with great unanimity amongst us, that our signal inequality of classes and property is expedient for our civilisation and welfare. But this assumption, of which the distinguished personages who adopt it seem so sure that they think it needless to produce grounds for it, is just what we have to examine.

Now, there is a sentence of Sir Erskine May, whom I have already quoted, which will bring us straight to the very point that I wish to raise. Sir Erskine May, after saying, as you have heard, that France has pursued social equality, and has come to fearful troubles, demoralisation, and intellectual stoppage by doing so, continues thus: 'Yet is she high, if not the first, in the scale of civilised nations.' Why, here is a curious thing, surely! A nation pursues social equality, supposed to be an utterly false and baneful ideal; it arrives, as might have been expected, at fearful misery and deterioration by doing so; and yet, at the same time, it is high, if not the first, in the scale of civilised nations. What do we mean by *civilised?* Sir Erskine May does not seem to have asked himself the question, so we will try to answer it for ourselves. Civilisation is the humanisation of man in society. To be humanised is to comply with the true law of our human nature: *servare modum, finemque tenere*, *Naturamque sequi*, says Lucan; 'to keep our measure, and to hold fast our end, and to follow Nature.' To be humanised is to make progress towards this, our true and full humanity. And to be civilised is to make progress towards this in civil society; in that civil society 'without which,' says Burke, 'man could not by any possibility arrive at the perfection of which his nature is capable, nor even make a remote and faint approach to it.' To be the most civilised of nations, therefore, is to be the nation which comes nearest to human perfection, in the state which that perfection essentially demands. And a nation which has been brought by the pursuit of social equality to moral deterioration, intellectual stoppage, and fearful troubles, is perhaps the nation which has come nearest to human perfection in that state which such perfection essentially demands! Michelet himself, who would deny the demoralisation and the stoppage, and call the fearful troubles a sublime expiation for the sins of the whole world, could hardly say more for France than this. Certainly Sir Erskine May never intended to say so much. But into what a difficulty has he somehow run himself, and what a good action would it be to extricate him from it! Let us see whether the performance of that good action may not also be a way of clearing our minds as to the uses of equality.

When we talk of man's advance towards his full humanity, we think of an advance, not along one line only, but several. Certain races and nations, as we know, are on certain lines pre-eminent and representative. The Hebrew nation was pre-eminent on one great line. 'What nation,' it was justly asked by their lawgiver, 'hath statutes and judgments so righteous as the law which I set before you this day? Keep therefore and do them; for this is your wisdom and your understanding in the sight of the nations which shall hear all these statutes and say: Surely this great nation is a wise and understanding people!' The Hellenic race was pre-eminent on other lines. Isocrates could say of Athens: 'Our city has left the rest of the world so far behind in philosophy and eloquence, that those educated by Athens have become the teachers of the rest of mankind; and so well has she done her part, that the name of Greeks seems no longer to stand for a race but to stand for intelligence itself, and they who share in our culture are called Greeks even before those who are merely of our own blood.' The power of intellect and science, the power of beauty, the power of social life and manners,—these are what Greece so felt, and fixed, and may stand for. They are great elements in our humanisation. The power of conduct is another great element;

and this was so felt and fixed by Israel that we can never with justice refuse to permit Israel, in spite of all his shortcomings, to stand for it.

So you see that in being humanised we have to move along several lines, and that on certain lines certain nations find their strength and take a lead. We may elucidate the thing yet further. Nations now existing may be said to feel or to have felt the power of this or that element in our humanisation so signally that they are characterised by it. No one who knows this country would deny that it is characterised, in a remarkable degree, by a sense of the power of conduct. Our feeling for religion is one part of this; our industry is another. What foreigners so much remark in us,—our public spirit, our love, amidst all our liberty, for public order and for stability,—are parts of it too. Then the power of beauty was so felt by the Italians that their art revived, as we know, the almost lost idea of beauty, and the serious and successful pursuit of it. Cardinal Antonelli, speaking to me about the education of the common people in Rome, said that they were illiterate indeed, but whoever mingled with them at any public show, and heard them pass judgment on the beauty or ugliness of what came before them,—'*è brutto*,' '*è bello*,'—would find that their judgment agreed admirably, in general, with just what the most cultivated people would say. Even at the present time, then, the Italians are pre-eminent in feeling the power of beauty. The power of knowledge, in the same way, is eminently an influence with the Germans. This by no means implies, as is sometimes supposed, a high and fine general culture. What it implies is a strong sense of the necessity of knowing *scientifically*, as the expression is, the things which have to be known by us; of knowing them systematically, by the regular and right process, and in the only real way. And this sense the Germans especially have. Finally, there is the power of social life and manners. And even the Athenians themselves, perhaps, have hardly felt this power so much as the French.

Voltaire, in a famous passage where he extols the age of Louis the Fourteenth and ranks it with the chief epochs in the civilisation of our race, has to specify the gift bestowed on us by the age of Louis the Fourteenth, as the age of Pericles, for instance, bestowed on us its art and literature, and the Italian Renascence its revival of art and literature. And Voltaire shows all his acuteness in fixing on the gift to name. It is not the sort of gift which we expect to see named. The great gift of the age of Louis the Fourteenth to the world, says Voltaire, was this: *l'esprit de société*, the spirit of society, the social spirit. And another French writer, looking for the good points in the old French nobility, remarks that this at any rate is to be said in their favour: they established a high and charming ideal of social intercourse and manners, for a nation formed to profit by such an ideal, and which has profited by it ever since. And in America, perhaps, we see the disadvantages of having social equality before there has been any such high standard of social life and manners formed.

We are not disposed in England, most of us, to attach all this importance to social intercourse and manners. Yet Burke says: 'There ought to be a system of manners in every nation which a well-formed mind would be disposed to relish.' And the power of social life and manners is truly, as we have seen, one of the great elements in our humanisation. Unless we have cultivated it, we are incomplete. The impulse for cultivating it is not, indeed, a moral impulse. It is by no means identical with the moral impulse to help our neighbour and to do him good. Yet in many ways it works to a like end. It brings men together, makes them feel the need of one another, be considerate of one another, understand one another. But, above all things, it is a promoter of equality. It is by the humanity of their manners that men are made equal. 'A man thinks to show himself my equal,' says Goethe, 'by being *grob*,—that is to say, coarse and rude; he does not show himself my equal, he shows himself *grob*.' But a community having humane manners is a community of equals, and in such a community great social inequalities have really no meaning, while they are at the same time a menace and an embarrassment to perfect ease of social intercourse. A community with the spirit of society is eminently, therefore, a community with the spirit of equality. A nation with a genius for society, like the French or the Athenians, is irresistibly drawn towards equality. From the first moment when the French people, with its congenital sense for the power of social intercourse and manners, came into existence, it was on the road to equality. When it had once got a high standard of social manners abundantly established, and at the same time the natural, material necessity for the feudal inequality of classes and property pressed upon it no longer, the French people introduced equality and made the French Revolution. It was not the spirit of philanthropy which mainly impelled the French to that Revolution, neither was it the spirit of envy, neither was it the love of abstract ideas, though all these did something towards it; but what did most was the spirit of society.

The well-being of the many comes out more and

more distinctly, in proportion as time goes on, as the object we must pursue. An individual or a class, concentrating their efforts upon their own well-being exclusively, do but beget troubles both for others and for themselves also. No individual life can be truly prosperous, passed, as Obermann says, in the midst of men who suffer; *passée au milieu des générations qui souffrent.* To the noble soul, it cannot be happy; to the ignoble, it cannot be secure. Socialistic and communistic schemes have generally, however, a fatal defect; they are content with too low and material a standard of well-being. That instinct of perfection, which is the master-power in humanity, always rebels at this, and frustrates the work. Many are to be made partakers of well-being, true; but the ideal of well-being is not to be, on that account, lowered and coarsened. M. de Laveleye, the political economist, who is a Belgian and a Protestant, and whose testimony therefore we may the more readily take about France, says that France, being the country of Europe where the soil is more divided than anywhere except in Switzerland and Norway, is at the same time the country where material well-being is most widely spread, where wealth has of late years increased most, and where population is least outrunning the limits which, for the comfort and progress of the working classes themselves, seem necessary. This may go for a good deal. It supplies an answer to what Sir Erskine May says about the bad effects of equality upon French prosperity. But I will quote to you from Mr. Hamerton what goes, I think, for yet more. Mr. Hamerton is an excellent observer and reporter, and has lived for many years in France. He says of the French peasantry that they are exceedingly ignorant. So they are. But he adds: 'They are at the same time full of intelligence; their manners are excellent, they have delicate perceptions, they have tact, they have a certain refinement which a brutalised peasantry could not possibly have. If you talk to one of them at his own home, or in his field, he will enter into conversation with you quite easily, and sustain his part in a perfectly becoming way, with a pleasant combination of dignity and quiet humour. The interval between him and a Kentish labourer is enormous.'

This is indeed worth your attention. Of course all mankind are, as Mr. Gladstone says, of our own flesh and blood. But you know how often it happens in England that a cultivated person, a person of the sort that Mr. Charles Sumner describes, talking to one of the lower class, or even of the middle class, feels, and cannot but feel, that there is somehow a wall of partition between himself and the other, that they seem to belong to two different worlds. Thoughts, feelings, perceptions, susceptibilities, language, manners,—everything is different. Whereas, with a French peasant, the most cultivated man may find himself in sympathy, may feel that he is talking to an equal. This is an experience which has been made a thousand times, and which may be made again any day. And it may be carried beyond the range of mere conversation, it may be extended to things like pleasures, recreations, eating and drinking, and so on. In general the pleasures, recreations, eating and drinking of English people, when once you get below that class which Mr. Charles Sumner calls the class of gentlemen, are to one of that class unpalatable and impossible. In France there is not this incompatibility. Whether he mix with high or low, the gentleman feels himself in a world not alien or repulsive, but a world where people make the same sort of demands upon life, in things of this sort, which he himself does. In all these respects France is the country where the people, as distinguished from a wealthy refined class, most lives what we call a humane life, the life of civilised man.

Of course, fastidious persons can and do pick holes in it. There is just now, in France, a *noblesse* newly revived, full of pretension, full of airs and graces and disdains ; but its sphere is narrow, and out of its own sphere no one cares very much for it. There is a general equality in a humane kind of life. This is the secret of the passionate attachment with which France inspires all Frenchmen, in spite of her fearful troubles, her checked prosperity, her disconnected units, and the rest of it. There is so much of the goodness and agreeableness of life there, and for so many. It is the secret of her having been able to attach so ardently to her the German and Protestant people of Alsace, while we have been so little able to attach the Celtic and Catholic people of Ireland. France brings the Alsatians into a social system so full of the goodness and agreeableness of life; we offer to the Irish no such attraction. It is the secret, finally, of the prevalence which we have remarked in other continental countries of a legislation tending, like that of France, to social equality. The social system which equality creates in France is, in the eyes of others, such a giver of the goodness and agreeableness of life, that they seek to get the goodness by getting the equality.

Yet France has had her fearful troubles, as Sir Erskine May justly says. She suffers too, he adds, from demoralisation and intellectual stoppage. Let us admit, if he likes, this to be true also. His error is that he attributes all this to equality. Equality, as we have seen, has brought France to a really admirable and enviable pitch of humanisation in one important line. And this, the work of equality, is so much a good in Sir Erskine May's eyes, that he has mistaken it for the whole of which it is a part, frankly identifies it with civilisation, and is inclined to pronounce France the most civilised of nations.

But we have seen how much goes to full humanisation, to true civilisation, besides the power of social life and manners. There is the power of conduct, the power of intellect and knowledge, the power of beauty. The power of conduct is the greatest of all. And without in the least wishing to preach, I must observe, as a mere matter of natural fact and experience, that for the power of conduct France has never had anything like the same sense which she has had for the power of social life and manners. Michelet, himself a Frenchman, gives us the reason why the Reformation did not succeed in France. It did not succeed, he says, because *la France ne voulait pas de réforme morale*—moral reform France would not have; and the Reformation was above all a moral movement. The sense in France for the power of conduct has not greatly deepened, I think, since. The sense for the power of intellect and knowledge has not been adequate either. The sense for beauty has not been adequate. Intelligence and beauty have been, in general, but so far reached, as they can be and are reached by men who, of the elements of perfect humanisation, lay thorough hold upon one only,—the power of social intercourse and manners. I speak of France in general; she has had, and she has, individuals who stand out and who form exceptions. Well then, if a nation laying no sufficient hold upon the powers of beauty and knowledge, and a most failing and feeble hold upon the power of conduct, comes to demoralisation and intellectual stoppage and fearful troubles, we need not be inordinately surprised. What we should rather marvel at is the healing and bountiful operation of Nature, whereby the laying firm hold on one real element in our humanisation has had for France results so beneficent.

And thus, when Sir Erskine May gets bewildered between France's equality and fearful troubles on the one hand, and the civilisation of France on the other, let us suggest to him that perhaps he is bewildered by his data because he combines them ill. France has not exemplary disaster and ruin as the fruits of equality, and at the same time, and independently of this, an exemplary civilisation. She has a large measure of happiness and success as the fruits of equality, and she has a very large measure of dangers and troubles as the fruits of something else.

We have more to do, however, than to help Sir Erskine May out of his scrape about France. We have to see whether the considerations which we have been employing may not be of use to us about England.

We shall not have much difficulty in admitting whatever good is to be said of ourselves, and we will try not to be unfair by excluding all that is not so favourable. Indeed, our less favourable side is the one which we should be the most anxious to note, in order that we may mend it. But we will begin with the good. Our people has energy and honesty as its good characteristics. We have a strong sense for the chief power in the life and progress of man,—the power of conduct. So far we speak of the English people as a whole. Then we have a rich, refined, and splendid aristocracy. And we have, according to Mr. Charles Sumner's acute and true remark, a class of gentlemen, not of the nobility, but well-bred, cultivated, and refined, larger than is to be found in any other country. For these last we have Mr. Sumner's testimony. As to the splendour of our aristocracy, all the world is agreed. Then we have a middle class and a lower class; and they, after all, are the immense bulk of the nation.

Let us see how the civilisation of these classes appears to a Frenchman, who has witnessed, in his own country, the considerable humanisation of these classes by equality. To such an observer our middle class divides itself into a serious portion and a gay or rowdy portion; both are a marvel to him. With the gay or rowdy portion we need not much concern ourselves; we shall figure it to our minds sufficiently if we conceive it as the source of that war-song produced in these recent days of excitement:

> We don't want to fight, but by jingo, if we do,
> We've got the ships, we've got the men, and we've got the money too.

We may also partly judge its standard of life, and the needs of its nature, by the modern English theatre, perhaps the most contemptible in Europe. But the real strength of the English middle class is in its serious portion. And of this a Frenchman, who was here some little time ago as the correspondent, I think, of the *Siècle* newspaper, and whose letters were afterwards published in a volume, writes as follows. He had been attending some of the Moody and Sankey meetings, and he says: 'To understand the success of Messrs. Moody and Sankey, one must be familiar with English manners, one must know the mind-deadening influence of a narrow Biblism, one must have experienced the sense of acute ennui which the aspect and the frequentation of this great division of English society produce in others, the want of elasticity and the chronic ennui which characterise this class itself, petrified in a narrow Protestantism and in a perpetual reading of the Bible.'

You know the French;—a little more Biblism, one may take leave to say, would do them no harm. But an audience like this,—and here, as I said, is the advantage of an audience like this,—will have no difficulty in admitting the amount of truth which there is in the Frenchman's picture. It is the picture of a class which, driven by its sense for the power of conduct, in the beginning of the seventeenth century entered,—as I have more than once said, and as I may more than once have occasion in future to say,—*entered the prison of Puritanism, and had the key turned upon its spirit there for two hundred years.* They did not know, good and earnest people as they were, that to the building up of human life there belong all those other powers also,—the power of intellect and knowledge, the power of beauty, the power of social life and manners. And something, by what they became, they gained, and the whole nation with them; they deepened and fixed for this nation the sense of conduct. But they created a type of life and manners, of which they themselves indeed are slow to recognise the faults, but which is fatally condemned by its hideousness, its immense ennui, and against which the instinct of self-preservation in humanity rebels.

Partisans fight against facts in vain. Mr. Goldwin Smith, a writer of eloquence and power, although too prone to acerbity, is a partisan of the Puritans, and of the Nonconformists who are the special inheritors of the Puritan tradition. He angrily resents the imputation upon that Puritan type of life, by which the life of our serious middle class has been formed, that it was doomed to hideousness, to immense ennui. He protests that it had beauty, amenity, accomplishment. Let us go to facts. Charles the First, who, with all his faults, had the just idea that art and letters are great civilisers, made, as you know, a famous collection of pictures,—our first National Gallery. It was, I suppose, the best collection at that time north of the Alps. It contained nine Raphaels, eleven Correggios, twenty-eight Titians. What became of that collection? The journals of the House of Commons will tell you. There you may see the Puritan Parliament disposing of this Whitehall or York House collection as follows: 'Ordered, that all such pictures and statues there as are without any superstition, shall be forthwith sold. . . . Ordered, that all such pictures there as have the representation of the Second Person in Trinity upon them, shall be forthwith burnt. Ordered, that all such pictures there as have the representation of the Virgin Mary upon them, shall be forthwith burnt.' There we have the weak side of our parliamentary government and our serious middle class. We are incapable of sending Mr. Gladstone to be tried at the Old Bailey because he proclaims his antipathy to Lord Beaconsfield. A majority in our House of Commons is incapable of hailing, with frantic laughter and applause, a string of indecent jests against Christianity and its Founder. But we are not, or were not, incapable of producing a Parliament which burns or sells the masterpieces of Italian art. And one may surely say of such a Puritan Parliament, and of those who determine its line for it, that they had not the spirit of beauty.

What shall we say of amenity? Milton was born a humanist, but the Puritan temper, as we know, mastered him. There is nothing more unlovely and unamiable than Milton the Puritan disputant. Some one answers his *Doctrine and Discipline of Divorce.* 'I mean not,' rejoins Milton, 'to dispute philosophy with this pork, who never read any.' However, he does reply to him, and throughout the reply Milton's great joke is, that his adversary, who was anonymous, is a serving-man. 'Finally, he winds up his text with much doubt and trepidation; for it may be his trenchers were not scraped, and that which never yet afforded corn of favour to his noddle,—the salt-cellar,—was not rubbed; and therefore, in this haste, easily granting that his answers fall foul upon each other, and praying you would not think he writes as a prophet, but as a man, he runs to the black jack, fills his flagon, spreads the table, and serves up dinner.' There you have the same spirit of urbanity and amenity, as much of it and as little, as generally informs the religious controversies of our Puritan middle class to this day.

But Mr. Goldwin Smith insists, and picks out his own exemplar of the Puritan type of life and manners; and even here let us follow him. He picks out the most favourable specimen he can find,—Colonel Hutchinson, whose well-known memoirs, written by his widow, we have all read with interest. 'Lucy Hutchinson,' says Mr. Goldwin Smith, 'is painting what she thought a perfect Puritan would be; and her picture presents to us not a coarse, crop-eared, and snuffling fanatic, but a highly accomplished, refined, gallant, and most amiable, though religious and seriously minded, gentleman.' Let us, I say, in this example of Mr. Goldwin Smith's own choosing, lay our finger upon the points where this type deflects from the truly humane ideal.

Mrs. Hutchinson relates a story which gives us a good notion of what the amiable and accomplished social intercourse, even of a picked Puritan family, was. Her husband was governor of Nottingham. He had occasion, she says, 'to go and break up a private meeting in the cannoneer's chamber;' and in the cannoneer's chamber 'were found some notes concerning pædobaptism, which, being brought into the governor's lodgings, his wife having perused them and compared them with the Scriptures, found not what to say against the truths they asserted concerning the misapplication of that ordinance to infants.' Soon afterwards she expects her confinement, and communicates the cannoneer's doubts about pædobaptism to her husband. The fatal cannoneer makes a breach in him too. 'Then he bought and read all the eminent treatises on both sides, which at that time came thick from the presses, and still was cleared in the error of the pædobaptists.' Finally, Mrs. Hutchinson is confined. Then the governor 'invited all the ministers to dinner, and propounded his doubt and the ground thereof to them. None of them could defend their practice with any satisfactory reason, but the tradition of the Church from the primitive times, and their main buckler of federal holiness, which Tombs and Denne had excellently overthrown. He and his wife then, professing themselves unsatisfied, desired their opinions.' With the opinions I will not trouble you, but hasten to the result: 'Whereupon that infant was not baptised.'

No doubt to a large division of English society at this very day, that sort of dinner and discussion, and, indeed, the whole manner of life and conversation here suggested by Mrs. Hutchinson's narrative, will seem both natural and amiable, and such as to meet the needs of man as a religious and social creature. You know the conversation which reigns in thousands of middle-class families at this hour, about nunneries, teetotalism, the confessional, eternal punishment, ritualism, disestablishment. It goes wherever the class goes which is moulded on the Puritan type of life. In the long winter evenings of Toronto Mr. Goldwin Smith has had, probably, abundant experience of it. What is its enemy? The instinct of self-preservation in humanity. Men make crude types and try to impose them, but to no purpose. '*L'homme s'agite, Dieu le mène*,' says Bossuet. 'There are many devices in a man's heart; nevertheless the counsel of the Eternal, that shall stand.' Those who offer us the Puritan type of life offer us a religion not true, the claims of intellect and knowledge not satisfied, the claim of beauty not satisfied, the claim of manners not satisfied.

In its strong sense for conduct that life touches truth; but its other imperfections hinder it from employing even this sense aright. The type mastered our nation for a time. Then came the reaction. The nation said: 'This type, at any rate, is amiss; we are not going to be all like *that*!' The type retired into our middle class, and fortified itself there. It seeks to endure, to emerge, to deny its own imperfections, to impose itself again;—impossible! If we continue to live, we must outgrow it. The very class in which it is rooted, our middle class, will have to acknowledge the type's inadequacy, will have to acknowledge the hideousness, the immense ennui of the life which this type has created, will have to transform itself thoroughly. It will have to admit the large part of truth which there is in the criticisms of our Frenchman, whom we have too long forgotten.

After our middle class he turns his attention to our lower class. And of the lower and larger portion of this, the portion not bordering on the middle class and sharing its faults, he says: 'I consider this multitude to be absolutely devoid, not only of political principles, but even of the most simple notions of good and evil. Certainly it does not appeal, this mob, to the principles of '89, which you English make game of; it does not insist on the rights of man; what it wants is beer, gin, and *fun.*'[1]

That is a description of what Mr. Bright would call the residuum, only our author seems to think the residuum a very large body. And its condition strikes him with amazement and horror. And surely well it may. Let us recall Mr. Hamerton's account of the most illiterate class in France; what an amount of civilisation they have notwithstanding! And this is always to be understood, in hearing or reading a Frenchman's praise of England. He envies our liberty, our public spirit, our trade, our stability. But there is always a reserve in his mind. He never means for a moment that he would like to change with us. Life seems to him so much better a thing in France for so many more people, that, in spite of the fearful troubles of France, it is best to be a Frenchman. A Frenchman might agree with Mr. Cobden, that life is good in England for those people who have at least 5,000*l.* a year. But the civilisation of that immense majority who have not 5,000*l.* a year, or 500*l.*, or even 100*l.*,—of our middle and lower class,—seems to him too deplorable.

And now what has this condition of our middle and lower class to tell us about equality? How is it, must

[1] So in the original.

we not ask, how is it that, being without fearful troubles, having so many achievements to show and so much success, having as a nation a deep sense for conduct, having signal energy and honesty, having a splendid aristocracy, having an exceptionally large class of gentlemen, we are yet so little civilised? How is it that our middle and lower classes, in spite of the individuals among them who are raised by happy gifts of nature to a more humane life, in spite of the seriousness of the middle class, in spite of the honesty and power of true work, the *virtus verusque labor*, which are to be found in abundance throughout the lower, do yet present, as a whole, the characters which we have seen?

And really it seems as if the current of our discourse carried us of itself to but one conclusion. It seems as if we could not avoid concluding, that just as France owes her fearful troubles to other things and her civilisedness to equality, so we owe our immunity from fearful troubles to other things, and our uncivilisedness to inequality. 'Knowledge is easy,' says the wise man, 'to him that understandeth;' easy, he means, to him who will use his mind simply and rationally, and not to make him think he can know what he cannot, or to maintain, *per fas et nefas*, a false thesis with which he fancies his interests to be bound up. And to him who will use his mind as the wise man recommends, surely it is easy to see that our shortcomings in civilisation are due to our inequality; or in other words, that the great inequality of classes and property, which came to us from the Middle Age and which we maintain because we have the religion of inequality, that this constitution of things, I say, has the natural and necessary effect, under present circumstances, of materialising our upper class, vulgarising our middle class, and brutalising our lower class. And this is to fail in civilisation.

For only just look how the facts combine themselves. I have said little as yet about our aristocratic class, except that it is splendid. Yet these, 'our often very unhappy brethren,' as Burke calls them, are by no means matter for nothing but ecstasy. Our charity ought certainly, Burke says, to 'extend a due and anxious sensation of pity to the distresses of the miserable great.' Burke's extremely strong language about their miseries and defects I will not quote. For my part, I am always disposed to marvel that human beings, in a position so false, should be so good as these are. Their reason for existing was to serve as a number of centres in a world disintegrated after the ruin of the Roman Empire, and slowly re-constituting itself. Numerous centres of material force were needed, and these a feudal aristocracy supplied. Their large and hereditary estates served this public end. The owners had a positive function, for which their estates were essential. In our modern world the function is gone ; and the great estates, with an infinitely multiplied power of ministering to mere pleasure and indulgence, remain. The energy and honesty of our race does not leave itself without witness in this class, and nowhere are there more conspicuous examples of individuals raised by happy gifts of nature far above their fellows and their circumstances. For distinction of all kinds this class has an esteem. Everything which succeeds they tend to welcome, to win over, to put on their side ; genius may generally make, if it will, not bad terms for itself with them. But the total result of the class, its effect on society at large and on national progress, are what we must regard. And on the whole, with no necessary function to fulfil, never conversant with life as it really is, tempted, flattered, and spoiled from childhood to old age, our aristocratic class is inevitably materialised, and the more so the more the development of industry and ingenuity augments the means of luxury. Every one can see how bad is the action of such an aristocracy upon the class of newly enriched people, whose great danger is a materialistic ideal, just because it is the ideal they can easiest comprehend. Nor is the mischief of this action now compensated by signal services of a public kind. Turn even to that sphere which aristocracies think specially their own, and where they have under other circumstances been really effective,—the sphere of politics. When there is need, as now, for any large forecast of the course of human affairs, for an acquaintance with the ideas which in the end sway mankind, and for an estimate of their power, aristocracies are out of their element, and materialised aristocracies most of all. In the immense spiritual movement of our day, the English aristocracy, as I have elsewhere said, always reminds me of Pilate confronting the phenomenon of Christianity. Nor can a materialised class have any serious and fruitful sense for the power of beauty. They may imagine themselves to be in pursuit of beauty ; but how often, alas, does the pursuit come to little more than dabbling a little in what they are pleased to call art, and making a great deal of what they are pleased to call love !

Let us return to their merits. For the power of manners an aristocratic class, whether materialised or not, will always, from its circumstances, have a strong sense. And although for this power of social life and manners, so important to civilisation, our English race has no special natural turn, in our aristocracy this power emerges, and marks them. When the day of general humanisation comes, they will have fixed the standard of manners. The English simplicity, too, makes the best of the English aristocracy more frank and natural than the best of the like class anywhere else, and even the worst of them it makes free from the incredible fatuities and absurdities of the worst. Then the sense of conduct they share with their countrymen at large. In no class has it such trials to undergo ; in none is it more often and more grievously overborne. But really the right comment on this is the comment of Pepys upon the evil courses of Charles the Second and the Duke of York and the court of that day : 'At all which I am sorry ; but it is the effect of idleness, and having nothing else to employ their great spirits upon.'

Heaven forbid that I should speak in dispraise of that unique and most English class which Mr. Charles Sumner extols,—the large class of gentlemen, not of the landed class or of the nobility, but cultivated and refined. They are a seemly product of the energy and of the power to rise in our race. Without, in general, rank and splendour and wealth and luxury to polish them, they have made their own the high standard of life and manners of an aristocratic and refined class. Not having all the dissipations and distractions of this class, they are much more seriously alive to the power of intellect and knowledge, to the power of beauty. The sense of conduct, too, meets with fewer trials in this class. To some extent, however, their contiguousness to the aristocratic class has now the effect of materialising them, as it does the class of newly enriched people. The most palpable action is on the young amongst them, and on their standard of life and enjoyment. But in general, for this whole class, established facts, the materialism which they see regnant, too much block their mental horizon, and limit the possibilities of things to them. They are deficient in openness and flexibility of mind, in free play of ideas, in faith and ardour. Civilised they are, but they are not much of a civilising force; they are somehow bounded and ineffective.

So on the middle class they produce singularly little effect. What the middle class sees is that splendid piece of materialism, the aristocratic class, with a wealth and luxury utterly out of their reach, with a standard of social life and manners, the offspring of that wealth and luxury, seeming utterly out of their reach also. And thus they are thrown back upon themselves,—upon a defective type of religion, a narrow range of intellect and knowledge, a stunted sense of beauty, a low standard of manners. And the lower class see before them the aristocratic class, and its civilisation, such as it is, even infinitely more out of *their* reach than out of that of the middle class; while the life of the middle class, with its unlovely types of religion, thought, beauty, and manners, has naturally, in general, no great attractions for them either. And so they too are thrown back upon themselves; upon their beer, their gin, and their *fun*. Now, then, you will understand what I meant by saying that our inequality materialises our upper class, vulgarises our middle class, brutalises our lower.

And the greater the inequality the more marked is its bad action upon the middle and lower classes. In Scotland the landed aristocracy fills the scene, as is well known, still more than in England; the other classes are more squeezed back and effaced. And the social civilisation of the lower middle class and of the poorest class, in Scotland, is an example of the consequences. Compared with the same class even in England, the Scottish lower middle class is most visibly, to vary Mr. Charles Sumner's phrase, *less* well-bred, *less* careful in personal habits and in social conventions, *less* refined. Let any one who doubts it go, after issuing from the aristocratic solitudes which possess Loch Lomond, let him go and observe the shopkeepers and the middle class in Dumbarton, and Greenock, and Gourock, and the places along the mouth of the Clyde. And for the poorest class, who that has seen it can ever forget the hardly human horror, the abjection and uncivilisedness of Glasgow?

What a strange religion, then, is our religion of inequality! Romance often helps a religion to hold its ground, and romance is good in its way; but ours is not even a romantic religion. No doubt our aristocracy is an object of very strong public interest. The *Times* itself bestows a leading article by way of epithalamium on the Duke of Norfolk's marriage. And those journals of a new type, full of talent, and which interest me particularly because they seem as if they were written by the young lion of our youth,—the young lion grown mellow and, as the French say, *viveur*, arrived at his full and ripe knowledge of the world, and minded to enjoy the smooth evening of his days,—those journals, in the main a sort of social gazette of the aristocracy, are apparently not read by that class only which they most concern, but are read with great avidity by other classes also. And the common people too have undoubtedly, as Mr. Gladstone says, a wonderful preference for a lord. Yet our aristocracy, from the action upon it of the Wars of the Roses, the Tudors, and the political necessities of George the Third, is for the imagination a singularly modern and uninteresting one. Its splendour of station, its wealth, show and luxury, is then what the other classes really admire in it; and this is not an elevating admiration. Such an admiration will never lift us out of our vulgarity and brutality, if we chance to be vulgar and brutal to start with; it will rather feed them and be fed by them. So that when Mr. Gladstone invites us to call our love of inequality 'the complement of the love of freedom or its negative pole, or the shadow which the love of freedom casts, or the reverberation of its voice in the halls of the constitution,' we must surely answer that all this mystical eloquence is not in the least necessary to explain so simple a matter; that our love of inequality is really the vulgarity in us, and the brutality, admiring and worshipping the splendid materiality.

Our present social organisation, however, will and must endure until our middle class is provided with some better ideal of life than it has now. Our present organisation has been an appointed stage in our growth; it has been of good use, and has enabled us to do great things. But the use is at an end, and the stage is over. Ask yourselves if you do not sometimes feel in yourselves a sense, that in spite of the strenuous efforts for good of so many excellent persons amongst us, we begin somehow to flounder and to beat the air; that we seem to be finding ourselves stopped on this line of advance and on that and to be threatened with a sort of standstill. It is that we are trying to live on with a social organisation of which the day is over. Certainly equality will never of itself alone give us a perfect civilisation. But, with such inequality as ours, a perfect civilisation is impossible.

To that conclusion, facts, and the stream itself of this discourse, do seem, I think, to carry us irresistibly. We arrive at it because they so choose, not because we so choose. Our tendencies are all the other way. We are all of us politicians, and in one of two camps, the Liberal or the Conservative. Liberals tend to accept the middle class as it is, and to praise the nonconformists; while Conservatives tend to accept the upper class as it is, and to praise the aristocracy. And yet here we are at the conclusion, that whereas one of the great obstacles to our civilisation is, as I have often said, British nonconformity, another main obstacle to our civilisation is British aristocracy! And this while we are yet forced to recognise excellent special qualities as well as the general English energy and honesty, and a number of emergent humane individuals, in both nonconformists and aristocracy. Clearly such a conclusion can be none of our own seeking.

Then again, to remedy our inequality, there must be a change in the law of bequest, as there has been in

France; and the faults and inconveniences of the present French law of bequest are obvious. It tends to over-divide property; it is unequal in operation, and can be eluded by people limiting their families; it makes the children, however ill they may behave, independent of the parent. To be sure, Mr. Mill and others have shown that a law of bequest fixing the maximum, whether of land or money, which any one individual may take by bequest or inheritance, but in other respects leaving the testator quite free, has none of the inconveniences of the French law, and is in every way preferable. But evidently these are not questions of practical politics. Just imagine Lord Hartington going down to Glasgow, and meeting his Scotch Liberals there, and saying to them: 'You are ill at ease, and you are calling for change, and very justly. But the cause of your being ill at ease is not what you suppose. The cause of your being ill at ease is the profound imperfectness of your social civilisation. Your social civilisation is indeed such as I forbear to characterise. But the remedy is not disestablishment. The remedy is social equality. Let me direct your attention to a reform in the law of bequest and entail.' One can hardly speak of such a thing without laughing. No, the matter is at present one for the thoughts of those who think. It is a thing to be turned over in the minds of those who, on the one hand, have the spirit of scientific inquirers, bent on seeing things as they really are; and, on the other hand, the spirit of friends of the humane life, lovers of perfection. To your thoughts I commit it. And perhaps, the more you think of it, the more you will be persuaded that Menander showed his wisdom quite as much when he said *Choose equality*, as when he assured us that *Evil communications corrupt good manners.*

IRISH CATHOLICISM AND BRITISH LIBERALISM.

All roads, says the proverb, lead to Rome; and one finds in like manner that all questions raise the question of religion. We say to ourselves that religion is a subject where one is prone to be too copious and too pertinacious, where it is easy to do harm, easy to be misunderstood; that what we felt ourselves bound to say on it we have said, and that we will discuss it no longer. And one may keep one's word faithfully so far as the direct discussion of religion goes; but then the irrepressible subject manages to present itself for discussion indirectly. Questions of good government, social harmony, education, civilisation, come forth and ask to be considered; and very soon it appears that we cannot possibly treat them without returning to treat of religion. Ireland raises a crowd of questions thus complicated.

Our nation is not deficient in self-esteem, and certainly there is much in our achievements and prospects to give us satisfaction. But even to the most self-satisfied Englishman, Ireland must be an occasion, one would think, from time to time of mortifying thoughts. We may be conscious of nothing but the best intentions towards Ireland, the justest dealings with her. But how little she seems to appreciate them! We may talk, with the *Daily Telegraph*, of our 'great and genial policy of conciliation' towards Ireland; we may say, with Mr. Lowe, that by their Irish policy in 1868 the Liberal Ministry, of whom he was one, 'resolved to knit the hearts of the empire into one harmonious concord, and knitted they were accordingly.' Only, unfortunately, the Irish themselves do not see the matter as we do. All that by our genial policy we seem to have succeeded in inspiring in the Irish themselves is an aversion to us so violent, that for England to incline one way is a sufficient reason to make Ireland incline another; and the obstruction offered by the Irish members in Parliament is really an expression, above all, of this uncontrollable antipathy. Nothing is more honourable to French civilisation than its success in attaching strongly to France,—France Catholic and Celtic,—the German and Protestant Alsace. What a contrast to the humiliating failure of British civilisation to attach to Germanic and Protestant Great Britain the Celtic and Catholic Ireland!

For my part, I have never affected to be either surprised or indignant at the antipathy of the Irish to us. What they have had to suffer from us in past times, all the world knows. And now, when we profess to practise 'a great and genial policy of conciliation' towards them, they are really governed by us in deference to the opinion and sentiment of the British middle class, and of the strongest part of this class, the Puritan community. I have pointed out this before, but in a book about schools, and which only those who are concerned with schools are likely to have read. Let me be suffered, therefore, to repeat it here. The opinion and sentiment of our middle class controls the policy of our statesmen towards Ireland. That policy does not represent the real mind of our leading statesmen, but the mind of the British middle class controlling the action of statesmen. The ability of our popular journalists and successful statesmen goes to putting the best colour they can upon the action so controlled. But a disinterested observer will see an action so controlled to be what it is, and will call it what it is. Now the great failure in our actual national life is the imperfect civilisation of our middle class. The great need of our time is the transformation of the British Puritan. Our Puritan middle class presents a defective type of religion, a narrow range of intellect and knowledge, a stunted sense of beauty, a low standard of manners. And yet it is in deference to the opinion and sentiment of such a class that we shape our policy towards Ireland. And we wonder at Ireland's antipathy to us! Nay, we expect Ireland to lend herself to the make-believe of our own journalists and statesmen, and to call our policy 'genial'!

The Irish Catholics, who are the immense majority in Ireland, want a Catholic university. Elsewhere both Catholics and Protestants have universities where their sons may be taught by persons of their own form of religion. Catholic France allowed the Protestants of Alsace to have the Protestant university of Strasburg. Protestant Prussia allows the Catholics of the Rhine Province to have the Catholic university of Bonn. True, at Strasburg men of any religious persuasion might be appointed to teach anatomy or chemistry; true, at Bonn there is a Protestant faculty of theology as well as a Catholic. But I call Strasburg a Protestant and Bonn a Catholic university in this sense: that religion and the matters mixed up with religion are taught in the one by Protestants and in the other by Catholics. This is the guarantee which ordinary parents desire, and this at Bonn and at Strasburg they get. The Protestants of Ireland have in Trinity College, Dublin, a university where the teachers in all those matters which afford debatable ground between Catholic and Protestant are Protestant. The Protestants of Scotland have universities of a like character. In England the members of the English Church have in Oxford and Cambridge universities where the teachers are almost wholly Anglican. Well, the Irish Catholics ask to be allowed the same thing.

There is extraordinary difficulty in getting this demand of theirs directly and frankly met. They are told that they want secondary schools even more than a university. That may be very true, but they do also want a university; and to ask for one institution is a simpler affair than to ask for a great many. They are told they have the Queen's Colleges, invented expressly for Ireland. But they do not want colleges invented expressly for Ireland; they want colleges such as those which the English and Scotch have in Scotland and England. They are told that they may have a university of the London type, an examining board, and perhaps a system of prizes. But all the world is not, like Mr. Lowe, enamoured of examining boards and prizes. The world in general much prefers to universities of the London type universities of the type of Strasburg, Bonn, Oxford; and the Irish are of the same mind as the world in general. They are told that Mr. Gladstone's government offered them a university without theology, philosophy, or history, and that they refused it. But the world in general does not desire universities with theology, philosophy, and history left out; no more did Ireland. They are told that Trinity College, Dublin, is now an unsectarian university no more Protestant than Catholic, and that they may use Trinity College. But the teaching in Trinity College is, and long will be (and very naturally), for the most part in the hands of Protestants; the whole character, tradition, and atmosphere of the place are Protestant. The Irish Catholics want to have on their side, too, a place where the university teaching is mainly in the hands of Catholics, and of which the character and atmosphere shall be Catholic. But then they are asked whether they propose to do away with all the manifold and deep-rooted results of Protestant ascendency in Ireland, and they are warned that this would be a hard, nay, impossible matter. But they are not proposing anything so enormous and chimerical as to do away with all the results of Protestant ascendency; they propose merely to put an end to one particular and very cruel result of it:—the result that they, the immense majority of the Irish people, have no university, while the Protestants in Ireland, the small minority, have one. For this plain hardship they propose a plain remedy, and to their proposal they want a plain and straightforward answer.

And at last they get it. It is the papal answer: *Non possumus.* The English Ministry and Parliament may wish to give them what they demand, may think their claim just, but they *cannot* give it them. In the mind and temper of the English people there is an unconquerable obstacle. 'The claims of the Irish Roman Catholics,' says the *Times*, 'are inconsistent with the practical conditions of politics. It is necessary to repeat the simple fact that the temper of the people of Great Britain will not admit of any endowment of Roman Catholic institutions. We should recognise the futility of contending against the most rooted of popular prejudices.' 'The demand for the State endowment of a Roman Catholic university, or of a Roman Catholic college,' says the *Saturday Review*, 'may be perfectly just, but it is at the same time perfectly impracticable. The determination not to grant it may be quite illogical, but it is very firmly rooted.' A radical and almost miraculous change in the mind and temper of the objectors is required, the *Saturday Review* adds, before such a thing can be granted. And in the House of Commons Mr. Lowe said: 'He would not argue whether it would be good or bad to found out of public funds a Catholic university in Ireland; all he said was that it was not in the power of that House to do so. Every one who knew the state of feeling in England, Scotland, and a part of Ireland, must know that if the Government were to attempt such a thing, it would be running its head against a wall, running upon its own destruction. It would be perfectly impossible to carry any such measure through the House.' So that in our 'genial policy of conciliation' towards Ireland we are fettered by a *non possumus.* And the *non possumus* has provided itself with a short formula which is everywhere current among us, and which is this: 'The Liberal party has emphatically condemned religious endowment; the Protestants of Great Britain are emphatically hostile to the endowment of Catholicism in any shape or form.'

Let us leave for a moment the Protestants of Great Britain, and let us think of the Liberal party only. Mr. Lowe has in the *Fortnightly Review,* not many months ago, admirably set forth the ideal of the Liberal party. 'The ideal of the Liberal party,' says Mr. Lowe, 'consists in a view of things undisturbed and undistorted by the promptings of interests or prejudice, in a complete independence of all class interests, and in relying for its success on the better feelings and higher intelligence of mankind.' Happier words could not well be found; such is indeed the true ideal of the Liberal party. Well, then, if the demand of the Irish for a Catholic university is perfectly just, if the refusal of it is perfectly illogical, how bitter it must be for a true Liberal to refuse it on the score of 'the futility of contending against the most rooted of popular prejudices'! To be undisturbed by the promptings of prejudice, and to rely for success on the better feelings and higher intelligence of mankind, is the very ideal which a true Liberal has to follow. And to the best and most reflecting Liberals, accordingly, it seems to have been given to see that, whether religious endowment be in itself good or bad, Great Britain cannot justly refuse Ireland's claim for a university of that kind which we ourselves, in England and Scotland, prefer and adopt, and that to withhold it in deference to popular prejudice is wrong. Mr. John Morley has recorded Mr. Mill's opinion, declared in the last conversation which Mr. Mill ever had with him. 'He seemed disposed to think that the most feasible solution of the Irish University question is a Catholic university, the restrictive and obscurantist tendencies of which you may expect to have checked by the active competition of life with men trained in more enlightened systems.'

Mr. Morley, who thus records Mr. Mill's opinion, has avowed that he himself shares it. But of still more importance was the practical adhesion given the other day in the House of Commons to Mr. Mill's opinion, by a certain number of English Liberals, on the occasion of the O'Conor Don's resolution affirming the claims of Ireland to a Catholic university. A certain number of English Liberal members, and amongst them men so prominent and so ardently Liberal as Mr. Chamberlain and Sir Charles Dilke, voted in favour of the O'Conor Don's resolution. True, there was after all a great majority against the resolution. The mass of Liberals, as well as the mass of Conservatives, were, like the *Times*, for 'recognising the futility of contending against the most rooted of popular prejudices.' The claims, the just claims, of Ireland were sacrificed, as they have been sacrificed so often, to the opinion and sentiment of the British middle class, of the British Puritan, who cries that if the State endows a Roman Catholic university, the State is, 'by force of the tax-gatherer, compelling us to teach as truth that which we before God assert without the slightest misgiving to be dismal error, and making us parties to a lie.' They were sacrificed to the prejudices of people whose narrowness and whose imperfect civilisation every cultivated man amongst us perceives and deplores. And the continued rule of these prejudices is presented as a fatality from which there can be no escape without a miracle. But perhaps when Liberals of such mark as Sir Charles Dilke and Mr. Chamberlain have the courage to set them at nought, and have the courage to set at nought also, at least for this one occasion, the formula that 'the Liberal party has emphatically condemned religious endowment,' the miracle has begun.

At all events, few things in politics have ever given me more pleasure than to see the aid courageously afforded to Irish Catholics by this little band of advanced English Liberals. I do not profess to be a politician, but simply one of a disinterested class of observers, who, with no organised and embodied set of supporters to please, set themselves to observe honestly and to report faithfully the state and prospects of our civilisation. But the ideal of the Liberal party, as we have seen it declared by Mr. Lowe, is certainly also the ideal of such a class of observers. However, the practice of Liberals has seemed to me to fall a good deal short of this ideal, and, instead of relying for its success on the better feelings and higher intelligence of mankind, to lend itself very often to the wishes of narrow and prejudiced people, in the hope of finding its account by so doing. And I have again and again, for a good many years past, being a humble follower of the true Liberal ideal, remarked that by their actual practice our Liberals, however prosperous they might seem, could not really succeed ;—that their doings wanted more of simple and sincere thought to direct them, that their performance was far less valuable than they supposed, and that it and they were more and more losing their charm for the nation. This I said in their prosperity. But in their present adversity I prefer to remember only that their cause is in a general way, at any rate, mine also ; that I serve and would fain follow the Liberal ideal.

And as we are told that, in the depressed days of Israel, 'they that feared the Eternal spake often one to another,' to confirm one another in a belief of the final triumph of their cause, so, in the present evil days, Liberals ought to speak often one to another of relying upon the better feelings and higher intelligence of mankind, that we may keep up our faith and spirits. Or if, in addressing advanced Liberals, it should seem out of place to cite the example of a set of antiquated Jewish religionists, let me quote the comfortable words of a blameless Liberal, Condorcet, who assures us that 'the natural order of things tends to bring general opinion more and more into conformity with truth.' *L'ordre naturel tend à rendre l'opinion générale de plus en plus conforme à la vérité.* And the politician who would be of real service must manage, Condorcet says, to get at this *vérité*, this truth. *Connaître la vérité pour y conformer l'ordre de la société, telle est l'unique source du bonheur public.* Therefore, when Mr. Chamberlain and Sir Charles Dilke and other Liberal politicians have just given a signal proof of their faith in justice and reason, and of their willingness to contend for them 'against the most rooted of popular prejudices,' let us seize the opportunity of fortifying them and ourselves in the conviction that 'the natural order of things tends to bring general opinion more and more into conformity with truth,' and that it is an excellent principle in government to believe that to what is reasonable one may always hope to make the majority of men at last come in. Let us see if this may not even lead us to recast entirely the programme of our practical Liberalism, and to use our present dull times for bringing it more into correspondence with the true Liberal ideal. Perhaps the weakness of Liberalism will be found to lie in its having followed hitherto with a too eager solicitude the wishes of a class narrow minded and imperfectly civilised; its strength in the future must lie more in complying with the order which for our progress appears the true one, and in co-operating with nature to bring general opinion into harmony with it.

For take the formula which is supposed to govern the action of British Liberalism towards Irish Catholicism, and which long has governed it, but which a small band of

Liberal heroes the other day set at nought. 'The Liberal party has emphatically condemned religious endowment; the Protestants of Great Britain are implacably hostile to the endowment of Catholicism in any shape or form.'

This may seem a convenient formula for Liberals to adopt, because it enables us to act in concert with English Nonconformity and Scotch Puritanism. But evidently it tends to divide British Liberals from Irish Liberals. It costs British Liberals the support of Liberalism in Ireland, which they can ill afford to do without. Therefore it extremely behoves them to examine the formula well, and to ascertain how far it corresponds with the natural truth of things; for this is always and surely tending, as we have seen, to prevail. And if the formula has natural truth on its side, then there is good reason for hoping that the Irish Catholics, however ignorant, may at last come into it and be reconciled to its operation. But if it has not natural truth on its side, then the irritation and estrangement which its operation must produce in Ireland will be perpetual. On the other hand, British Puritanism, however prejudiced, may be trusted to resign itself at some distant day to the abandonment of the formula if it is false, because time and nature will beneficently help towards such abandonment.

'The Liberal party has emphatically condemned

religious endowment.' This maxim is not even now quite true in fact, for many members of the Liberal party favour religious endowment. And if that view of things out of which the maxim arises turns out to be erroneous, there is no reason why even those Liberals who have adopted the maxim should not drop it; their cause, and their work, and their reason for existing are in no wise bound up with it. But it is not denied that 'the Protestants,' or at any rate the Puritans, 'of Great Britain, are implacably hostile to the endowment of Catholicism in any shape or form.' And however that view out of which their hostility arises may be shown to be erroneous, there is every reason why they should long and obstinately shut their minds to the thought of abandoning that view and that hostility, because their cause, and their work, and their reason for existing are in great measure bound up with it. Still, if there appears to be no rational ground for objecting to the endowment of Catholicism in particular, any more than to religious endowment in general, but, on the contrary, rational ground for allowing both the one and the other, Liberals ought not to set themselves stubbornly against even the endowment of Catholicism.

As to the Church of England there are special errors of their own into which our Liberals are apt to fall, but as to Catholicism their usual and grand error is one which they have in common with Continental Liberals. This error consists in always regarding what is prodigious, mischievous, impossible in Catholicism, rather than what is natural, amiable, likely to endure. It is by this natural and better side that we should accustom ourselves to consider Catholicism, and we cannot conceive this side too simply. We should begin with Catholicism at that elementary stage when it is not yet even in conscious conflict with Protestantism. Let us take a Protestant example of the power of religion, since with Protestant examples we ourselves are naturally most familiar, and let us see on what it hinges, and we shall be satisfied that the true power of religion in all forms of Christianity hinges at bottom on the same thing. Here is a letter written the other day by a common soldier in Walmer barracks to a lady whom he had met at a Methodist prayer-meeting, and who had interested herself in him :—

A few weeks ago I was thoroughly tired of Deal, but since I found my Saviour I thank God most heartily that ever I enlisted. I had been going on loosely for years. From the death of a sister I left off for a time, but soon relapsed, and went from bad to worse until I came here, when one day walking by the chapel in a most miserable state of mind, I heard singing and was induced to go in. There I was powerfully wrought upon, resolved at once to give up sin, and am now happy in the enjoyment of God's love. God bless you, madam, and may God spare your useful life many years!

Here, then, to what Epictetus calls 'the madness and the misery of one who has been using as his measure of things that which *seems* to the senses and appetites, and misusing it,' the influence of the religion of Jesus Christ has been applied, and has operated as a cure. Cases of exactly the same sort of emotion and conversion may be witnessed among the Breton mariners, hanging on the lips of an impassioned Jesuit preacher in one of the crowded churches of Brittany. And no wonder. Men conscious of a bent for being modest, temperate, kindly, affectionate, find themselves shameless, dissolute, living in malice and envy, hateful and hating one another. The experience is as old as the world, and the misery of it. And it is no cure whatever to be told that the Pope is not infallible, or that miracles do not happen; but a cure, a divine cure, for the bondage and the misery, has been found for nearly two thousand years to lie in the word, the character, the influence of Jesus. In this cure resides the power and the permanence of the Christian religion.

Liberals who have no conception of the Christian religion as of a real need of the community, which the community has to satisfy, should learn to fix their view upon this simple source, common to Catholics and Protestants alike, of Christianity's power and permanence. The power and permanence come from Christianity's being a real source of cure for a real bondage and misery. Men have adapted the source to their use according to their lights, often very imperfect;—have piled fantastic buildings around it, carried its healing waters by strange and intricate conduits, done their best to make it no longer recognisable. But, in their fashion, they have used and they do still use it; and whenever their religion is treated, often because of their mishandling and disfigurement of it, as an obsolete nuisance to be discouraged and helped to die out, a profound sentiment in them rebels against such an outrage, because they are conscious not of their vain disfigurements of the Christian religion, but of its genuine curativeness.

Catholicism is that form of Christianity which is fullest of human accretions and superstitions, because it is the oldest, the largest, the most popular. It is the religion which has most reached the people. It has been the great popular religion of Christendom, with all the accretions and superstitions inseparable from such a character. The bulk of its superstitions come from its having really plunged so far down into the multitude, and spread so wide among them. If this is a cause of error, it is also a cause of attachment. Who has seen the poor in other churches as they are seen in Catholic churches? Catholicism, besides, enveloped human life, and Catholics in general feel themselves to have drawn not only their religion from the Church, they feel themselves to have drawn from her, too, their art and poetry and culture. Her hierarchy, again, originally stamped in their imaginations with the character of a beneficent and orderly authority springing up amidst anarchy, appeared next as offering a career where birth was disregarded and merit regarded, and the things of the mind and the soul were honoured, in the midst of the iron feudal age which worshipped solely birth and force. So thus Catholicism acquired on the imagination a second hold. And if there is a thing specially alien to religion, it is divisions; if there is a thing specially native to religion, it is peace and union. Hence the original attraction towards unity in Rome, and hence the great charm and power for men's minds of that unity when once attained. All these spells for the heart and imagination has Catholicism to Catholics, in addition to the spell for the conscience of a divine cure for vice and misery. And whoever treats Catholicism as a nuisance, to be helped to die out as soon as possible, has the heart, the imagination, and the conscience of Catholics, in just revolt against him.

True, the accretions and superstitions, gathered round the curative religious germ, are dense; true, the system of the Romish hierarchy carried with it the seeds of a thousand temptations and dangers, which have abundantly struck root; true, as the individuality of the European nations has ripened, and unity in one's nation has become a dominant habit and idea, the collisions between this unity and the unity in Rome have become a matter for just disquietude. Here are hindrances to be combated by us undoubtedly, and if possible to be removed; nevertheless, even in combating and removing them we should always remember that to the mass of Catholics they present themselves by a good side, not by their bad one. However, they are hindrances to civilisation, and we ought to regard them as such. But in a modern community they meet with natural counteractions of great power. And the power of those counteractions is greater, the more the community has education, good government, happiness; it is least when the community is misgoverned, sunk in ignorance and misery. The national sense, in a free and high-spirited modern nation, may be trusted to assert itself, as time goes on, against that dependence on a government of foreigners, that meddling and intrigue by a government of foreigners, which is what the Ultramontane system, judged by practice, not theory, is seen really to bring with it. The family spirit, in a nation prosperous, educated, and of sound morals, may be trusted to assert itself against the excessive intervention of the priest. Finally and above all, religion, like human society itself, follows a law of progress and growth; and this law may be trusted, in a well-governed, sound, and progressive community, advancing in intelligence and culture, to clear away the accretions and the superstitions which have gathered round religion. In short, to the retention and aggravation of the mischiefs of the Catholic system,—its Ultramontanism, sacerdotalism, superstition,—the great auxiliaries are ill-government, vice, ignorance. Ultramontanism, sacerdotalism, and superstition a good statesman must desire and hope to be rid of; but he cannot extirpate them offhand, he must let their natural counteractors have play. And their natural counteractors are freedom, good government, sound morals, intelligence. With the help of these they may be got rid of, but not without.

But when Ultramontanism, sacerdotalism, and superstition are gone, Catholicism is not, as some may suppose, gone too. Neither is it left with nothing further but what it possesses in common with all the forms of Christianity, —the curative power of the word, character, and influence of Jesus. It is, indeed, left with this, which is the root of the matter, but it is left with a mighty power besides. It is left with the beauty, the richness, the poetry, the infinite charm for the imagination, of its own age-long growth, a growth such as we have described,—unconscious, popular, profoundly rooted, all-enveloping.

It is the sure sign of a shallow mind, to suppose that the strength of the Catholic Church is really in its tone of absolute certainty concerning its dogmas, in its airs of omniscience. On the contrary, as experience widens, as the scientific and dogmatic pretensions of the Church become more manifestly illusory, its tone of certitude respecting them, so unguarded, so reiterated, and so grossly calculated for immediate and vulgar effect, will be an embarrassment to it. The gain to-day, the effect upon a certain class of minds, will be found to be more than counterbalanced by the embarrassment to-morrow. No doubt there are pious souls to-day which are edified and fortified at being told by Cardinal Manning that 'whoever does not in his heart receive and believe the doctrine of the Immaculate Conception, as defined by the supreme authority of the Church, does by that very fact cease to be a Catholic;' and that 'in the Encyclical *Ineffabilis Deus*, of the 8th of December, 1854, the Sovereign Pontiff, the supreme authority of the Church, defined that the most blessed Virgin Mary was, by a singular grace and privilege of Almighty God, and by reason of the merits of Jesus Christ, the Saviour of mankind, preserved in the first moment of her conception free from all stain of original sin.' But even in Catholics the irrepressible question will soon arise: 'How can he possibly know?' Then the solemnity of the assurance will turn out to be a weakness, not a strength. Monsignor Capel may elate his auditory to-day by telling them that Protestants are more and more discovering that their Bible, which they used to oppose to the Catholic's Church, is not infallible. How delightful, think his devout hearers, to have an infallible Church, since the Bible is not infallible! But sooner or later will come the irrepressible question: 'Is there, can there be, either an infallible Bible or an infallible Church?' What a ridiculous argument will the argument, *Because there exists no infallible Bible, there must exist an infallible Church*, be then perceived to be! It is like arguing: Because there are no fairies, therefore there must be gnomes. There are neither fairies nor gnomes, but nature and the course of nature.

Its dogma and its confident assertion of its dogma are no more a real source of strength and permanence to the Catholic Church, than its Ultramontanism. Its real superiority is in its charm for the imagination,—its poetry. I persist in thinking that Catholicism has, from this superiority, a great future before it; that it will endure while all the Protestant sects (in which I do not include the Church of England) dissolve and perish. I persist in thinking that the prevailing form for the Christianity of the future will be the form of Catholicism ; but a Catholicism purged, opening itself to the light and air, having the consciousness of its own poetry, freed from its sacerdotal despotism and freed from its pseudo-scientific apparatus of superannuated dogma. Its forms will be retained, as symbolising with the force and charm of poetry a few cardinal facts and ideas, simple indeed, but indispensable and inexhaustible, and on which our race could lay hold only by materialising them.

From this ideal future of Catholicism, truly, few countries can be farther removed than the Ireland of the present day. All the mischiefs of Catholicism are rampant there. Irish Catholicism is Ultramontane, priest-governed, superstitious, self-confident. It could hardly be otherwise. The Irish Catholic has no public education beyond the elementary school. His priests are educated in the closest of seminaries. The national sense has been so managed in him by us, with our oppression and ill-government, that national sense as a member of our nation and empire he has none. His national sense is that of a conquered people, held down by a superior force of aliens, and glad to conspire against them with Rome or with any one else. If we want the Irish to be less superstitious, less priest-governed, less Ultramontane, let us do what is likely to serve this end. The Irish will use Catholic schools and no other. Let us give them secondary and higher Catholic schools with a public character. They have at present no secondary schools with a public character. As public higher schools the Queen's Colleges have been offered to them; but they will not use the Queen's Colleges, any more than we, either, are disposed to use colleges of that type. The Catholic layman has, therefore, neither secondary nor higher school; the priest has for a higher school Maynooth, a close seminary. What an admirable and likely cure is this for Irish ignorance, sacerdotalism, Ultramontanism, and disaffection!

Let us try, at any rate, a more hopeful treatment. Let us make no needless difficulties for ourselves by pulling to pieces what is established and what is working well. The distinguished past and the honourable present of Trinity College, Dublin, as well as the large proportion of the wealth and property of Ireland which belongs to Protestants, amply justify its continuance. The endowed secondary schools of Ireland are Protestant. It is alleged that the endowments are wasted, and that a share in some of them, at any rate, belongs by right to Catholics Let waste and abuse be put an end to, and let Catholics have that share in the endowments which belongs to them; but here, too, let us be unwilling to disturb what is established, what is consonant with the terms of the endowment, and what is working well. Their legal share in the actual endowed schools of Ireland is not likely to afford to Catholics the supply of education needed; while schools of the type of those old endowed schools are, besides, not so desirable for them as schools of a more directly public institution and character. Let us give them public schools.

A clearing and enlarging spirit is in the air; all the influences of the time help it. Wherever the pressure of the time and of collective human life can make itself felt, and therefore in all public and national institutions for education, the spirit works. The one way to prevent or adjourn its working is to keep education what is called a hole-and-corner affair, cut off from the public life of the nation and the main current of its thoughts, in the hands of a clique who have been narrowly educated themselves. Irish Catholicism has been entirely dissociated from the public life of the country, has been left to be an entirely private concern of the persons attached to it. Its education has been kept a hole-and-corner thing, with its teachers neither of public appointment nor designated by public opinion as eminent men. We have prevented all access of the enlarging influences of the time to either teacher or taught. Well, but what has been the consequence? Has Irish Catholicism died out because of this wholesome neglect by the State? Among no people is their religion so vigorous and pervasive. Has it fewer faults and disadvantages than Catholicism in countries where Catholic education is publicly instituted? In no country, probably, is Catholicism so crude, blind, and unreasoning as in Ireland. The public institution of Catholic education in Ireland is not only, therefore, what the Irish themselves want; it is also just the very thing to do them good.

The public institution of Catholic education with the proper and necessary guarantees. Our newspapers always assume that Catholic education must be 'under complete clerical control." We are reminded that the Irish bishops claimed from Lord Mayo the entire government of their Irish university, the right of veto on the appointment of professors, the right of dismissing professors. This would make the university simply a religious seminary with a State payment. But the State has no right, even if it had the wish, to abandon its duties towards a national university in this manner. The State, in such a university, is proctor for the nation. The appointment and dismissal of the professors belong to no corporation less large and public than the nation itself; and it is best in the hands of the nation, and not made over to any smaller and closer corporation like the clergy, however respectable. The professors should be nominated and removed, not by the bishops, but by a responsible minister of State acting for the Irish nation itself. They should be Catholics, but he should choose them; exercising his choice as a judicious Catholic would be disposed to exercise it, who had to act in the name and for the benefit of the whole community. While the bishops, if they have the appointment of professors in a Catholic university, will be prone to ask: 'Who will suit the bishops?' the community, or the minister representing it, is interested in asking solely: 'Who is the best and most distinguished Catholic for the chair?'

In the interest of the Irish themselves, therefore, the professors in a publicly instituted Catholic university ought to be nominated by a minister of State, acting under a public responsibility, and proctor for the Irish nation. Would Ireland reject a Catholic university offered with such a condition? I do not believe it. At any rate, if we offered it, and if Ireland refused it, our conscience would be clear; for only with such a condition can the State fairly and rightly bestow a university. At present the Roman Catholic hierarchy perceive that the

Government cannot seriously negotiate with them, because it is controlled by popular prejudice and unreason. In any parleyings, therefore, they feel themselves free to play at a mere game of brag, and to advance confidently pretensions the most exorbitant, because they are sure that nothing reasonable can be done. But once break resolutely with the prejudice and unreason; let it be clear that the Government can and will treat with the Irish Catholics for the public institution of a Catholic university such as they demand, such as they have a right to, such as in other Protestant countries Catholics enjoy. Would the Irish bishops prove impracticable *then*, or would Ireland allow them to be so, even if they were so inclined? I do not believe it. I believe that a wholesome national feeling, thus reasonably appealed to, would be found to spring up and respond; and that here we should have the first instalment of the many ameliorations which the public establishment of Catholic education is calculated to produce in Ireland.

This is so evident, that no one in Great Britain with clear and calm political judgment, or with fine perception, or with high cultivation, or with large knowledge of the world, doubts it. Statesmen see it, the aristocracy see it, the important class which we have to thank Mr. Charles

Sumner for noting,—the large class of gentlemen, not of the squirearchy or nobility, but cultivated and refined,—they see it too. The populace know and care nothing about the matter. And yet there is in one quarter,—in the British middle class,—a force of prejudice on this subject so strong and so rooted, that we are bidden to recognise the futility of contending with it, and to treat the claims of the Irish Catholics for a Catholic university as inconsistent with the practical conditions of politics.

This it is which is, indeed, calculated to drive the Irish to rage and despair. If the English race may be said, by one speaking favourably of it but not extravagantly, to be characterised by energy and honesty, the Irish race may be described, in like manner, as being characterised by sentiment and perception. And they find themselves sacrificed to the prejudices of a class which they see, as the rest of the world sees it, to be, in its present state, imperfectly civilised and impossible; a class ill-educated as the Irish middle class itself, knowing how to make money, but not knowing how to live when they have made it; and in short, of the powers which, as we saw when we were discussing Equality, go to constitute civilisation,—the powers of conduct, intellect, beauty, manners,—laying hold upon one only, the power of conduct. But for this factor in civilisation the Irish, in the first place, have by nature not sufficient sympathy, and it comes up in our middle class so strangely misgrown and disguised that strangers may easily fail to recognise it; and then besides, of the sense for conduct in our middle class, though the sense is there, the Irish have really had no experience at all, but have had a long experience of this class as unjust, hard, and cruel. And they see that our government and upper class quite share their opinions about this class, but that we have a system which requires that the upper class should be cultivated and attractive and should govern, and that the middle class should be, as it is, impossible, but that it should be flattered and humoured; and therefore to the deep-rooted prejudices of the middle class against Catholicism Ireland must be sacrificed. But the Irish are quite out of this singular game, which our notorious passion for inequality makes us play with such zest in England; they cannot appreciate its ways and laws. All they feel is that they are kept from having what they want, and what is fair, and what we have ourselves, because the British middle class, being such as we have described it, pronounces their religion to be *a lie* and *heathenish superstition*.

Now I am here pouring out my heart to advanced Liberals, in my joy at their sound and hopeful vote on the O'Conor Don's resolution. I am sure that Sir Charles

Dilke does not suppose that Mr. Arthur or Mr. Spurgeon is in possession of *the truth* in some eminent way, compared with which the tenets of Lacordaire, for instance, were *a lie* and *heathenish superstition.* Each, Sir Charles Dilke would probably say, can at most but be pronounced free from some bondage still confining the mind of the other; Mr. Arthur and Mr. Spurgeon from the delusion of an infallible church, and Lacordaire from the jungle of the justification theology. But then I, on my part, must ask leave to say that they all, nevertheless, possess as their foundation, however overlaid, a germ of inestimable power for lifting human life out of misery and servitude, and for assuring its felicity. And Sir Charles Dilke, again, is thereupon likely to rejoin that this may possibly be so, but that the whole natural history of that germ, the whole philosophy of the thing, as they and theirs have constructed it for themselves, is, with all of them alike, a construction utterly fantastic and hollow; the *Quicunque vult* like the Westminster Confession, and the Tridentine Decrees like the Thirty-nine Articles. Bits, he will say, the Protestant may have more right than the Catholic, and in other bits, again, the Catholic may have the advantage; and the being right on some points may happen to contribute more help towards making progress on the line of liberty, let us say, or industry, than the being right on others. But the whole philosophy of the thing is fantastic in both. And if Sir Charles Dilke chooses to say this, I shall not contend with him; for I hate contention, and besides, I do not know that I much disagree with him.

So I shall acquiesce and say: Well, then, let us be agreed. Both Catholic and Protestant have the germ, both Catholic and Protestant have a false philosophy of the germ. But Catholicism has the germ invested in an immense poetry, the gradual work of time and nature, and of that great impersonal artist, Catholic Christendom. And here it has the superiority over Protestantism. So that when the British Puritan prevents our doing justice to the Irish Catholic because his religion is, says the Puritan, *a lie* and *heathenish superstition*, the Irish Catholic is conscious that he has the germ like the Puritan; that the philosophy of the germ those who prate of such things would allow neither that he nor that the Puritan has, but he has it, they would allow, quite as much as the Puritan; while in the beauty and poetry of his clothing of the germ he has an immeasurable superiority. And he is not to have a Catholic university because, though this is so, and though all the world except the British middle class see it to be so, this class must be humoured and flattered by the governing class in England, and its mail of prejudice is impenetrable! Let Sir Charles Dilke ask himself with what feelings this state of things would fill him, if he were an Irishman affected by it. But he *has* asked himself, and hence his vote. It would be likely to fill him, he saw, with rage and despair; and when his mind dwelt on it he might even be inclined, instead of marvelling at the extravagance of Mr. Biggar and Mr. Parnell and the other obstructionists, rather to chafe at their moderation.

But then, if Sir Charles Dilke and his friends wish to have truth and nature on their side in their political labours, and to bring them to a happy end, they ought to proceed boldly and unwaveringly in the excellent course which by their vote on the O'Conor Don's resolution they have begun. The present government leans naturally for its support upon the feeling of the upper class, and to the just claims of Ireland in the matter of education the feeling of this class is not opposed. If the present government, therefore, should show a disposition to do justice to Ireland in this matter, let the advanced Liberals, who have so well begun, steadily support the government in such a disposition, and steadily refuse in this question, for the sake of snatching a party advantage, to trade upon the baneful fund of middle-class prejudice, which is so easy and so tempting to use even while one despises it. There will be plenty of other occasions on which the pursuit of the true Liberal ideal must inevitably bring Liberals into conflict with the present government, and with the feeling of the upper class. But on this particular question for a Liberal to thwart the government, if the government were inclined to do what Ireland justly desires, would be to put himself into conflict with truth and nature, and, therefore, with the Liberal ideal itself.

And how can I forbear adding,—though the space which remains to me is short, and though on this subject Mr. Chamberlain will be hard to persuade, and he may still be under the spell, besides, of that recent article by Mr. Jenkins in the *Fortnightly Review*,—yet how can I forbear adding that the same considerations of the sure loss and defeat at last, from coming into conflict with truth and nature, ought to govern the action of Liberals as to the disestablishment of the Church of England, and to make this action other than what it now is? For if to the building up of human life and civilisation there go these four powers, the power of conduct, the power of intellect and knowledge, the power of beauty, and the power of social life and manners, and if to the disengagement and strengthening and final harmony of these powers we are pushed by the instinct of self-preservation in humanity then to go against any one of them is to go against truth and nature. And the case for the Church of England is really, in respect of its Puritan reproachers and attackers, just like that of the Church of Rome, and has the same sort of natural strength. The Church of England has the germ of Christianity like its attackers; the philosophy of the germ (so we understood Sir Charles Dilke to say) neither the Church nor its attackers have; in the beauty and poetry of its clothing of the germ, the Church has an immeasurable superiority. Joseph de Maistre, that ardent Catholic, remarked that the Church of England was the only one of the Reformation Churches which still showed promise and vitality; and he attributed this superiority to its retention of bishops. Sir Charles Dilke will probably say that this is one of those explanations which explain nothing. But suppose we fill out the term bishops a little, and understand the retention of bishops to mean that the Church of England, while getting rid of Ultramontanism, and of many other things plainly perceived to be false or irksome, yet kept in great measure the traditional form of Catholicism, and thus preserved its link with the past, its share in the beauty and the poetry and the charm for the imagination of Catholicism,—its inheritance in all that work of ages, and of nature, and of popular instinct, and of the great impersonal artist whom we can only name Catholic

Christendom. Then in the retention of bishops, thus explained, we arrive at a real superiority,—a superiority in beauty.

And if one man's notion of beauty were as good as another's, and there were not an instinct of self-preservation in humanity working upwards towards a real beauty, then this superiority would be of no avail. But now nature herself fights against the Puritan, with his services of religion such as they visibly are,—free from all touch or suspicion of the great impersonal artist, but just what the British middle class, left to itself, might be expected to make them; while his intellectual conception of religion is no more adequate than the conception current in the Church, or indeed is even less adequate, since a great public body is more open to the enlarging influences of the time. And so the Church of England is likely to grow stronger rather than weaker. The desire to keep it a public institution will grow stronger rather than weaker. The more its superiority to the sects is perceived, and the source of this superiority, the stronger will be the desire to continue that public institution of it which gives more weight, solemnity, and grandeur to religion, which makes religion less like a thing of private fancy or invention. The community will wish religion to be a thing which may grow according to their needs, and be administered according to their needs; and also to be a thing of public institution, removed from the freaks of private caprice, ignorance, and vulgarity.

People, therefore, will use the germ of curative power which lies in Christianity, because they cannot do without it; and the intellectual conception they will shape for themselves as they can; and for beauty and poetry of religious service they will go to the Church. There have been a few Liberals, such as Sir John Lubbock, in whom the scientific spirit was so strong that they wanted fairly to know how things stood and how many adherents the Church numbered even now, and to get a religious census taken. But in general it fared with the religious census as it fared with the Catholic university for Ireland; Liberals recognised the futility of contending against rooted Puritan prejudice. However, if the present government remain in office, a religious census will, one may hope, be taken; and that is one good reason, at any rate, for wishing stability to the present government. It is dangerous to prophesy; yet I will venture to prophesy, and to say that if a religious census is taken, the majority in England ranging themselves with the Church will be found to be overwhelming, and the Dissenters will be found much less numerous than they give themselves out to be.

But I must end. Out of gratitude for the pleasure

given to me by the Liberal votes for the O'Conor Don's resolution, I have been endeavouring to caution my benefactors against the common Liberal error of supposing that all the influences of truth and nature are against Catholicism, whether on the Continent or in Ireland, and against the Established Church in England. On the contrary, they are, many of them, in their favour. They are, many of them, against the Puritan and Nonconformist cause, which, in this country, Liberals are always tempted to think themselves safe in supporting. The need for beauty is a real and now rapidly growing need in man; Puritanism cannot satisfy it, Catholicism and the English Church can. The need for intellect and knowledge in him, indeed, neither Puritanism, nor Catholicism, nor the English Church, can at present satisfy. That need has to seek satisfaction nowadays elsewhere,—through the modern spirit, science, literature. But, as one drops the false science of the Churches, one perceives that what they had to deal with was so simple that it did not require science. Their beauty remains, investing certain elementary truths of inestimable depth and value, yet of extreme simplicity. But the Puritan Churches have no beauty. This makes the difficulty of maintaining the Established Church of Scotland. Once drop the false science on which successive generations of Scotchmen have so vainly valued themselves, once convince oneself that the Westminster Confession, whatever Principal Tulloch may think, is a document absolutely antiquated, sterile, and worthless, and what remains to the Church of Scotland? Besides the simple elementary truths present in all forms of Christianity, there remains to the Church of Scotland merely that which remains to the Free Church, to the United Presbyterians, to Puritanism in general, — a religious service which is perhaps the most dismal performance ever invented by man. It is here that Catholicism and the Church of England have such a real superiority; and nothing can destroy it, and the present march of things is even favourable to it. Let Liberals do their best to open Catholicism and the Church of England to all the enlarging influences of the time, to make tyranny and vexatiousness on the part of their clergy impossible; but do not let them think they are to be destroyed, nor treat them as their natural enemies.

Perhaps Lord Granville has come a little late in life to the consideration of these matters, and assumes over-hastily that because the alliance with the Dissenters persecuted was valuable for the Liberal party, the alliance with the Dissenters aggressive must be valuable for them too. Let him bring his acute mind to see the thing as it really is. He is for admitting, in a public rite, the services of Dissent on the same footing as the services of the Church of England. But let him accustom himself to attend both, and he will perceive what the difference between the services is. The difference is really very much the difference between a reading from Milton and a reading from Eliza Cook,—a poetess, I hasten to add, of wide popularity, full of excellent sentiments, of appeals to the love of liberty, country, home. And for a long while the English Church, with the State to back her, committed the fatal mistake of trying to compel everybody to forsake the reading of Eliza Cook and come to the reading of Milton; nay, to declare that they utterly abjured Eliza Cook, and that they preferred Milton. And sometimes, when it would have suited a man to come to the reading of Milton, they would not let him, if he and his family had ever preferred Eliza Cook. This was the time of the strong and fruitful alliance of the Whigs with Dissent. It may be said to have closed with the death of a man whom we all admired, Lord Russell. He established the right of the Dissenters to be not cross-questioned and persecuted about the preferability of Milton to Eliza Cook; they were to be free to prefer which they pleased. Yet Milton remains Milton, and Eliza Cook remains Eliza

Cook. And a public rite, with a reading of Milton attached to it, is another thing from a public rite with a reading from Eliza Cook. The general sentiment has gone heartily with Lord Russell in leaving the Dissenters perfectly free to prefer and use Eliza Cook as much as they please; but is it certain that it will be found equally to go with Lord Granville in letting them import her into a public rite?

Not in this direction, I think, shall we do well to seek to extend the conquests of Liberalism. They are to be extended on other lines, some of them hardly entered upon at present. It is a long time since last February, and things are easily forgotten; let me, therefore, recall to my Liberal benefactors what I said at the Royal Institution last February, that the excesses to which our love of inequality has carried us have ended in materialising our upper class, vulgarising our middle class, and brutalising our lower class; and that they do this, if we will look at the thing simply, by a kind of necessary and fatal operation, throwing the middle class,—to speak now of that one class only,—in upon itself, and giving it over to the narrownesses, and prejudices, and hideousnesses, which many people regard as incurable, but which are not. And therefore, for the good of the whole community, and by no means from any enmity to the upper class,—who are indeed better than one could have thought their circumstances would allow them to be, and who are much more pricked by an uneasy consciousness of being materialised, than the middle class are of being vulgarised, or the lower of being brutalised, —Liberals would do well to set seriously about the reform of our law of bequest and inheritance. Another object for them is the establishment of a system of public schools for the middle class, such as in all other civilised countries it enjoys, but which alike in England and in Ireland is wanting. The *Times* itself, though too prone to 'recognise the futility of contending against rooted prejudices,' is yet 'convinced that one of the best guarantees for the stability and progress of society is the influence of an educated middle class.' The *Times* is indeed here speaking of Ireland, but this influence is just what in England, no less than in Ireland, is so sadly wanting; and the Irish, if they are to be ruled by our middle class, have at least a right to supplicate us, in Mr. Lowe's words, to 'educate their masters.' And the real obstacle to the establishment of public schools for the middle class is, that both the upper and the middle class have a lurking sense that by such schools the middle class would be transformed; and the upper class do not care to be disturbed in their preponderance, or the middle class in their vulgarity. To convince the one resistance of its selfishness, and the other of its folly, should be the aim of all true Liberals. Finally, Liberals should remember that the country districts throughout England have their municipal organisation still to get; that they have at present only the feudal and ecclesiastical organisation of the Middle Ages. Nothing struck me more than this, on my return to England after seeing the Continental schools for the people, and the communal basis on which everything there rested. Our agricultural labourer will doubtless have the franchise, and that is well; but how much more constant and sure a training for him than that of the franchise is the public life in common of a true municipal system universally diffused! To this, rather than to the institution in our country churchyards of readings from Eliza Cook, Liberals might with much advantage turn their thoughts. Still the great work to be done in this country, and at this hour, is not with the lower class, but with the middle; a work of raising its whole level of civilisation, and, in order to do this, of transforming the British Puritan.

Hume relates that the well-known Praise God Barebones had a brother less famous than himself, but with a yet more singular name. He was called: 'If Christ had not died for thee thou wert damned Barebones.'

But to go through all this was a terribly long business, and so the poor man came to be called simply: *Damned Barebones.* And the misfortune of this poor owner of an edifying name comes to one's mind when one thinks of what is happening now to the Puritan middle class. After all its sermons, all its victories, all its virtues, all its care for conduct, all its zeal for righteousness, to be told that it must transform itself, that the body of which it is the nerve and sinew is at a low level of civilisation! But so great and wide a thing is human progress; tentatives, approximations, hold good only for a certain time, and bring us only a certain way on our road; then they have to be changed. Happy the workers whose way and work have to be changed only, not abolished! The Puritan middle class, with all its faults, is still the best stuff in this nation. Some have hated and persecuted it, many have flattered and derided it,—flattered it that while they deride it they may use it; I have believed in it. It is the best stuff in this nation, and in its success is our best hope for the future. But to succeed it must be transformed.

PORRO UNUM EST NECESSARIUM.

An acute French critic says that a wise man's best happiness is to be found, perhaps, in his having the sense *de ne pas être dupe*, of not being taken in. At any rate, we may allow that such happiness is better than none at all, and sometimes it is the only happiness within our reach. Certainly it is the only happiness to which the would-be reformer of secondary instruction in England can at present pretend.

There has just appeared in the French *Journal Officiel* a report by M. Bardoux, the Minister of Public Instruction, on the present state of the secondary schools in France, and on their movement since 1865, the date of a like decennial report on them by M. Duruy. With an interest not unmixed with the sense of defeat and weakness, I have studied this picture of the schools of that immense class of society, which in France has even more greatness and extent than with us,—the middle class. Yes, the schools for this class are indeed, as the

French themselves say, the key-stone of a country's whole system of public instruction : they are what fixes and maintains the intellectual level of a people. And in our country they have been left to come forth as they could and to form themselves at haphazard, and are now, as a whole, in the most serious degree inadequate and unsatisfactory. For some twenty years I have been full of this thought, and have striven to make the British public share it with me ; but quite vainly. At this hour, in Mr. Gladstone's programme of the twenty-two engagements of the Liberal party, there is not a word of middle-class education. Twenty-two Liberal engagements, and the reform of middle-class education not one of them ! What a blow for the declining age of a sincere but ineffectual Liberal, who so long ago as 1859 wrote with faith and ardour the words following,—buried in a blue-book, and now disinterred to show the vanity of human wishes :—

Let me be permitted to call the attention of Englishmen to the advantage which France possesses in its vast system of public secondary instruction ; in its 63 lyceums and 244 communal colleges, inspected by the State, aided by the State ; drawing from this connexion with the State both efficiency and dignity ; and to which, in concert with the State, the departments and the communes and private benevolence all co-operate to provide free admission for poor and deserving scholars. M. de Talleyrand said that the education of the great English public schools was the best in the world. He added, to be sure, that even this was detestable. But allowing it all its merits ; how small a portion of the population does it embrace ! It embraces the aristocratic class, it embraces the higher professional class, it embraces a certain number from the richer families of the commercial class ; from the great body of the commercial class and of the immense middle class of this country, it embraces hardly one. They are left to an education which, though among its professors are many excellent and honourable men, is deplorable. Our middle classes are among the worst educated in the world. But it is not this only ; although, when I consider this, all the French commonplaces about the duty of the State to protect children from the charlatanism and cupidity of individual speculation seem to me to be justified. It is far more that a great opportunity is missed of fusing all the upper and middle classes into one powerful whole, elevating and refining the middle classes by the contact and stimulating the upper. In France this is what the system of public secondary education effects ; it effaces between the middle and upper classes the sense of social alienation ; it gives to the boy of the middle class the studies, the superior teaching, the sense of belonging to a great school, which the Eton or Harrow boy has with us ; it tends to give to the middle classes precisely what they most want, and their want of which makes the great gulf between them and the upper,—it tends to give them personal dignity. The power of such an education is seen in what it has done for the professional classes in England. The clergy, and barristers, and officers of both services, who have commonly passed through the great public schools, are nearly identified in thought, feeling, and manners with the aristocratic class. They have not been unmixed gainers by this identification; it has too much isolated them from a class to which by income and social position they, after all, naturally belong; while towards the highest class it has made them, not vulgarly servile, certainly, but intellectually too deferential, too little apt to maintain entire mental independence on questions where the prepossessions of that class are concerned. Nevertheless they have, as a class, acquired the unspeakable benefit of that elevation of the mind and feelings which it is the best office of superior education to confer. But they have bought this elevation at an immense money-price,—at a price which they can no better than the commercial classes afford to pay; which they who have paid it long, and who know what it has bought for them, will continue to pay while they must, but which the mass of the middle classes will never even begin to pay. Either the education of this mass must remain what it is, vulgar and unsound; or the State must create by its legislation, its aid, its inspection, institutions honourable because of their public character, and cheap because nationally frequented, in which they may receive a better. The French middle classes may well be taxed for the education of the poor, since public provision has already been made for their own education. But already there are complaints among the lower middle classes of this country that the Committee of Council is providing the poor with better schools than those to which they themselves have access. The Education Commissioners would excite, I am convinced, in thousands of hearts a gratitude of which they little dream, if in presenting the result of their labours on primary instruction they were at the same time to say to the government: 'Regard the necessities of a not distant future, and *organise your secondary instruction.*'

The emotions of gratitude here promised were suffered to slumber on unawakened. This was in 1859. In 1865, having again been sent to visit the schools of the Continent, I struck the same note once more:—

Neither is the secondary and superior instruction given in England so good on the whole, if we regard the whole number of those to whom it is due, as that given in Germany or France, nor is it given in schools of so good a standing. Of course, what good instruction there is, and what schools of good standing there are to get it in, fall chiefly to the lot of the upper class. It is on the middle class that the injury, such as it is, of getting inferior instruction, and of getting it in schools of inferior standing, mainly comes. This injury, as it strikes one after seeing attentively the schools of the Continent, has two aspects. It has a social aspect, and it has an intellectual aspect.

The social injury is this. On the Continent the upper and middle class are brought up on one and the same plane. In England the middle class, as a rule, *is brought up on the second plane.* One hears many discussions as to the limits between the middle and the upper class in England. From a social and educational point of view these limits are perfectly clear. Ten or a dozen famous schools, Oxford or

Cambridge, the church or the bar, the army or navy, and those posts in the public service supposed to be posts for gentlemen,—these are the lines of training, all or any of which give a cast of ideas, a stamp or habit, which make a sort of association of all those who share them; and this association is the upper class. Except by one of these modes of access, an Englishman does not, unless by some special play of aptitude or of circumstances, become a vital part of this association, for he does not bring with him the cast of ideas in which its bond of union lies. This cast of ideas is naturally in the main that of the most powerful and prominent part of the association,—the aristocracy. The professions furnish the more numerous but the less prominent part; in no country, accordingly, do the professions so naturally and generally share the cast of ideas of the aristocracy as in England. Judged from its bad side, this cast of ideas is characterised by over-reverence for things established, by an estrangement from the powers of reason and science. Judged from its good side, it is characterised by a high spirit, by dignity, by a just sense of the greatness of great affairs,—all of them governing qualities; and the professions have accordingly long recruited the governing force of the aristocracy, and assisted it to rule. But they are separate, to a degree unknown on the Continent, from the commercial and industrial classes with which in social standing they are naturally on a level. So we have amongst us the spectacle of a middle class cut in two in a way unexampled anywhere else; of a professional class brought up on the first plane, with fine and governing qualities, but disinclined to rely on reason and science; while that immense business class, which is becoming so important a power in all countries, on which the future so much depends, and which in the great public schools of other countries fills so large a place, is in England brought up on the second plane, cut off from the aristocracy and the professions, and without governing qualities.

If only, in compensation, it had science, systematic knowledge, reason! But here comes in the intellectual mischief of the bad condition of the mass of our secondary schools. In England the business class is not only inferior to the professions and aristocracy in the social stamp of its places of training; it is actually inferior to them, maimed and incomplete as their development of reason is, in its development of reason. Short as the offspring of our public schools and universities come of the idea of science and systematic knowledge, the offspring of our middle-class academies probably come, if that be possible, even shorter. What these academies fail to give in social and governing qualities, they do not make up for in intellectual power. Their intellectual result is as faulty as their social result.

If this be true, then that our middle class does not yet itself see the defects of its own education, is not conscious of the injury to itself from them, and is satisfied with things as they are, is no reason for regarding this state of things without disquietude.

Alas, in 1865, it was hardly permissible even to be disquieted at the state of middle-class education! 'We must confess to a feeling of shame,' cried one newspaper, 'at the nonsense which is being uttered on this subject.

It might be thought from what is said, that this section of the community, which has done everything else so well, which has astonished the world by its energy, enterprise, and self-reliance, which is continually striking out new paths of industry and subduing the forces of nature, cannot, from some mysterious reason, get their children properly educated!' 'All the world knows,' cried another, 'that the great middle class of this country supplies the mind, the will, and the power, for all the great and good things that have to be done, and it is not likely that that class should surrender its powers and privileges in the one case of the training of its own children. How the idea of such a scheme can have occurred to anybody, how it can have been imagined that parents and schoolmasters in the most independent and active and enlightened class of English society, how it can have been supposed that the class which has done al the great things that have been done in all departments, will beg the government to send inspectors through the schools, when it can itself command whatever advantages exist, seems almost unintelligible.'

This dithyrambic style about the middle class and its schools has, it is true, been dropped for the last few years. It seems even a little grotesque as one surveys it now; not 'unintelligible' perhaps, but somewhat ridiculous. In this respect there is progress; but still middle-class education remains just as it was. The commercial travellers or the licensed victuallers have the happy thought of making a school entirely for children of commercial travellers or of licensed victuallers, and royal dukes and ministerial earls are still found to go down and bless the young institution, and to glorify the energy and self-reliance of the commercial travellers and the licensed victuallers. A satisfactory system of public secondary schools nobody calls for. It finds, as we have seen, no place among the twenty-two engagements of the Liberal party. The newspapers never touch the subject. Both upper and middle class appear content that their schools should stay as they are. And the enthusiast who has had a vision of better things is left to console himself with what is alleged, certainly, to be the wise man's true satisfaction,—the sense *de ne pas être dupe*, of not being taken in. He has the pleasure, such as it is, of knowing that our body of secondary schools is suffered to remain the most imperfect and unserviceable in civilised Europe, because our upper class does not care to be disturbed in its preponderance, or our middle class in its vulgarity.

A report like that of M. Bardoux is calculated, however, to make the poor enthusiast restless and impatient, to set him asking himself whether the middle class in England is really always to be ruled by the fatal desire not to be disturbed in its vulgarity, whether that class is always to be taken in by grandees extolling this desire as energy and self-reliance, and whether his own only comfort for ever is to consist in not being taken in too. The impulse is irresistible to seek to communicate his impatience to others, and for this end nothing can be more useful, one would think, than simply to retrace the main lines of the picture drawn by M. Bardoux.

The public secondary schools of France are of two kinds,—*lycées*, or lyceums, and communal colleges. The *lycées* are maintained by the State. The communal colleges are maintained by the municipalities, but may be aided by the State. The instruction in both is of the same type, as to its general features, with the instruction given in the great grammar-schools of this country. It is classical, with a side or department called by us modern, by the French special, by the Germans real, intended to suit the requirements of practical life in the present day, by teaching the natural sciences and the modern languages in place of Greek and Latin. Alike in the *lycées* and in the communal colleges, all the teaching staff have to furnish guarantees of their capacity to teach the matters of instruction confided to them. The guarantee takes generally the form of a university degree, varying in kind and in rank according to the post to be filled by the holder.

At the end of 1865, the date to which the report of M. Duruy,—the last report previous to M. Bardoux's,—goes down, France had at work 77 *lycées* and 251 communal colleges. Three of the 77 *lycées* (those of Strasburg, Metz, and Colmar), and 15 of the 251 communal colleges, have been lost to France in consequence of the war of 1870. But new ones have in the meanwhile been added, so that on the 31st of December, 1876, the date to which M. Bardoux's report comes down, France had 81 *lycées* at work, with 5 others building, and 252 communal colleges. If we deduct Strasburg, Metz, and Colmar, which are not now part of the territory of France, the French *lycées*, in 1865, had 31,321 pupils. At the end of 1876 they had, for the same extent of territory, 40,995 pupils,—an average of 506 pupils to each *lycée*, about half of whom are boarders and half day-boys. The communal colleges had in 1865 a total number of 32,881 pupils, with an average of 131 pupils to each college; at the end of 1876 they had 38,236 pupils, with an average of 152 for each college.

Eighty-one great secondary schools of the first class, two hundred and fifty-two of the second, all of them with a public character, all of them under inspection, all of them offering guarantees of the capacity of their teaching staff! and in these schools a total of 79,241 scholars!

Let us note, in passing, that the modern or special instruction in these schools is constantly growing. The *lycées* are the stronghold of the classics; yet in the *lycées* the number of boys on the modern side had risen from 5,002 at the end of 1865 to 8,628 at the end of 1876, and the average number of such scholars for each *lycée* from 71 to 107. The teaching of the natural sciences, of the living languages, of geography, modern history, and literature, is being continually strengthened. The class of pupils receiving special preparation in the *lycées* for schools such as the Polytechnic, Saint Cyr, the Naval, Central, and Forest Schools, steadily increases. In the communal colleges the development of the modern side is much greater still, and is extremely remarkable. Of the 38,236 pupils in these colleges at the end of 1876, 9,232 are little boys not yet going beyond primary instruction; of the remainder, 14,992 are on the classical side, and very nearly as many, 14,012, are on the modern. The number of teacherships for the modern languages has more than doubled in these colleges since 1865.

But I am not here writing for schoolmasters and specialists, for whose benefit, indeed, I have formerly given a full account of the French secondary schools, of their organisation and teaching. I am writing now for that great public which is interested in the provision of secondary schools for its children; the broad plain lines of the subject are all that they will care for, and are what I shall keep to. I repeat, then: 81 *lycées*, 252 communal colleges, with a total of nearly 80,000 scholars; a modern side established, and constantly growing; all the schools under inspection, and of all their teachers guarantees of capacity required.

As to the quality of the instruction, it is at the same general level as the instruction in our great secondary schools which are called public. In Greek it is not so strong. In Latin it is much on a par with ours, though with a nearer sense of the Latin language, because of its affinity with the French. In modern languages it is, again, much on a par with our instruction. In arithmetic and mathematics, in the natural sciences, in modern history, and above all in knowledge of the mother-tongue and its literature, it is stronger. The boarders are fed and lodged in a different mode from the boarders of our public schools, but, in my opinion, quite as well. They are, however, more confined and harder worked, and have less freedom, air, and exercise. This is a disadvantage. But it comes from the dangers of confinement and study for boys being less apprehended, the good of play for them less valued, in the whole body of Continental schools, whether public or private, than they are by us all in England.

I pass from the public secondary schools to the private,—the *écoles libres*, as the French call them. This part of the subject has a peculiar interest for us in England, because our secondary instruction is in so large a measure supplied by private adventure schools. In France the private secondary schools are of two kinds, lay and ecclesiastical. There were 803 of them at the end of 1876. But in these schools, as a whole, we do not find the progressive advance in numbers which we find in the public schools; we find, on the contrary, a progressive diminution. In 1854 the private secondary schools in France numbered 1,081; in 1865 they numbered 935; in 1876 their number had fallen to 803. And it is in the lay establishments that the diminution has taken place; the ecclesiastical establishments are more in number than formerly. But whereas the lay establishments in 1854 were as many as 825,—more than the whole number of private secondary schools at the present day,—in 1865 they had fallen to 657, in 1876 to 494. The ecclesiastical establishments in 1854 numbered 256; in 1865, 278; in 1876, 309. From 1806, when the University of France was instituted, down to 1850, private establishments for secondary instruction could not exist. All the secondary schools belonged to the University, a State-institution, and all the teachers in them were its functionaries. The law of March the 15th, 1850, the organic law which at present governs public instruction in France, was conceived in a spirit of dissatisfaction with this exclusive rule of the University, and permitted the opening, upon certain conditions, of private schools. The result has been, as we have seen, favourable especially to the growth of ecclesiastical establishments, and it disquiets French Liberals exceedingly. It deserves investigation and discussion, but I must abstain from everything of that kind here. The lay private schools had in 1865, eleven years after the passing of the new law, 43,009 scholars to the 34,897 of their ecclesiastical rivals. The proportion is now reversed, and the ecclesiastical private schools have 46,816 pupils, while the lay private schools have but 31,249.

The ecclesiastical schools are either under episcopal control, or they belong to one of the teaching orders, amongst whom the Jesuits have the chief place. Both the episcopal schools and the *congreganist* schools, as they are called, have increased in number, but the congreganist schools are by far the more numerous and important division. They have nearly 20,000 pupils.

The episcopal schools have 12,300. A third class of establishments under ecclesiastical direction is formed by schools under the secular Catholic clergy or under ministers of other religious denominations. Of these schools the non-Catholic form a quite insigificant proportion; they are but 13 out of 165. But this whole class of schools has decreased in number since 1865, while the episcopal and congreganist schools keep increasing. And this, again, is a matter of disquietude to French Liberals, who consider the influence of the secular clergy as less unfavourable to independence of thought than episcopal influence or the influence of the teaching orders. And strong discontent is expressed with the law of March, 1850, which has rendered such a development of episcopal and congreganist schools possible.

For the present, however, let us not be diverted by this contest between liberalism and clericalism from what is the central point of interest for us,—the actual supply in France of a sound secondary instruction, apart from all question of the religious bias given. In these private establishments for instruction of which we have been speaking, no less than in the public, guarantees are taken for its soundness. A private or free school in France is not free in the sense that any man may keep one who likes. The head of such a school must be at least twenty-five years old, must have had five years' practice in school-keeping, and must hold either the University degree of bachelor, or a certificate which is given after an examination of the same nature as the examination required for the degree of bachelor. His school is, moreover, under government inspection as regards its state of commodiousness, healthiness, and repair. These are serious guarantees. And, in fact, by them and by other causes which co-operate with them, the soundness of the secular instruction in the *écoles libres* is sufficiently secured. The secular instruction, having the degree of bachelor or the admission to government schools, such as the Polytechnic, in view, cannot but follow in general the same line as that of the public secondary schools. Some of the schools of the religious, such as the Jesuits' school at Vaugirard, and the school in the Rue des Postes, are in direct competition with the Paris *lycées*, and in very successful competition. They employ, along with their own teachers, the best lay instructors accessible, often the very same whom the *lycées* employ. Whatever clerical influence may be superadded to it, the secular instruction in the schools of the teaching orders, and in the *écoles libres* in general, does not fall below the ordinary level of this instruction in the public schools.

It is true that, owing to a recent law permitting the formation of free Catholic universities and recognising their degrees, the degree required for those who conduct free secondary schools can now be obtained from bodies not of public appointment or public responsibility. Undoubtedly, new and denominational universities, in which the professors are not of public appointment, ought not to be entrusted with power to confer degrees. The law in question is said to have been obtained by accident; an overwhelming majority of the Legislative Assembly are for its repeal, and after the next elections to the Senate it will certainly, people say, be repealed. But whatever the demerits of that law may be, it has not been in operation long enough to affect injuriously the standard of secular instruction. Secular instruction in the private schools remains in general, as I have said already, at the same level as in the public schools. Before the level can have been lowered by the inferior standard for degrees (if it is inferior) of the free Catholic universities, those universities will have lost the power of granting them.

But I grudge every word which is here given to these questions of religious politics, so attractive to the middle-class Englishman, so fatally apt to divert his mind from what is the point of cardinal importance for him, the one thing needful. For him the point to be seized and set in clear light, and again and again to be insisted upon until seized and set in clear light it is, is this: that while we have not more than 20,000 boys in Great Britain and Ireland receiving a secondary instruction which can in any possible sense be said to offer guarantees for its efficiency, France has 79,231 boys receiving secondary instruction in inspected public schools, and 78,065 more who are receiving it in schools giving public guarantees for their efficiency. It is this: that whereas in England the middle class is brought up on the second plane, in France the middle class is brought up on the first plane.

In 1865 there was published a statement by which it appeared that we had in England, counting not only the nine great public schools which formed the subject of an inquiry by a Royal Commission, but counting also all the important endowed schools of the country, and all the important schools of recent foundation, such as Cheltenham and Marlborough,—that we had in all these taken together a total number of scholars amounting, in round figures, to 16,000. Let us consider all these schools as being sufficiently in the public eye to afford, through that very publicity, guarantees for their efficiency. Let us add 4,000 scholars more. We remember the picture which was the other day officially drawn for us of the secondary schools of Ireland. In Scotland, deservedly celebrated for its elementary schools, the secondary schools of high standing and character are few in number. But both Ireland and Scotland make considerable use of the English secondary schools. If we add 4,000 for increase in England since 1865, and for Scotland and Ireland, and put at 20,000 our total number of boys under secondary instruction which may be called guaranteed, we make a liberal estimate. In France they have 157,296.

The middle class in France has, in consequence, a homogeneity, an extent, and an importance, which it has nowhere else. 'It is our middle class in France,' says M. Bardoux, 'which makes the *grandeur et originalité*, the greatness and originality, of the nation.' Above the peasant and artisan, the class who live by the labour of their hands and who are the subjects for elementary instruction, the rest of the nation consists, for all intents and purposes, of one immense class who are subjects for secondary instruction, and who receive it of one equal quality and in schools of one equal standing. The professions and that whole class which Mr. Charles Sumner distinguishes as the class of gentlemen are in England separated from the great bulk of the middle class, and are brought up along with the aristocracy in a superior order of schools. In France the professions and the great bulk of the middle class are brought up in schools of one equal standing. This creates a middle class larger, more homogeneous, and better educated than ours. The French aristocracy are chiefly brought up at Vaugirard and at schools under ecclesiastics. I have no prejudice against schools under ecclesiastics, and Vaugirard is an excellent school. But Vaugirard is not a school with better instruction and of higher standing than the great public schools used by the middle class. It stands to them not as with us Eton and Harrow stand to a middle-class academy, but rather as Stonyhurst stands to Eton and Harrow. The aristocracy in France, therefore, is not a class which, in addition to its advantages of birth and wealth over the middle class, has received a higher training than the middle class, in schools of a superior standing. Aristocracy and middle class are brought up in schools of one equal standing. The French aristocracy has, it is true, the spirit of caste; it strives to separate itself, to assert its superiority, to give effect to its prepossessions. But the immense homogeneous middle class in France is too strong for it. The mind and imagination of this class is not subjugated by aristocracy like the mind and imagination of the middle class in our country. The mere comparison of the governments of the two countries at the present moment is evidence enough of the truth of what I say. In England the government is composed of a string of aristocratical personages, with one or two men from the professional class who are engaged with them, and a man of genius of whom it is not easy to say whether he is engaged with them or they with him. In France the government is composed entirely of men from the professional and middle class. True, the difference between the two aristocracies in property and standing, since the French Revolution, accounts for much of the difference in political influence. But the training of the middle class in France counts for more. Its great mass has not, as with us, the sense of an inferior training. It is not cut in two, as with us; it is homogeneous. And this immense homogeneous class is brought up in schools of as good standing as those of the aristocracy; it is brought up on the first plane. It is possible and producible.

The Exhibition has this year drawn English people over to Paris in great numbers. They have had the astonishing beauty of Paris, and the civilisation and prosperity of the French people, brought close before their eyes, and they have been struck by it. Prince Bismarck says, we know, that the French nation has a social solidity such as no other nation of Europe enjoys. This can only come from the broad basis of well-being, and of cause for satisfaction with life, which in France, more than in other European countries, exists. We have the testimony of the Belgian economist, M. de Laveleye, to the superior well-being of the French peasant, and we ought not to be tired of repeating it to ourselves over and over again, that we may get it well fixed in our minds. 'France is the country of Europe,' says M. de Laveleye, 'where the soil is more divided than anywhere else except in Switzerland and Norway, and it is at the same time the country where material well-being is most widely spread, where wealth has of late years increased most, and where population is least outrunning the limits which, for the comfort and progress of the working classes themselves, seem necessary.' And Mr. Hamerton, an acute observer, and an Englishman to boot, has remarked on 'the enormous interval,' as he calls it, by which the French peasant is raised above the Kentish labourer. Thus much for the lower class in France, and for its causes of satisfaction with life. And if we consider the beauty and the ever-advancing perfection of Paris,—nay, and the same holds good, in its degree, of all the other great French cities also,—if we consider the theatre there, if we consider the pleasures, recreations, even the eating and drinking, if we consider the whole range of resources for instruction and for delight and for the conveniences of a humane life generally, and if we then think of London, and Liverpool, and Glasgow, and of the life of English towns generally, we shall find that the advantage of France arises from its immense middle class making the same sort of demands upon life which only a small upper class makes elsewhere.

Delicate and gifted single natures are sown in all countries. The French aristocracy will not bear a moment's comparison for splendour and importance with ours, neither have the French our exceptional class, registered by Mr. Charles Sumner, of gentlemen. But these are, after all, only two relatively small divisions broken off from the top of that whole great class which does not live by the labour of its hands. These small divisions make upon life the demands of humane and civilised men. But they are too small and too weak to create a civilisation, to make a Paris. The great bulk of the class from which they are broken off makes, as is well known, no such demands upon life. London, Liverpool, and Glasgow, with their kind of building, physiognomy, and effects, with their theatres, pleasures, recreations, and resources in general of delight and convenience for a humane life, are the result. But in France the whole middle class makes, I say, upon life the demands of civilised men, and this immense demand creates the civilisation we see. And the joy of this civilisation creates the passionate delight and pride in France which we find in Frenchmen. Life is so good and agreeable a thing there, and for so many.

French society has, in my opinion, whatever Prince Bismarck may say, sources of great danger as well as of great strength. English society has its sources of great strength as well as its sources of danger. But I am calling attention now to one single point in the social condition of the two nations,—to the demand which the middle class, in each of them, makes upon life, and to the results which flow from it. It is surely impossible to deny that the whole immense middle class in France makes upon life the demands which are elsewhere those of a limited upper class only, and that French civilisation gains enormously in both volume and quality by this being so. It is not difficult, of course, in England, for one of the aristocratic class, or for one of the class of gentlemen, to see that our middle class rests satisfied with a defective type of religion, a narrow range of intellect and knowledge, a stunted sense of beauty, a low standard of manners. But an ordinary Frenchman of the middle class sees it just as clearly as any great lord or refined gentleman sees it with us, because his standard of civilisation is so comparatively high. It is not the French aristocracy and professions, it is the whole French middle class, which is astonished at the pleasures of the gay and pleasure-seeking portion of our middle class. It is not the French aristocracy and professions, it is the whole French middle class, which is astonished at the hideousness and immense ennui of the life of the graver portion. 'The sense of acute ennui which the aspect and frequentation of this great division of English society produce in others, the want of elasticity and the chronic ennui which characterise this class itself'—that is not an expression of the feeling merely of a fastidious upper class or of a superfine individual, it is the genuine sentiment of the mass of middle-class France.

The French middle class is called Voltairian, as the French University and its schools, in which the middle class is educated, are called Voltairian too. Voltairian the French middle class in the main is. A great deal may be said in dispraise of Voltaire. But this is his centenary year; it is a hundred years ago this year since he died. *Il avait beaucoup travaillé dans ce monde*, as Michelet says of our own Henry the Fifth;—'he had done a big spell of work in this world;' and of the indefatigable worker let us on this occasion speak good rather than evil. He looked at things straight, and he had a marvellous logic and lucidity. The *Morning Star*, I remember, which has passed away from amongst us, used to say that what characterises Englishmen, and, above all, Englishmen of the middle class, is 'clear, manly intelligence, which penetrates through sophisms, ignores commonplaces, and gives to conventional illusions their true value.' And the French, in like manner, the French middle class above all, pique themselves on their logic and lucidity. The French mind craves it, the French language almost compels it; Voltaire, the French Luther of the eighteenth century, was a splendid professor and propagator of it. And to a middle-class Frenchman it seems a matter of the plainest reasoning in the world, that the civilisation of the middle class must suffer in England and thrive in France. 'Equality,' he thinks with M. Gambetta, 'is in France the source of all our strength in the present, of all our good hope for the future.' England has, in Mr. Gladstone's famous words, the religion of inequality. 'With your enormous inequality of conditions and property,' our Frenchman would say, 'a middle class is naturally thrown back upon itself and upon an inferior type of social life and of civilisation. Add to this your want of public schools for this class, and that it is brought up anyhow, brought up in hugger-mugger, brought up on the second plane ;--its being thrown back upon an inferior type of social life and of civilisation is an irresistible necessity. In France we have got equality, and we bring up our middle class on the first plane ; hence French civilisation.' And the *Morning Star*, which should have answered this man of logic and lucidity, and should have shown why it is the part of the clear manly intelligence of Englishmen, which penetrates through sophisms, ignores commonplaces, and gives to conventional illusions their true value, rather to insist on introducing readings from Eliza Cook into our public churchyards, or on legalising marriage with a deceased wife's sister, than to abate our enormous in-equality of conditions and property, or to provide schools for bringing up our middle class on the first plane instead of the second,—the *Morning Star*, I say, is unhappily defunct.

And if, in the regretted absence of that powerful dis-putant, our man of logic and lucidity were to be told by some ingenuous person that after all we were not all of us, in England, satisfied with the state of our secondary in-struction, although our aristocratic class and our middle class itself apparently were, but that there was a project on foot for bettering it, and if our Frenchman were then to ask what it was,—what should we say? We should say that a generous and humane soul, a lover of light and perfection, detached from the prepossessions both of the aristocratic and of the middle class, and not willing that our middle class should continue to be the worst schooled in civilised Europe, had adopted a bill which he found waiting for some one to take charge of it and to put it forward, and which he hoped might improve matters if it could become law; that his name was Playfair, and that he was member for the University of Edinburgh. And Dr. Playfair's bill proposes, we should say, to form a Council of Public Instruction such as exists in France, and to give power to this council to send its inspectors into endowed schools, and to offer to send its inspectors into schools which are not endowed, if the schools like to receive them. For not even a generous and humane soul, we should have to say, such as Dr. Playfair, thinks it possible to attempt in England, for the rescue of the middle class from its state of inferior schooling, more than this. And our man of logic and lucidity would certainly reply, that this was like attempting to cure our enormous inequality of conditions and property by the Real Estates Intestacy Bill; that the real *objective* for us, as the military phrase is, was the bringing up of the middle class on the first plane, not the second, and that this is not to be done by inspecting a certain number of schools whether they will or no, and offering to inspect others if they like it, but by creating a system of public secondary schools.

And certainly, as a matter of fact, a plan of annual examination of secondary schools by inspectors, such as that which we have in elementary schools, does not seem likely in itself to work well and smoothly, while at the same time it fails, as the Frenchman says, to bring us to what is our real objective. The examination of secondary schools by inspectors is a matter of far greater difficulty and delicacy than the examination of elementary schools, is far more likely to produce impatience and opposition among the schoolmasters subjected to it, and is really far less necessary. All our good secondary schools have at present some examination proceeding from the universities; and if this kind of examination, customary and admitted already, were generalised and regularised, it would be sufficient for the purpose. What is really needed is to follow the precedent of the Elementary Education Act, by requiring the provision throughout the country of a proper supply of secondary schools, with proper buildings and accommodations, at a proper fee, and with proper guarantees given by the teachers in the shape either of a university degree or of a special certificate for secondary instruction. An inquiry, as under that Act, would have to be made as to the fulfilment of the necessary conditions by the actual schools now professing to meet the demand for secondary instruction, and as to the correspondence of the supply of schools fulfilling those conditions with the supply fixed after due calculation as requisite. The existing resources for secondary instruction, if judiciously co-ordered and utilised, would prove to be immense; but undoubtedly gaps would have to be filled, an annual State grant and municipal grants would be necessary. That is to say, the nation would perform, as a corporate and co-operative work, a work which is now never conceived and laid out as a whole, but is done sporadically, precariously, and insufficiently. We have had experience how elementary instruction gains by being thus conceived and laid out, instead of being left to individual adventure or individual benevolence. The middle class who contribute so immense a share of the cost incurred for the public institution of elementary schools, while their own school supply is so miserable, would be repaid twenty times over for their share in the additional cost of publicly instituting secondary instruction by the direct benefit which they and theirs would get from its system of schools. The upper class, which has bought out the middle class at so many of the great foundation schools designed for its benefit, and which has monopolised what good secondary instruction we have, owes to the middle class the reparation of contributing to a public system of secondary schools. Perhaps *secondary* is a bad word to use, because it is equivocal. Intermediate is a better. A system of public intermediate schools we require to have throughout the country, of two grades, the classical side predominating in the schools of one grade, the modern side in the other; where for a fee of from 30*l.* to 50*l.* a year for boarders, and from 10*l.* to 20*l.* a year for day boys, the middle class might obtain education. All existing schools which give, under proper guarantees, secondary instruction, should be classed as public intermediate schools. Nor should their scale of fees be interfered with. But it should be calculated for what proportion of the class requiring secondary instruction schools with such fees can be considered to make provision. For the proportion remaining,—for the great bulk, that is, of the middle class,—provision ought to be found or made at the lower rates.

The intervention and inspection of government should be limited to the following points mainly. First, to inquiring and announcing what is the provision requisite, to taking care that within a certain time it is supplied, and that when supplied it is maintained. Secondly, to ascertaining that the teaching staff is provided with the degrees or certificates prescribed as a public guarantee of efficiency, that some examination of the schools by other teachers than their own, an examination proceeding either from the universities or from some recognised scholastic authority, takes place in them every year, and that the school premises are sufficient, suitably fitted and kept, and wholesome. Inspection of this kind is the function of a ministerial department rather than of a council, and it is not of a nature to irritate schoolmasters' susceptibilities.

The function of a council is consultative: to consider and advise as to methods and studies. The function is a very important one. But a Council of Public Instruction is generally a body framed so as to represent several great interests. It is so in France, at any rate. And the consequence is, I believe, that instead of there being much consideration of school methods and studies, the interests generally break out and begin a war, religious, professional, or administrative, amongst themselves; and the minister finds it expedient to convoke and consult his council as little as possible.

It is not always quite easy to follow our French friends, men of logic and lucidity though they may be, when they are singing the glories of the ideas of 1789. But the French system of public secondary instruction is one of the real, one of the best conquests of 1789 and of the Revolution. Decreed and begun by the Convention, organised by Fourcroy's law in 1802, secured by the establishment of the University in 1806, this system provides effective schooling, and on one common plane, for the whole class requiring an instruction more than elementary; while with the elementary schools it connects itself in an unbroken order, offering a second stage by which the new social strata, as M. Gambetta calls them, may move onward, if they are worthy, and may rise. And our want of any such system in England is like the want of any municipal system for our country parishes, where the mode of government by vestry answers to that in use formerly in the rural districts of France, and described by Turgot: a kind of mass-meeting of the parishioners held by the curé in the churchyard after service. Both wants are due to what Thiers was never weary of pointing out as matter for remark and reflexion: the purely political character of our revolutions; the absence from them,—the unavoidable and irreproachable absence it may be, but still the absence,—of all aim at social renovation.

Schools for the licensed victuallers, schools for the

commercial travellers, schools for the Wesleyans, schools for the Quakers,—to educate a middle class in this way is to doom it to grow up on an inferior plane, with the claims of intellect and knowledge not satisfied, the claim of beauty not satisfied, the claim of manners not satisfied. At a very great money-price the upper class has got possession of what public secondary schools of good standing there are, and does not feel bound to lend its endeavours towards stripping itself of the advantage which this higher training gives to it. That an upper class should not care to be disturbed in its preponderance is perhaps natural; that a middle class should acquiesce in a state of things which dooms it to inferiority does at first sight seem astonishing. Yet we ought not to be too much astonished at it, for human nature resists instinctively any change in its habits. And an English middle class brought up in public schools and on the first plane, an English middle class homogeneous, intelligent, civilised, would undergo more than some slight and partial change of habits. It would undergo transformation. A transformation devoutly to be wished, indeed, yet so vast a one that the wise man may be inclined to shrink from the toil of trying single-handed to bring it to pass,—may content himself with not being made a dupe of, not being taken in, when he is told that it is undesirable and impossible.

And yet if all those generous and humane souls, free from the prepossessions of class, who are scattered about in every society, were to turn their thoughts this way, and to see what is the truth, that perhaps our chief and gravest want in this country at present, our *unum necessarium*, is a middle class homogeneous, intelligent, civilised, brought up in good public schools and on the first plane, something surely might be done!

Mr. Lowe says that 'an English government should be guided simply by the consideration how to produce for the country the greatest amount of happiness of which the condition of its existence admits.' Mr. Gladstone says that 'with the true Liberal statesman, England's first care is held to be the care of her own children within her own shores, the redress of wrongs, the supply of needs, the improvement of laws and institutions.' If there is one thing more certain than another, it is this: that the middle class is in France *happier* than with us. If there is one need more crying than another, it is the need of the English middle class to be rescued from a defective type of religion, a narrow range of intellect and knowledge, a stunted sense of beauty, a low standard of manners. And what could do so much to deliver them and to render them happier, as to give them proper education, public education, to bring them up on the first plane; to make them a class homogeneous, intelligent, civilised? Nay, and our upper class itself, though it may be supposed to be not naturally inclined to lend a hand to deprive itself of preponderance, has far too much public spirit not to be concerned and disquieted if it really comes to see that our civilisation is maimed by our middle class being left as it is, and that the whole country, the whole English nation, suffers by it. Where is there in the world an upper class which has in it so many who know well that it will not do for a man simply to think of himself,—to aggrandise himself; that a man must be *in commune bonus*, good with a goodness serviceable to the common cause? And this is just what is required of every worthier soul amongst our upper classes; that in the matter of middle-class education he should be *in commune bonus*, good with a goodness serviceable to the common cause:—

> Nec sibi, sed toti genitum se credere mundo . . .
> Justitiæ cultor, rigidi servator honesti,
> *In commune bonus.*

A GUIDE TO ENGLISH LITERATURE.

PEOPLE repeat, till one is almost tired of hearing it, the story of the French Minister of Instruction who took out his watch and said complacently to a foreigner, that at that moment, in all the public grammar-schools of France, all boys of the same class were saying the same lesson. In England the story has been eagerly used to disparage State-meddling with schools. I have never been able to see that it was in itself so very lamentable a thing that all these French boys should be saying the same lesson at the same time. Everything, surely, depends upon what the lesson was. Once secure what is excellent to be taught, and you can hardly teach it with too much insistence, punctuality, universality. The more one sees of the young, the more one is struck with two things: how limited is the amount which they can really learn, how worthless is much of what goes to make up this amount now. Mr. Grant Duff, misled by his own accomplishments and intelligence, is, I am convinced, far too encyclopædic in his requirements from young learners. But the heart-breaking thing is, that what they *can* be taught and *do* learn is often so ill-chosen. 'An apple has a stalk, peel, pulp, core, pips, and juice; it is odorous and opaque, and is used for making a pleasant drink called cider.' There is the pedant's fashion of using the brief lesson-time, the soon-tired attention, of little children. How much, how far too much, of all our course of tuition, early and late, is of like value!

For myself, I lament nothing more in our actual instruction than its multiformity,—a multiformity, too often, of false direction and useless labour. I desire nothing so much for it as greater uniformity,—but uniformity in good. Nothing is taught well except what is known familiarly and taught often The Greeks used to say: Δὶς ἢ τρὶς τὰ καλά,—Give us a fine thing two and three times over! And they were right.

In literature we have present, and waiting ready to form us, the best which has been thought and said in the world. Our business is to get at this best and to know it well. But even to understand the thing we are dealing with, and to choose the best in it, we need a guide, a clue. The literature most accessible to all of us, touching us most nearly, is our own literature, English literature. To get at the best in English literature and to know that best well, nothing can be more helpful to us than a guide who will show us, in clear view, the growth of our literature, its series of productions, and their relative value. If such a guide is good and trustworthy, his instructions cannot be too widely brought into use, too diligently studied, too thoroughly fixed in the mind.

But to deserve such universal acceptance and such heedful attention our guide ought to have special qualifications. He ought to be clear. He ought to be brief,—as brief as is consistent with not being dry. For dry he must not be; but we should be made to feel, in listening to him, as much as possible of the power and charm of the literature to which he introduces us. His discourse, finally, ought to observe strict proportion and to observe strict sobriety. He should have one scale and should keep to it. And he should severely eschew all violence and exaggeration; he should avoid, in his judgments, even the least appearance of what is arbitrary, personal, fantastic.

Mr. Stopford Brooke has published a little book entitled *A Primer of English Literature.* I have read it with the most lively interest and pleasure. I have just been saying how very desirable is a good guide to

English literature, and what are a good guide's qualifications. Mr. Stopford Brooke seems to me to possess them all. True, he has some of them in a higher degree than others. He is never dry, never violent; but occasionally he might, I think, be clearer, shorter, in more perfect proportion, more thoroughly true of judgment. To say this is merely to say that in a most difficult task, that of producing a book to serve as a guide to English literature, a man does not reach perfection all at once. The great thing was to produce a primer so good as Mr. Stopford Brooke's. It is easy to criticise it when it has once been produced, easy to see how in some points it might have been made better. To produce it at all, so good as it is, was not easy. On the whole, and compared with other workmen in the same field, Mr. Stopford Brooke has been clear, short, interesting, observant of proportion, free from exaggeration and free from arbitrariness Yet with the book lying before one as a whole, one can see, I think, that with respect to some of these merits the work might be brought to a point of excellence higher than that at which it now stands. Mr. Stopford Brooke will not, I am sure, take it amiss if an attentive and gratified reader of his book, convinced of the great importance of what it attempts, convinced of its merits, desirous to see it in every one's hands,—he will not take it ill, I say, if such a reader asks his leave to go rapidly through the book with him, to point out what seem imperfections, to suggest what might bring his book yet nearer towards the ideal of what such a book should be.

I will begin at the beginning, and will suggest that Mr. Stopford Brooke should leave out his first two pages, the pages in which he lays down what literature is, and what its two main divisions (as he calls them), prose and poetry, are. His primer is somewhat long, longer than most primers. It is a gain to shorten it by expunging anything superfluous. And the reader does not require to be told what literature is, and what prose and poetry are. For all practical purposes he knows this sufficiently well already. Or even if he were in doubt about it, Mr. Stopford Brooke's two pages would not make the matter much clearer to him; they are a little embarrassed themselves, and tend to embarrass the attentive reader. And a primer, at any rate, should be above all things quite plain and clear; it should contain nothing to embarrass its reader, nothing not perfectly thought out and lucidly laid down. So I wish Mr. Stopford Brooke would begin his primer with what is now the fourth section: 'The history of English literature is the story of what English men and women thought and felt, and then wrote down in good prose or beautiful poetry in the English language. The story is a long one. It begins about the year 670 and it is still going on in the year 1875. Into this little book, then, is to be put the story of 1,200 years.' Nothing can be better.

The sentence which follows is questionable :—

> No people that have ever been in the world can look back so far as we English can to the beginnings of our literature ; no people can point to so long and splendid a train of poets and prose-writers, no nation has on the whole written so much and so well.

The first part of this sentence makes an assertion of very doubtful truth ; the second part is too much to the tune of *Rule Britannia.* Both parts offend against sobriety. The four cardinal virtues which are, as I have said, to be required in the writer of a primer of English literature are these : clearness, brevity, proportion, sobriety. Sobriety needs to be insisted upon, perhaps, the most, because in things meant, and rightly meant, to be popular, there is such danger of sinning against it. Anything of questionable and disputed truth, even though we may fairly hold it and in a longer performance might fairly lay it down and defend it, is out of place in a primer. It is an offence against sobriety to insert it there. And let Mr. Stopford Brooke ask himself what foreigner, or who except an Englishman, would admit that 'no people can point to so long and splendid a train of poets and prose-writers as the English people, no nation has on the whole written so much and so well?' Nay, it is not every Englishman who, with Greece before his eyes, would admit it. What follows is in a truer strain, in the right strain for a guide to take :—

Every English man and woman has good reason to be proud of the work done by their forefathers in prose and poetry. Every one who can write a good book or a good song may say to himself: 'I belong to a great company which has been teaching and delighting men for more than a thousand years.' And that is a fact in which those who write and those who read ought to feel a noble pride.

This is unquestionable, and it is sufficient.

Nothing, in a task like Mr. Stopford Brooke's, is more difficult than the start, and it was natural, therefore, that his first page or two should be peculiarly open to criticism. Once started, Mr. Stopford Brooke proceeds safely and smoothly, and page after page is read with nothing but acquiescence. His first chapter is excellent, and has that great merit for which his primer is, as I have said, conspicuous : the merit of so touching men and works of which the young reader, and the general reader, knows and can be expected to know very little, as to make them cease to be mere names ;—as to give a real sense of their power and charm. His manner of dealing with Cædmon and Bede is a signal instance of this. I shall not quote the passage, because I wish to quote presently another passage with the like merit, in which Mr. Stopford Brooke is even happier: the passage where he treats of Chaucer.

In the second chapter there is in several places a want of clearness, due to a manner of writing which leaves something to be filled out and completed by the reader himself. This task should not be thrown upon readers of a primer. 'The last memoranda of the Peterborough Chronicle are of the year 1154, the last English Charter can scarcely be earlier than 1155.' Mr. Stopford Brooke gives these words as a quotation, but it is not fully clear how they relate themselves to the context, or exactly what is to be deduced from them. In another instance, the want of clearness arises from an attempt to give a piece of information by the way, and because the piece of information seems to be a part of the argument, but is not. 'The first friars were foreigners, and they necessarily used many French words in their English teaching, and Normans as well as English now began to write religious works in English.' The point to be made out is that English came into greater use because even foreigners had for certain purposes to adopt it. Mr. Stopford Brooke wishes to inform by the way his young reader, that the foreigners in doing so used many French words. But the manner in which he throws this in must cause puzzle; for the young reader imagines it to lead up somehow to the main point that English came into more general use, and it does not. Or the want of clearness arises from something being put forward, about which Mr. Stopford Brooke, after he has put it forward, feels hesitation. 'The poem marks the close of the religious influence of the friars. They had been attacked before in a poem of 1320; but in this poem there is not a word said against them. It is true, the author living far in the country may not have been thrown much with them.' Mr. Stopford Brooke means here, so far as I understand him, to imply that there not being a word said against the friars in the poem in question marks the close of their religious influence. That is rather a subtle inference for a young reader to follow. Mr. Stopford Brooke, however, seems to feel (for I am really not quite sure that I understand him) that he may have been too subtle; and he adds: 'It is true, the author living far in the country may not have been thrown much with them.' That is to say: 'If you consider the thing more subtly, perhaps you had better not make the inference I have suggested.' A subtlety requiring immediately to be relieved by another subtlety, is rather too much for a young reader. The writer of a primer should attempt to convey nothing but what can be conveyed in a quite plain and straightforward fashion.

But presently we come to Layamon's *Brut*, and here we see how admirably Mr. Stopford Brooke understands his business. It is not difficult to be dull in speaking of Layamon's *Brut*, or even in quoting from it. But what Mr. Stopford Brooke says of Layamon and his work is just what every one will feel interested in hearing of them; and what he quotes is exactly what will complete and enhance this feeling of interest :—

'There was a priest in the land,' Layamon writes of himself, 'whose name was Layamon; he was son of Leovenath; may the Lord be gracious unto him! He dwelt at Earnley, a noble church on the bank of Severn, near Radstone, where he read books. It came in mind to him and in his chiefest thought that he would tell the noble deeds of England, what the men were named, and whence they came, who first had English land.'

Freshness of touch, a treatment always the very opposite of the pedant's treatment of things, make the great charm of Mr. Stopford Brooke's work. He owes them, no doubt, to his genuine love for nature and poetry :—

In 1300 we meet with a few lyric poems, full of charm. They sing of spring-time with its blossoms, of the woods ringing with the thrush and nightingale, of the flowers and the seemly sun, of country work, of the woes and joy of love, and many other delightful things.

No such secret of freshness as delight in all these 'delightful things' and in the poetry which tells of them!

This second chapter, giving the history of English literature from the Conquest to Chaucer, is admirably proportioned. The personages come in due order, the humblest not without his due word of introduction; the chief figures pause awhile and stand clear before us, each in his due degree of prominence. To do justice to the charm of Mr. Stopford Brooke's primer, let the reader turn to the pages on Chaucer. Something I must quote from them; I wish I could quote all!

Chaucer's first and great delight was in human nature, and he makes us love the noble characters in his poems, and feel with kindliness towards the baser and ruder sort. He never sneers, for he had a wide charity, and we can always smile in his pages at the follies and forgive the sins of men. He had a true and chivalrous regard for women, and his wife and he must have been very happy if they fulfilled the ideal he had of marriage. He lived in aristocratic society, and yet he thought him the greatest gentleman who was 'most vertuous alway, Privé and pert (open), and most entendeth aye To do the gentil dedes that he can.' He lived frankly among men, and, as we have seen, saw many different types of men, and in his own time filled many parts as a man of the world and of business. Yet with all this active and observant life, he was commonly very quiet and kept much to himself. The Host in the Tales japes at him for his lonely, abstracted air. 'Thou lookest as thou wouldest find a hare, And ever on the ground I see thee stare.' Being a good scholar, he read morning and night alone, and he says that after his office-work he would go home and sit at another book as dumb as a stone, till his look was dazed. While at study and when he was making of songs and ditties, 'nothing else that God had made' had any interest for him. There was but one thing that roused him then, and that too he liked to enjoy alone. It was the beauty of the morning and the fields, the woods, the streams, the flowers, and the singing of the little birds. This made his heart full of revel and solace, and when spring came after winter, he rose with the lark and cried, 'Farewell my book and my devotion.' He was the first who made the love of nature a distinct element in our poetry. He was the first who, in spending the whole day gazing alone on the daisy, set going that lonely delight in natural scenery which is so special a mark of our later poets. He lived thus a double life, in and out of the world, but never a gloomy one. For he was fond of mirth and good-living, and when he grew towards age was portly of waist, 'no poppet to embrace.' But he kept to the end his elfish countenance, the shy, delicate, half-mischievous face which looked on men from its grey hair and forked beard, and was set off by his light grey-coloured dress and hood. A knife and inkhorn hung on his dress, we see a rosary in his hand, and when he was alone he walked swiftly.

I could not bring myself to make the quotation shorter, although Mr. Stopford Brooke may ask me, indeed, why I do not observe in a review the proportion which I demand in a primer.

The third and fourth chapters bring us to the Renascence and the Elizabethan age. Spenser is touched by Mr. Stopford Brooke almost as charmingly as Chaucer. The pages on Shakspeare are full of interest, and the great poet gains by the mode in which we are led up to him. Mr. Stopford Brooke has remembered that Shakspeare is, as Goethe said, not truly seen when he is regarded as a great single mountain rising straight out of the plain; he is truly seen when seen among the hills of his *Riesen-Heimath*, his giant home,—among them, though towering high above them. Only one or two sentences I could wish otherwise. Mr. Stopford Brooke says of Shakspeare's last plays:—

All these belong to and praise forgiveness, and it seems, if we may conjecture, that looking back on all the wrong he had suffered and on all that he had done, Shakspeare could say in the forgiveness he gave to men and in the forgiveness he sought of heaven the words he had written in earlier days: *The quality of mercy is not strained.*

Perhaps that might not be out of place in a volume of lectures on Shakspeare. But it is certainly somewhat far-fetched and fanciful;—too fanciful for our primer. Nor is it quite sound and sober criticism, again, to say of Shakspeare: 'He was altogether, from end to end, an artist, and the greatest artist the modern world has known.' Or again: 'In the unchangeableness of pure art-power Shakspeare stands entirely alone.' There is a peculiarity in Mr. Stopford Brooke's use of the words *art*, *artist*. He means by an artist one whose aim in writing is not to reveal himself, but to give pleasure; he says most truly that Shakspeare's aim was to please, that Shakspeare 'made men and women whose dramatic action on each other and towards a catastrophe was intended to please the public, not to reveal himself.' This is indeed the true temper of the artist. But when we call a man emphatically *artist*, a *great artist*, we mean something more than this temper in which he works; we mean by art, not merely an aim to please, but also, and more, a law of pure and flawless workmanship. As living always under the sway of *this* law, and as, therefore, a perfect artist, we do not conceive of Shakspeare. His workmanship is often far from being pure and flawless.

> Till that Bellona's bridegroom, lapp'd in proof,
> Confronted him with self-comparisons—

There is but one name for such writing as that, if Shakspeare had signed it a thousand times,—it is detestable. And it is too frequent in Shakspeare. In a book, therefore, where every sentence should be sure, simple, and solid, not requiring mental reservations nor raising questions, we ought not to speak of Shakspeare as 'altogether, from end to end, an artist;' as 'standing entirely alone in the unchangeableness of pure art-power.' He is the richest, the most wonderful, the most powerful, the most delightful of poets; he is not altogether, nor even eminently, an artist.

In the fifth chapter we reach Milton. Mr. Stopford Brooke characterises Milton's poems well, when he speaks of 'their majestic movement, their grand style, and their grave poetry.' But I wonder at his designating Milton *our greatest poet.* Nor does the criticism of *Paradise Lost* quite satisfy me. I do not think that 'as we read the great epic, we feel that the lightness and grace of Milton's youthful time are gone.' True, the poet of *Paradise Lost* differs from the poet of *L'Allegro* and *Il Penseroso*; but the feeling raised by *Paradise Lost* is not a feeling that lightness and grace are gone. That would be a negative feeling, a feeling of disappointment; and the feeling raised by *Paradise Lost* is far other. Yet neither is it a feeling which justifies Mr. Stopford Brooke in saying that 'at last all thought and emotion centre round Adam and Eve, until the closing lines leave us with their lonely image in our minds.' The personages have no growing, absorbing interest of this kind; when we finish the poem, it is not with our minds agitated by them and full of them. The power of *Paradise Lost* is to be sought elsewhere. Nor is it true to say that Milton 'summed up in himself all the higher influences of the Renascence.' The disinterested curiosity, the *humanism* of the Renascence, are not characteristics of Milton,—of Milton, that is to say, when he is fully formed and has taken his ply. Nor again can it rightly be said that Milton 'began that pure poetry of natural description which has no higher examples to show in Wordsworth, or Scott, or Keats, than his *L'Allegro* and *Il Penseroso*.' *L'Allegro* and *Il Penseroso* are charming, but they are not pure poetry of natural description in the sense in which the *Highland Reaper* is, or the *Ode to Autumn*. The poems do not touch the same chords or belong to the same order. Scott is altogether out of place in the comparison. His natural description in verse has the merits of his natural description in prose, which are very considerable. But it never has the grace and felicity of Milton, or the natural magic of Wordsworth and Keats. As poetical work, it is not to be even named with theirs.

Shakspeare and Milton are such prominent objects in a primer of English literature that one dwells on them, strives to have them presented quite aright. After Milton we come to a century whose literature has no figures of this grandeur. The literary importance of the eighteenth century lies mainly in its having wrought out a revolution begun in the seventeenth,—no less a revolution than the establishment of what Mr. Stopford Brooke well calls 'the second period of English prose, in which the style is easy, unaffected, moulded to the subject, and the proper words are put in their proper places.' With his strong love of poetry, Mr. Stopford Brooke could not, perhaps, feel the same sympathy and delight in dealing with this prose century as in dealing with the times of Chaucer or Elizabeth. Still his account of its writers does not fail in interest, and is in general just. But his arrangement is here not quite satisfactory. The periods of time covered by his chapters should be literary periods, not merely periods in political history. His sixth chapter has for its title: *From the Restoration to George III.* The period from the Restoration to George the Third is a period in political history only. George the Third has nothing to do with literature; his accession marks no epoch in our civilisation or in our literature, such as is marked by the Conquest or by the reign of Elizabeth. I wish that Mr.

Stopford Brooke would change the title of this chapter, and make it: *From the Restoration to the Death of Pope and Swift.* Pope died in 1744, Swift in 1745. The following chapter should be: *From* 1745 *to the French Revolution.* The next and last: *From the French Revolution to the Death of Scott.*

These are real periods in our literature. Mr. Stopford Brooke enumerates, at the beginning of his seventh chapter, causes which from the early part of the eighteenth century were at work to influence literature.

The long peace after the accession of the House of Hanover had left England at rest and given it wealth. The reclaiming of waste tracts, the increased wealth and trade, made better communication necessary; and the country was soon covered with a network of highways. The leisure gave time to men to think and write; the quicker interchange between the capital and the country spread over England the literature of the capital, and stirred men everywhere to write. The coaching services and the post carried the new book and the literary criticism to the villages. Communication with the Continent had increased during the peaceable times of Walpole.

By the middle of the century, by a time well marked by the death of Pope and Swift, these influences had been in operation long enough to form a second period in the eighteentn century, sufficiently distinguishable from the period of Addison and Pope, and lasting down to a period of far more decisive change, the period of the French Revolution.

Prose and poetry, within these periods, should not have each their separate chapter ; it is unnecessary, and leads to some confusion. Sir Walter Scott is at present noticed in one of Mr. Stopford Brooke's chapters as a poet, in another as a prose writer. And the limits of each period should be observed ; authors and works should not be mentioned out of their order of date. At present Mr. Stopford Brooke mentions the *Rivals* and *School for Scandal* of Sheridan in his sixth chapter, a chapter which professes to go from the Restoration to the accession of George the Third. At the very beginning of the following chapter, which goes from 1760 to 1837, he introduces his mention of the *Morning Chronicle*, the *Post*, the *Herald*, and the *Times*, of the *Edinburgh* and the *Quarterly Review*, and of *Blackwood's Magazine*. By being freed from all such defects in lucid and orderly arrangement, the primer would gain in clearness.

It would gain in brevity and proportion by ending with the death of Scott in 1832. I wish I might prevail upon Mr. Stopford Brooke to bring his primer to an end with Scott's death in that year. I wish he would leave out every word about his contemporaries, and about publications which have appeared since 1832. The death of Sir Walter Scott is a real epoch; it marks the end of one period and the beginning of another,—of the period in which we are ourselves now living. No man can trust himself to speak of his own time and his own contemporaries with the same sureness of judgment and the same proportion as of times and men gone by; and in a primer of literature we should avoid, so far as we can, all hindrances to sureness of judgment and to proportion. The readers of the primer, also, are not likely to hear too little of contemporary literature, if its praises are unrehearsed in their primer; they are certain, under all circumstances, to hear quite enough of it, probably too much.

Charlotte Brontë revived in *Jane Eyre* the novel of Passion, and Miss Yonge set on foot the religious novel in support of a special school of theology. Miss Martineau and Mr. Disraeli carried on the novel of political opinion and economy, and Charles Kingsley applied the novel to the social and theological problems of our own day.

Let Mr. Stopford Brooke make a clean sweep of all this, I entreat him. And if his date of 1832 compels him to include Rogers and his poetry, let him give to them, not a third part of a page, but one line. I reckon that these reductions would shorten the last part of the primer by five pages. A little condensation in the judgments on

Wordsworth, Byron, and Shelley would abridge it by another page; the omission of the first pages of the volume by two more. Our primer shortened by eight pages! no small gain in a work of this character.

The last three chapters of the book, therefore, I could wish recast, and one or two phrases in his criticism Mr. Stopford Brooke might perhaps revise at the same time. He says most truly of Addison that his *Spectator* 'gave a better tone to manners and a gentler one to political and literary criticism.' He says truly, too, of Addison's best papers: 'No humour is more fine and tender; and, like Chaucer's, it is never bitter.' He has a right to the conclusion, therefore, that 'Addison's work was a great one, lightly done.' But to say of Addison's style, that 'in its varied cadence and subtle ease it has never been surpassed,' seems to me to be going a little too far. One could not say more of Plato's. Whatever his services to his time, Addison is for us now a writer whose range and force of thought are not considerable enough to make him interesting; and his style cannot equal in varied cadence and subtle ease the style of a man like Plato, because without range and force of thought all the resources of style, whether in cadence or in subtlety, are not and cannot be brought out.

Is it an entirely accurate judgment, again, on the

poems of Gray and Collins, to call them 'exquisite examples of perfectly English work wrought in the spirit of classic art'? I confess, this language seems to me to be too strong. Much as I admire Gray, one feels, I think, in reading his poetry never quite secure against the false poetical style of the eighteenth century. It is always near at hand, sometimes it breaks in; and the sense of this prevents the security one enjoys with truly classic work, the fulness of pleasure, the cordial satisfaction.

> Thy joys no glittering female meets—

or even things in the *Elegy*:

> He gave to misery all he had—a tear;
> He gain'd from Heaven ('twas all he wish'd) a friend—

are instances of the sort of drawback I mean. And the false style, which here comes to the surface, we are never very far from in Gray. Therefore, to call his poems 'exquisite examples of perfectly English work wrought in the spirit of classic art' seems to me an exaggeration.

Mr. Stopford Brooke's Cowper is excellent, but again there seems to me to be some want of sobriety in the praise given. Philanthropy, no doubt, animated Cowper's heart and shows itself in his poetry. But it is too much to say of the apparition of Cowper and of his philanthropy in English poetry: 'It is a wonderful change, a change so wonderful that it is like a new world. It is, in fact, the concentration into our retired poet's work of all the new thought upon the subject of mankind which was soon to take so fierce a form in Paris.' Cowper, with his morbid religion and lumbering movement, was no precursor, as Mr. Stopford Brooke would thus make him, of Byron and Shelley. His true praise is, that by his simple affections and genuine love of nature he was a precursor of Wordsworth.

Of Wordsworth's philosophy of Nature Mr. Stopford Brooke draws out, I think, a more elaborate account than we require in a primer. No one will be much helped by Wordsworth's philosophy of Nature, as a scheme in itself and disjoined from his poems. Nor shall we be led to enjoy the poems the more by having a philosophy of Nature abstracted from them and presented to us in its nakedness. Of the page and a quarter which Mr. Stopford Brooke has given to Wordsworth's philosophy of Nature, all might with advantage, perhaps, be dropped but this :—

> Nature was a person to Wordsworth, distinct from himself, and capable of being loved. He could brood on her character, her ways, her words, her life. Hence arose his minute and loving observation of her, and his passionate description of all her forms.

There might be some condensation, too, in the criticism of Byron as the poet of *Don Juan* and as the poet of Nature. But some touches in the criticism of Byron are admirable. 'We feel naturally great interest in this strong personality, put before us with such obstinate power; but it wearies at last. *Finally it wearied himself.*' Or again: 'It is his colossal power and the ease which comes from it, in which he resembles Dryden, that marks him specially.' Nothing could be better.

On Shelley, also, Mr. Stopford Brooke has an excellent sentence. He says of his lyrics: 'They form together the most sensitive, the most imaginative, and the most musical, but the least tangible lyrical poetry we possess.' But in the pages on Shelley, yet more than in those on Byron, condensation is desirable. Shelley is a most interesting and attractive personage; but in a work of the dimensions of this primer, neither his *Queen Mab*, nor his *Alastor*, nor his *Revolt of Islam*, nor his *Prometheus Unbound*, deserve the space which Mr. Stopford Brooke gives to them. And finally, as the sentence which I have last quoted is just a sentence of the right stamp for a primer, so a passage such as the following is just of the sort which is unsuitable:—

Shelley wants the closeness of grasp of nature which Wordsworth and Keats had, but he had the power in a far greater degree than they of describing a vast landscape melting into indefinite distance. In this he stands first among English poets, and is in poetry what Turner was in landscape painting. Along with this special quality of vastness his colour is as true as Scott's, but truer in this that it is full of half tones, while Scott's is laid out in broad yellow, crimson, and blue, in black and white.

Very clever, but also very fantastic; and at all events quite out of place in a primer!

Mr. Stopford Brooke will forgive me for my plain-speaking. It comes from my hearty esteem and admiration for his primer, and my desire to clear it of every speck and flaw, so that it may win its way into every one's hands. I hope he will revise it, and then I shall read it again with a fresh pleasure. But indeed, whether he revises it or no, I shall read it again: δὶς ἢ τρὶς τὰ καλά.

FALKLAND.

'THE English are just, but not amiable.' A well-bred Frenchman, who has recently travelled in India, and who published in the *Revue des Deux Mondes* an interesting account of what he saw and heard there, ends with this criticism. The criticism conveys, he says, as to the English and their rule, the real mind of the best informed and most intelligent of the natives of India with whom he conversed. They admitted the great superiority of the English rule in India to every other which had preceded it. They admitted the good intentions of the English rule; they admitted its activity, energy, incorruptibility, justice. Still, the final impression was this: something wanting in the English, something which they were not. *Les Anglais sont justes, mais pas bons.* 'The English are just, but not kind and good.'

It is proposed to raise, on the field of Newbury, a monument to a famous Englishman who was amiable. A meeting was held at Newbury to launch the project, and Lord Carnarvon made there an excellent speech. I believe the subscription to the monument does not grow very rapidly. The unamiable ones amongst us, the vast majority, naturally perhaps keep their hands in their pockets. But let us take the opportunity, as others, too, have taken it, for at least recalling Falkland to memory. Let us give our attention for a moment to this phenomenon of an amiable Englishman.

Clarendon says :—

At the battle of Newbury was slain the Lord Viscount Falkland; a person of such prodigious parts of learning and knowledge, of that inimitable sweetness and delight in conversation, of so glowing and obliging a humanity and goodness to mankind, and of that primitive simplicity and integrity of life, that if there were no other brand upon this odious and accursed Civil War than that single loss, it must be most infamous and execrable to all posterity. *Turpe mori, post te, solo non posse dolore.*

Clarendon's style is here a little excessive, a little Asiatic. And perhaps a something Asiatic is not wholly absent, either, from that famous passage,—the best known, probably, in all the *History of the Rebellion*,—that famous passage which describes Lord Falkland's longing for peace.

Sitting among his friends, often, after a deep silence and frequent sighs, he would with a shrill and sad accent ingeminate the word *Peace, Peace*; and would passionately profess that the very agony of the war, and the view of the calamities and desolation the kingdom did and must endure, took his sleep from him, and would shortly break his heart.

Clarendon's touch, where in his memoirs he speaks of Falkland, is simpler than in the *History*. But we will not carp at this great writer and faithful friend. Falkland's life was an uneventful one, and but a few points in it are known to us. To Clarendon he owes it that each of those points is a picture.

In his speech at Newbury Lord Carnarvon said: 'When we look back to the history of the Civil War, I can think of no character that stands out in higher, purer relief, than Falkland.' 'Of all the names,' says Lord Carnarvon again, 'which have come down to us from the Great Rebellion, none have come invested with higher respect and greater honour than the name of Lord Falkland.' One asks oneself how this comes to be so. Falkland wrote both in verse and in prose. Both his verse and his prose have their interest, yet as a writer he scarcely counts. He was a gallant soldier, but gallant soldiers are not uncommon. He was an unsuccessful politician, and was reproached with deserting his party. He was Secretary of State for but two years, and in that office he accomplished, and could then accomplish, nothing remarkable. He was killed in the four-and-thirtieth year of his age. Horace Walpole pronounces him a much overrated man. But let us go through the scanty records of his life a little more deliberately.

Lucius Cary, Lord Falkland, was born in 1610 His father, Sir Henry Cary, the first Lord Falkland, went to Ireland as Lord Deputy in 1622, and remained there until 1629. 'The son was bred,' says Clarendon, 'in the court and in the university, but under the care, vigilance, and direction of such governors and tutors, that he learned all his exercises and languages better than most men do in more celebrated places.' In 1629 the father, who appears to have been an able man, but violent and unfortunate, returned with broken fortunes to England. Shortly afterwards the son inherited from his maternal grandfather, the Lord Chief Baron Tanfield, who in his will passed over his daughter and her husband the ex-Lord Deputy, a good estate at Burford and Great Tew, in Oxfordshire. At nineteen, then, the young Lucius Cary came into possession of 'all his grandfather's land, with two very good houses very well furnished (worth about 2,000*l.* per annum), in a most pleasant country, and the two most pleasant places in that country, with a very plentiful personal estate.' But, adds Clarendon:—

With these advantages he had one great disadvantage

(which in the first entrance into the world is attended with too much prejudice) in his person and presence, which was in no degree attractive or promising. His stature was low, and smaller than most men; his motion not graceful, and his aspect so far from inviting, that it had somewhat in it of simplicity; and his voice the worst of the three, and so untuned that instead of reconciling, it offended the ear, so that nobody would have expected music from that tongue; and sure no man was ever less beholden to nature for its recommendation into the world. But then no man sooner or more disappointed this general and customary prejudice. That little person and small stature was quickly found to contain a great heart, a courage so keen, and a nature so fearless, that no composition of the strongest limbs and most harmonious and proportioned presence and strength ever more disposed any man to the greatest enterprise; it being his greatest weakness to be too solicitous for such adventures. And that untuned tongue and voice easily discovered itself to be supplied and governed by a mind and understanding so excellent, that the wit and weight of all he said carried another kind of admiration in it, and even another kind of acceptation from the persons present, than any ornament of delivery could reasonably promise itself, or is usually attended with. And his disposition and nature was so gentle and obliging, so much delighted in courtesy, kindness, and generosity that all mankind could not but admire and love him.

For a year or two Falkland moved in the gay life of London, rich, accomplished, popular, with a passion for soldiering, with a passion for letters. He was of Ben Jonson's society at the 'Apollo'; he mixed with Suckling, Carew, Davenant, Waller, Sandys, Sir Kenelm Digby; with Selden and Hobbes; with Hales of Eton and Chillingworth,—great spirits in little bodies, these two last, like Falkland himself. He contracted a passionate friendship with a young man as promising and as universally beloved as himself, Sir Henry Morison. Ben Jonson has celebrated it; and it was on Morison's early death that Jonson wrote the beautiful lines which every one knows, beginning—

> It is not growing like a tree,
> In bulk, doth make men better be.

Falkland married, before he was of age, Morison's sister. The marriage gave mortal offence to his father. His father had projected for the young Lucius, says Clarendon, a marriage which might mend his own broken fortunes and ruined credit at court. The son behaved admirably. He offered to resign his whole estate to his father, and to rely entirely upon his father's pleasure for his own maintenance. He had deeds of conveyance prepared to that effect, and brought them to his father for signature:—

But his father's passion and indignation so far transported him (though he was a gentleman of excellent parts), that he refused any reconciliation and rejected all the offers that were made him of the estate, so that his son remained still in the possession of his estate against his will, for which he found great reason afterwards to rejoice. But he was for the present so much afflicted with his father's displeasure that he transported himself and his wife into Holland, resolving to buy some military command, and to spend the remainder of his life in that profession. But being disappointed in the treaty he expected, and finding no opportunity to accommodate himself with such a command, he returned again into England; resolving to retire to a country life and to his books, that since he was not like to improve himself in arms he might advance in letters.

So began the *convivium philosophicum*, or *convivium theologicum*, of Falkland's life at Great Tew. With a genuine thoroughness of nature, with the high resolve to make up his mind about the matters of most vital concernment to man, and to make it up on good grounds, he plunged into study. The controversy with Rome was at that moment keen. Agents of conversion to the Romish Church, *corner-creepers* as they were called, penetrated everywhere. Two young brothers of Falkland himself were won over by them. More and more, therefore, his thoughts and his studies took a theological turn. On his first retirement to the country he had declared, says Clarendon, that 'he would not see

London in many years, which was the place he loved of all the world.' But his father's death from the effects of an accident, soon afterwards, forced him back for a time to London. Then, on his return to Oxfordshire, he surrounded himself with friends from the university, who led with him the life which Clarendon's description has made memorable :—

His house where he usually resided (Tew or Burford, in Oxfordshire), being within ten or twelve miles of the university, looked like the university itself by the company that was always found there. There were Dr. Sheldon, Dr. Morley, Dr. Hammond, Dr. Earles, Mr. Chillingworth, and indeed all men of eminent parts and faculties in Oxford, besides those who resorted thither from London; who all found their lodgings there as ready as in the colleges; nor did the lord of the house know of their coming or going, nor who were in his house, till he came to dinner or supper where all still met. Otherwise there was no troublesome ceremony or constraint, to forbid men to come to the house, or to make them weary of staying there. So that many came thither to study in a better air, finding all the books they could desire in his library, and all the persons together whose company they could wish, and not find in any other society. Here Mr. Chillingworth wrote and formed and modelled his excellent book against the learned Jesuit Mr. Nott (*The Religion of Protestants a Safe Way to Salvation*), after frequent debates upon the most important particulars; in many of which he suffered himself to be overruled by the judgment of his friends, though in others he still adhered to his own fancy, which was sceptical enough even in the highest points.

From 'this happy and delightful conversation and restraint' Falkland was in 1639 called away by 'the first alarum from the north,' Charles the First's expedition to suppress the disturbances in Scotland. After the return of that expedition Falkland sate in the Short Parliament of 1640, which preceded the Long Parliament. The 'Short Parliament' sate but a few weeks. Falkland was born a constitutionalist, a hater of all that is violent and arbitrary. What he saw in the Short Parliament made a favourable and deep impression upon him. 'From the debates which were there managed with all imaginable gravity and solemnity, he contracted' (says Clarendon) 'such a reverence to Parliaments that he thought it really impossible they could ever produce mischief or inconvenience to the kingdom, or that the kingdom could be tolerably happy in the intermission of them.'

In the next Parliament this faith in Parliaments was destined to be roughly shaken. The Long Parliament met at the end of 1640. Falkland had a warm admiration for Hampden, and a strong disapprobation of the violent proceedings of the court. He acted with the popular party. He made a powerful speech against ship-money. He was convinced of Strafford's guilt, and joined in his prosecution. He spoke vigorously for the bill to remove the bishops from the House of Lords. But the reason and moderation of the man showed itself from the first. Alone among his party he raised his voice against pressing forward Strafford's impeachment with unfair and vindictive haste. He refused to consider, like the Puritans, the order of bishops as a thing by God's law either appointed or forbidden. He treated it as a thing expedient or inexpedient. And so foolish had been the conduct of the High Church bishops and clergy, so much and so mischievously had they departed from their true province, that it was expedient at that moment, Falkland thought, to remove the bishops from the House of Lords. 'We shall find them,' he said of the High Church clergy, 'to have tithed mint and anise, and have left undone the weightier works of the law. The most frequent subjects, even in the most sacred auditories, have been the *jus divinum* of bishops and tithes, the sacredness of the clergy, the sacrilege of impropriations, the demolishing of Puritanism.' But he was careful to add: 'We shall make no little compliment to those to whom this charge belongs, if we shall lay the faults of these men upon the *order* of the bishops.' And even against these misdoing men he would join in no injustice. To his clear reason sacerdotalism was repulsive. He disliked Laud, moreover; he had a natural antipathy to his heat, fussiness, and arbitrary temper. But he refused to concur in Laud's impeachment.

The Lords threw out the bill for the expulsion of the bishops. In the same session, a few months later, the bill was reintroduced in the House of Commons. But, during this time the attitude of the popular party had been more and more declaring itself. The party had professed at first that the removal of the bishops from Parliament was all they wanted; that they had no designs against episcopacy and the Church of England. The strife deepened, and new and revolutionary designs emerged. When, therefore, the bill against the bishops was reintroduced, Falkland voted against it. Hampden reproached him with inconsistency. Hampden said, that 'he was sorry to find a noble lord had changed his opinion since the time the last bill to this purpose had passed the House; for he then thought it a good bill, but now he thought this an ill one.' But Falkland answered, that 'he had been persuaded at that time by that worthy gentleman to believe many things which he had since found to be untrue, and therefore he had changed his opinion in many particulars as well as to things as persons.'

The king's party availed themselves eagerly of this changed disposition in a man so much admired and respected. They pressed Falkland to come to the aid of the Crown, and to take office. He was extremely loth to comply. He disapproved of the policy of the court party. He was for great reforms. He disliked Charles's obstinacy and insincerity. So distasteful, indeed, were they to him, that even after he had taken office it was difficult to him,—to him, the sweetest mannered of men,—to maintain towards Charles the same amenity which he showed towards everyone else. Compliant as he was to others, yet towards the king, says Clarendon, 'he did not practise that condescension, but contradicted him with more bluntness and by sharp sentences; and in some particulars (as of the Church) to which the king was in conscience most devoted; and of this his majesty often complained.' Falkland feared that, if he took office, the king would require a submission which he could not give. He feared, too, and to a man of his high spirit this thought was most galling, that his previous opposition to the court might be supposed to have had for its aim to heighten his value and to insure his promotion. He had no fancy, moreover, for official business, and believed himself unfit for it. Hyde at last, by earnestly pleading the considerations which, he thought, made his friend's acceptance of office a duty, overcame his reluctance. At the beginning of 1642 Falkland became a member of the King's Council, and Secretary of State.

We approach the end. Falkland 'filled his place,' says Clarendon, 'with great sufficiency, being well versed in languages, to understand any that are used in business and to make himself understood.' But in August, 1642, the Civil War broke out. With that departure of the public peace fled for ever Falkland's own. He exposed himself at Edge-hill with even more than his ordinary carelessness of danger. As the war continued, his unhappiness grew upon him more and more. But let us quote Clarendon, who is here admirable :—

From his entrance into this unnatural war, his natural cheerfulness and vivacity grew clouded, and a kind of sadness and dejection of spirit stole upon him which he had never been used to. Yet being one of those who believed that one battle would end all differences, and that there would be so great a victory on one side that the other would be compelled to submit to any conditions from the victor (which supposition and conclusion generally sank into the minds of most men, and prevented the looking after many advantages that might then have been laid hold of), he resisted those indispositions, *et in luctu, bellum inter remedia erat.* But after the king's return from Brentford, and the furious resolution of the two Houses not to admit any treaty for peace, those indispositions, which had before touched him, grew into a perfect habit of uncheerfulness. And he who had been so exactly easy and affable to all men that his face and countenance was always present and vacant to his company, and held any cloudiness and less pleasantness of the visage a kind of rudeness or incivility, became on a sudden less communicable, and thence very sad, pale, and exceedingly affected with the spleen. In his clothes and habits, which he had minded before always with more industry and neatness and expense than is usual to so great a soul, he was now not only incurious, but too negligent.

In this mood he came to Newbury. Before the battle he told one of his friends that 'he was weary of the times and foresaw much misery to his country, and did believe he should be out of it ere night.' But now, as always, the close contact with danger reanimated him :—

In the morning before the battle, as always upon action, he was very cheerful, and put himself into the first rank of the Lord Byron's regiment, then advancing upon the enemy, who had lined the hedges on both sides with musketeers ; from whence he was shot with a musket in the lower part of the belly, and in the instant falling from his horse, his body was not found till the next morning ; till when there was some hope he might have been a prisoner, though his nearest friends, who knew his temper, received small comfort from that imagination. Thus fell that incomparable young man in the four-and-thirtieth year of his age, having so much despatched the true business of life that the eldest rarely attain to that immense knowledge, and the youngest enter not into the world with more innocency. Whosoever leads such a life, needs be the less anxious upon how short warning it is taken from him.

Falkland fell on the 20th of September, 1643. His body was carried to Great Tew and buried in the churchyard there. But his grave is unmarked and unknown. The house, too, in which he lived, is gone and replaced by a new one. The stables and dovecot, it is thought, existed in his time; and in the park are oaks and limes on which his eyes must have rested. He left his estates, and the control of his three children, all of them sons, to his wife, with whom he had lived happily and in great affection. But the lands of Tew and Burford have long passed away from his family.

And now, after this review of Falkland's life, let us ask whence arose that exalted esteem of him whereof Lord Carnarvon speaks, and whether it was deserved. In the first place, then, he had certainly, except personal beauty, everything to qualify him for a hero to the imagination of mankind in general. He had rank, accomplishment, sweet temper, exquisite courtesy, liberality, magnanimity, superb courage, melancholy, misfortune, early death. Of his accomplishment we have spoken. And he was accomplished, nay learned, 'with the most dexterity and address,' says Clarendon, 'and the least pedantry and affectation, that ever men who knew so much was possessed with, of what quality soever.' Of his amenity we have spoken also; of 'his disposition so gentle and obliging, so much delighting in courtesy, that all mankind could not but admire and love him;' of 'his gentleness and affability so transcendent and obliging, that it drew reverence, and some kind of compliance, from the roughest and most unpolished and stubborn constitutions, and made them of another temper of debate, in his presence, than they were in other places.' Equally charming was his generosity and delicacy to all who stood in need of help, but especially to those 'whose fortunes required, and whose spirits made them superior to, ordinary obligations.' Such is Clarendon's euphemistical phrase for poor and proud men of letters. His high-mindedness is well shown in his offer, which we have already mentioned, to resign his fortune to his father. Let me quote another fine instance of it. He never would consent, while he was Secretary of State, to two practices which he found established in his office,—the employment of spies and the opening of letters:—

For the first, he would say, such instruments must be void of all ingenuousness and common honesty before they could be of use, and afterwards they could never be fit to be credited; and no single preservation could be worth so general a wound and corruption of human society, as the cherishing such persons would carry with it. The last he thought such a violation of the law of nature that no qualification by office could justify him in the trespass.

His courage, again, had just the characters which charm the imagination:—

Upon any occasion of action, he always engaged his person in those troops which he thought, by the forwardness of the commanders, to be most like to be farthest engaged. And in all such encounters he had about him an extraordinary cheerfulness, without at all affecting the execution that usually attended them, in which he took no delight, but took pains to prevent it where it was not by resistance made necessary. Insomuch that at Edge-hill, when the enemy was routed, he was like to have incurred great peril by interposing to save those who had thrown away their arms, and against whom, it may be, others were more fierce for their having thrown them away. So that a man might think, he came into the field chiefly out of curiosity to see the face of danger, and charity to prevent the shedding of blood.

At the siege of Gloucester, when Hyde

passionately reprehended him for exposing his person unnecessarily to danger, as being so much beside the duty of his place (of Secretary of State) that it might be understood rather to be against it, he would say merely that his office could not take away the privilege of his age, and that a *secretary*, in war, might be present at the greatest *secret* of danger; but withal alleged seriously, that it concerned him to be more active in enterprises of hazard than other men, that all might see that his impatiency for peace proceeded not from pusillanimity or fear to adventure his own person.

To crown all, Falkland has for the imagination the indefinable, the irresistible charm of one who is and must be, in spite of the choicest gifts and graces, unfortunate, —of a man in the grasp of fatality. Like the Master of Ravenswood, that most interesting by far of all Scott's heroes, he is surely and visibly touched by the finger of doom. And he knows it himself; yet he knits his forehead, and holds on his way. His course must be what it must, and he cannot flinch from it; yet he loves it not, hopes nothing from it, foresees how it will end.

He had not the court in great reverence, and had a presaging spirit that the king would fall into great misfortune; and often said to his friend that he chose to serve the king because honesty obliged him to it, but that he foresaw his own ruin by doing it.

Yes, for the imagination Falkland cannot but be a

figure of ideal, pathetic beauty. But for the judgment, for sober reason? Here opinions differ.

Lord Carnarvon insisted on the salutary example of Falkland's moderation. The Dean of Westminster, who could not go to the Newbury meeting, wrote to say that in his opinion Falkland 'is one of the few examples of political eminence unconnected with party, or rather equally connected with both parties; and he is the founder, or nearly the founder, of the best and most enlightening tendencies of the Church of England.' And Principal Tulloch, whose chapter on Falkland is perhaps the most delightful chapter of his delightful book,[1] calls him 'the inspiring chief of a circle of rational and moderate thinkers amidst the excesses of a violent and dogmatic age.'

On the other hand, the *Spectator* pronounces Falkland to have been capricious and unstable, rather than truly moderate. It thinks that 'he was vacillating, and did not count the cost of what he undertook.' It judges his life to have been wasted. It says that 'the heart of moderation is strength,' and that 'it seems to us easier to maintain that either Cromwell, or Pym, or Hampden, or Fairfax, presented the true type of moderation, than Falkland.' Falkland recoiled, and changed sides; the others recognised the duty for a man 'to take strong

[1] *Rational Theology in England in the Seventeenth Century.*

measures, if none less strong will secure an end which he deems of supreme importance.'

Severe, too, upon Falkland, as might be expected, is the *Nonconformist.* It talks of his 'amiable and hesitating inconsistency.' It says that he was moved by 'intellectual perception and spiritual sentiment' rather than by 'moral impulse,' while the Puritan leaders were 'moved mainly by moral impulse.' It adds that 'the greatest reformers have always been those who have been swayed by moral feeling rather than by intellectual conceptions, and the greatest reforming movements have been those accomplished not by the enlightened knowledge of a few, but by the moral enthusiasm of the many.' The Puritan leaders had faith. 'They drew no complete picture of the ideal to be arrived at. But they were firmly and fixedly resolved, that, come what might, the wrongs of which they were conscious should not be endured.' They followed, then, the voice of conscience and of duty; 'and, broadly speaking, the voice of conscience is the voice of God.' And therefore, while Falkland's death 'has a special sadness as the end of an inconsistent and in a certain sense of a wasted life, on the other hand the death of Hampden was a martyr's seal to truths assured of ultimate triumph.'

Truths assured of ultimate triumph! Let us pause

upon those words. The Puritans were victors in the Civil War, and fashioned things to their own liking. How far was their system at home an embodiment of 'truth'? Let us consult a great writer, too little read. *Who now reads Bolingbroke?* asked Burke scornfully. And the right answer is, so far as regards, at any rate, the historical writings of Bolingbroke: 'Far too few of us; the more's the pity!' But let us hear Bolingbroke on the success of Puritanism at home:—

Cavaliers and Roundheads had divided the nation, like Yorkists and Lancastrians. To reconcile these disputes by treaty became impracticable, when neither side would trust the other. To terminate them by the sword was to fight, not for preserving the constitution, but for the manner of destroying it. The constitution might have been destroyed under pretence of prerogative. It was destroyed under pretence of liberty. We might have fallen under absolute monarchy. We fell into absolute anarchy.

And to escape from that anarchy, the nation, as everyone knows, swung back into the very hands from which Puritanism had wrested it, to the bad and false system of government of the Stuarts.

But the Puritan government, though it broke down at home, was a wise and grand government abroad. No praise is more commonly heard than this. But it will not stand. The Puritan government, Cromwell's government, was a *strong* government abroad ; a wise and true-sighted government abroad it was not. Again let us hear Bolingbroke :—

Our Charles the First was no great politician, and yet he seemed to discern that the balance of power was turning in favour of France, some years before the treaties of Westphalia. He refused to be neuter, and threatened to take part with Spain. Cromwell either did not discern this turn of the balance of power, long afterward when it was much more visible ; or, discerning it, he was induced by reasons of private interest to act against the general interest of Europe. Cromwell joined with France against Spain ; and though he got Jamaica and Dunkirk, he drove the Spaniards into a necessity of making a peace with France, that has disturbed the peace of the world almost fourscore years, and the consequences of which have well nigh beggared in our times the nation he enslaved in his.

Bolingbroke deals in strong language, but there can be no doubt that the real imminent danger for Europe, in Cromwell's time, was French ambition and French aggrandisement. There can be no doubt that Cromwell either did not discern this, or acted as if he did not discern it; and that Europe had to bear, in consequence, the infliction of the Grand Monarch and of all he brought with him.

But is it meant that the Puritan triumph was the

triumph of religion,—of conduct and righteousness? Alas! it was its defeat. So grossly imperfect, so false, was the Puritan conception and presentation of righteousness, so at war with the ancient and inbred integrity, piety, good nature, and good humour of the English people, that it led straight to moral anarchy, the profligacy of the Restoration. It led to the court, the manners, the stage, the literature, which we know. It led to the long discredit of serious things, to the dryness of the eighteenth century, to the 'irreligion' which vexed Butler's righteous soul, to the aversion and incapacity for all deep inquiries concerning religion and its sanctions, to the belief so frequently found now among the followers of natural science that such inquiries are unprofitable. It led, amongst that middle class where religion still lived on, to a narrowness, an intellectual poverty, almost incredible. They 'entered the prison of Puritanism, and had the key turned upon their spirit there for two hundred years.' It led to that character of their steady and respectable life which makes one shiver: its hideousness, its immense ennui.

But is it meant, finally, that, after all, political liberty re-emerged in England, seriousness re-emerged: that they re-emerged and prevail, and that herein, and in the England of to-day, is the triumph of Puritanism? Yes, this is what is really meant. It is very commonly believed and asserted. But let us imitate the society of Great Tew, and make it our business 'to examine and refine those grosser propositions which laziness and consent make current in vulgar conversation.' Undoubtedly there has been a result from the long travail which England has passed through between the times of the Renascence and our own. *Something* has come of it all; and that something is the England of to-day, with its seriousness, such as it is, with its undeniable political liberty. Let us be thankful for what we have, and to the Puritans for their share in producing it. But, in the first place, is it certain that the England of to-day is the best imaginable and possible result from the elements with which we started at the Renascence? Because, if not, then by some other shaping of events, and without the Puritan triumph, we might conceivably have stood even yet better than we stand now. In the second place, is it certain that of the good which we admittedly have in the England of to-day,—the seriousness and the political liberty,—the Puritans and the Puritan triumph are the authors? The assumption that they are so is plausible,—it is current; it pervades, let me observe in passing, Mr. Green's fascinating History. But is the assumption sound? When one considers the strength, the boldness, the self-assertion, the instincts of resistance and independence in the English nature, it is surely hazardous to affirm that only by the particular means of the Puritan struggle and the Puritan triumph could we have become free in our persons and property. When we consider the character shown, the signal given, in the thinking of Thomas More and Shakspeare, of Bacon and Harvey, how shall we say that only at the price of Puritanism could England have had free thought? When we consider the seriousness of Spenser, that ideal Puritan before the fanatical Puritans and without their faults; when we consider Spenser's seriousness and pureness, in their revolt against the moral disorder of the Renascence, and remember the allies which they had in the native integrity and piety of the English race, shall we even venture to say that only at the price of Puritanism could we have had seriousness? Puritanism has been one element in our seriousness; but it is not the whole of our seriousness, nor the best in it.

Falkland himself was profoundly serious. He was 'in his nature so severe a lover of justice and so precise a lover of truth, that he was superior to all possible temptations for the violation of either.' Far from being a man flighty and unstable, he was a man, says Clarendon, *constant and pertinacious*; 'constant and pertinacious, and not to be wearied with any pains.' And he was, as I have said, a born constitutionalist, a hater of 'exorbitances' of all kinds, governmental or popular. He 'thought no mischief so intolerable as the presumption of ministers of state to break positive rules for reasons of state, or judges to transgress known laws upon the title of conveniency or necessity; which made him so severe against the Earl of Strafford and the Lord Finch, contrary to his natural gentleness and temper.' He had the historic sense in politics; an aversion to root-and-branch work, to what he called 'great mutations.' He was for using compromise and adjustment, for keeping what had long served and what was ready to hand, but amending it and turning it to better account. 'I do not believe bishops to be *jure divino*,' he would say; 'nay, I believe them not to be *jure divino*.' Still, he was not disposed to 'root up this ancient tree.' He had no superstition about it. 'He had in his own judgment,' says Clarendon, 'such a latitude in opinion, that he did not believe any part of the order or government of it to be so essentially necessary to religion, but that it might be parted with and altered for a notable public benefit or convenience.' On the other hand: 'He was never in the least degree swayed or moved by the objections which were made against that government (episcopacy) in the Church, holding them most ridiculous; or affected to the other which those men (the Puritans) fancied to themselves.' There Episcopacy and the Church of England had been for ages, and it was the part of a statesman, Falkland thought, rather to use them than to destroy them. All this is in the very spirit of English political liberty, as we now conceive it, and as, by the Revolution of 1688, it triumphed. But it is not in the spirit of the Puritans. The *truths assured of ultimate triumph* were, then, so far as political liberty is concerned, rather with Falkland than with the Puritans.

It was his historic sense, again, which made him, when compromise was plainly impossible, side with the king. Things had come, and by no fault of Falkland, to that pass, when the contention, as Bolingbroke truly says, was 'not for preserving the constitution but for the manner of destroying it.' In such a juncture Falkland looked for the best *power* or *purchase*, to use Burke's excellent expression, that he could find. He thought he found it in the Crown. He thought the Parliament a less available *power* or *purchase* than the Crown. He thought renovation more possible by means of the triumph of the Crown than by means of the triumph of the Parliament. He thought the triumph of the Parliament the greater leap into chaos. He may have been wrong.

Whether a better result might have been got out of the Parliament's defeat than was got out of its triumph, we can never know. What is certain is that the Parliament's triumph did bring things to a dead-lock, that the nation reverted to the monarchy, and that the final victory was neither for Stuarts nor Puritans. And it could not be for either of them, for the cause of neither was sound. Falkland had lucidity enough to see it. He gave himself to the cause which seemed to him least unsound, and to which 'honesty,' he thought, bound him; but he felt that the truth was not there, any more than with the Puritans,—neither the truth nor the future. This is what makes his figure and situation so truly tragic. For a sound cause he could not fight, because there was none; he could only fight for the least bad of two unsound ones. 'Publicans and sinners on the one side,' as Chillingworth said; 'Scribes and Pharisees on the other.' And Falkland had, I say, the lucidity of mind and the largeness of temper to see it.

Shall we blame him for his lucidity of mind and largeness of temper? Shall we even pity him? By no means. They are his great title to our veneration. They are what make him ours; what link him with the nineteenth century. He and his friends, by their heroic and hopeless stand against the inadequate ideals dominant in their time, kept open their communications with the future, lived with the future. Their battle is ours too; and that we pursue it with fairer hopes of success than they did, we owe to their having waged it and fallen. To our English race, with its insularity, its profound faith in action, its contempt for dreamers and failers, inadequate ideals in life, manners, government, thought, religion, will always be a source of danger. Energetic action makes up, we think, for imperfect knowledge. We think that all is well, that a man is following 'a moral impulse,' if he pursues an end which he 'deems of supreme importance. We impose neither on him nor on ourselves the duty of discerning whether he is *right* in deeming it so.

Hence our causes are often as small as our noise about them is great. To see people busy themselves about Ritualism, that question of not the most strong-minded portion of the clergy and laity, or to see them busy themselves about that 'burning question' of the fierce and acrimonious political Dissenters, the Burials Bill, leading up to the other 'burning question' of dis-establishment,—to see people so eager about these things, one might sometimes fancy that the whole English nation, as in Chillingworth's time it was divided into two great hosts of publicans and sinners on the one side, scribes and Pharisees on the other, so in ours it was going to divide itself into two vast camps of Simpletons here, under the command, suppose, of Mr. Beresford Hope, and of Savages there, under the command of Mr. Henry Richard. And it is so notorious that great movements are always led by aliens to the sort of people who make the mass of the movement,—by gifted outsiders,—that I shall not, I hope, be suspected of implying that Mr. Beresford Hope is a simpleton or Mr. Henry Richard a savage. But what we have to do is to raise and multiply in this country a third host, with the conviction that the ideals both of Simpletons and Savages are profoundly inadequate and profoundly unedifying, and with the resolve to win victory for a better ideal than that of either of them.

Falkland and his friends had in their day a like task. On the one hand was the Royalist party, with its vices, its incurable delusions; on the other, the Puritans, with their temper, their false, old-Jewish mixture of politics with an ill-understood religion. I should have been glad to say not one word against Hampden in his honourable grave. But the lovers of Hampden cannot forbear to extol him at Falkland's expense. Alas! yet with what benign disdain might not Jesus have whispered to that exemplary but somewhat Philistine Buckinghamshire squire, *seeking the Lord* about militia or ship-money: 'Man, who made me a judge or a divider over you?'

No, the true martyr was not Hampden. If we are to find a martyr in the history of the Great Civil War, let it be Falkland. He was the martyr of lucidity of mind and largeness of temper, in a strife of imperfect intelligences and tempers illiberal. Like his friend Hales of Eton, who in our century will again, he too, emerge, after having been long obscured by the Lauds and the Sheldons, by the Owens and the Baxters,—like Hales, Falkland in that age of harsh and rancorous tempers was 'of a nature so kind, so sweet, that it was near as easy a task for anyone to become so knowing as so obliging.' Like Hales, too, Falkland could say: 'The pursuit of truth hath been my only care ever since I fully understood the meaning of the word. For this I have forsaken all hopes, all friends, all desires which might bias me, and hinder me from driving right at what I aimed.' Like Hales, and unlike our nation in general, Falkland concerned himself with the *why* of things as well as the *what*. 'I comprise it all,' says Hales, in two words: '*what* and *wherefore*. That part of your burden which contains *what*, you willingly take up. But that other, which comprehends *why*, that is either too hot or too heavy; you dare not meddle with it. But I must add that also to your burden, or else I must leave you for idle persons; for without the knowledge of why, of the grounds or reasons of things, there is no possibility of not being deceived.' How countless are the deceived and deceiving from this cause! Nay, and the fanatics of the *what*, the neglecters of the *why*, are not unfrequently men of genius; they have the temperament which influences, which prevails, which acts magnetically upon men. So we have the Philistine of genius in religion,—Luther; the Philistine of genius in politics,—Cromwell; the Philistine of genius in literature,—Bunyan. All three of them, let us remark, are Germanic, and two of them are English. Mr. Freeman must be enchanted.

But let us return to Falkland,—to our martyr of sweetness and light, of lucidity of mind and largeness of temper. Let us bid him farewell, not with compassion for him and not with excuses, but in confidence and pride. Slowly, very slowly, his ideal of lucidity of mind and largeness of temper conquers; but it conquers. In the end it will prevail; only we must have patience. The day will come when this nation shall be renewed by it. But, O lime-trees of Tew, and quiet Oxfordshire field-banks where the first violets are even now raising their heads!—how often, ere that day arrive for Englishmen, shall your renewal be seen!

A FRENCH CRITIC ON MILTON.

MR. TREVELYAN'S Life of his uncle must have induced many people to read again Lord Macaulay's *Essay on Milton.* With the *Essay on Milton* began Macaulay's literary career, and, brilliant as the career was, it had few points more brilliant than its beginning. Mr. Trevelyan describes with animation that decisive first success. The essay appeared in the *Edinburgh Review* in 1825. Mr. Trevelyan says, and quite truly :—

The effect on the author's reputation was instantaneous. Like Lord Byron, he awoke one morning and found himself famous. The beauties of the work were such as all men could recognise, and its very faults pleased. . . . The family breakfast-table in Bloomsbury was covered with cards of invitation to dinner from every quarter of London. . . . A warm admirer of Robert Hall, Macaulay heard with pride how the great preacher, then wellnigh worn out with that long disease, his life, was discovered lying on the floor, employed in learning by aid of grammar and dictionary enough Italian to enable him to verify the parallel between Milton and Dante.

But the compliment that, of all others, came most nearly home, —the only commendation of his literary talent which even in the innermost domestic circle he was ever known to repeat, —was the sentence with which Jeffrey acknowledged the receipt of his manuscript: 'The more I think, the less I can conceive where you picked up that style.'

And already, in the *Essay on Milton*, the style of Macaulay is, indeed, that which we know so well. A style to dazzle, to gain admirers everywhere, to attract imitators in multitude! A style brilliant, metallic, exterior; making strong points, alternating invective with eulogy, wrapping in a robe of rhetoric the thing it represents; not, with the soft play of life, following and rendering the thing's very form and pressure. For, indeed, in rendering things in this fashion, Macaulay's gift did not lie. Mr. Trevelyan reminds us that in the preface to his collected Essays Lord Macaulay himself 'unsparingly condemns the redundance of youthful enthusiasm' of the *Essay on Milton.* But the unsoundness of the essay does not spring from its 'redundance of youthful enthusiasm.' It springs from this: that the writer has not for his aim to see and to utter the real truth about his object. Whoever comes to the *Essay on Milton* with the desire to get at the real truth about Milton, whether as a man or as a poet, will feel that the essay in nowise helps him. A reader who only wants rhetoric, a reader who wants a panegyric on Milton, a panegyric on the Puritans, will find what he wants. A reader who wants criticism will be disappointed.

This would be palpable to all the world, and every-one would feel, not pleased, but disappointed, by the *Essay on Milton*, were it not that the readers who seek for criticism are extremely few; while the readers who seek for rhetoric, or who seek for praise and blame to suit their own already established likes and dislikes, are extremely many. A man who is fond of rhetoric may find pleasure in hearing that in *Paradise Lost* 'Milton's conception of love unites all the voluptuousness of the Oriental haram, and all the gallantry of the chivalric tournament, with all the pure and quiet affection of an English fireside.' He may glow at being told that 'Milton's thoughts resemble those celestial fruits and flowers which the Virgin Martyr of Massinger sent down from the gardens of Paradise to the earth, and which were distinguished from the productions of other souls not only by superior bloom and sweetness, but by miraculous efficacy to invigorate and to heal.' He may imagine that he has got something profound when he reads that, if we compare Milton and Dante in their management of the agency of supernatural beings,—'the exact details of Dante with the dim intimations of Milton,'—the right conclusion of the whole matter is this :—

Milton wrote in an age of philosophers and theologians. It was necessary, therefore, for him to abstain from giving such a shock to their understandings as might break the charm which it was his object to throw over their imaginations. It was impossible for him to adopt altogether the material or the immaterial system. He therefore took his stand on the debateable ground. He left the whole in ambiguity. He has doubtless, by so doing, laid himself open to the charge of inconsistency. But though philosophically in the wrong he was poetically in the right.

Poor Robert Hall, 'wellnigh worn out with that long disease, his life,' and, in the last precious days of it, 'discovered lying on the floor, employed in learning, by aid of grammar and dictionary, enough Italian to enable him to verify' this ingenious criticism! Alas! even had his life been prolonged like Hezekiah's, he could not have verified it, for it is unverifiable. A poet who, writing 'in an age of philosophers and theologians,' finds it 'impossible for him to adopt altogether the material or the immaterial system,' who, therefore, 'takes his stand on the debateable ground,' who 'leaves the whole in ambiguity,' and who, in doing so, 'though philosophically in the wrong, was poetically in the right'! Substantial meaning such lucubrations have none. And in like manner, a distinct and substantial meaning can never be got out of the fine phrases about 'Milton's conception of love uniting all the voluptuousness of the Oriental haram, and all the gallantry of the chivalric tournament, with all the pure and quiet affection of an English fireside;' or about 'Milton's thoughts resembling those celestial fruits and flowers which the Virgin Martyr of Massinger sent down from the gardens of Paradise to the earth;' the phrases are mere rhetoric. Macaulay's writing passes for being admirably clear, and so externally it is; but often it is really obscure, if one takes his deliverances seriously, and seeks to find in them a definite meaning. However, there is a multitude of readers, doubtless, for whom it is sufficient to have their ears tickled with fine rhetoric; but the tickling makes a serious reader impatient.

Many readers there are, again, who come to an Essay on Milton with their minds full of zeal for the Puritan cause, and for Milton as one of the glories of Puritanism. Of such readers the great desire is to have the cause and the man, who are already established objects of enthusiasm for them, strongly praised. Certainly Macaulay will satisfy their desire. They will hear that the Civil War was 'the great conflict between Oromasdes and Arimanes, liberty and despotism, reason and prejudice;' the Puritans being Oromasdes, and the Royalists Arimanes. They will be told that the great Puritan poet was worthy of the august cause which he served. 'His radiant and beneficent career resembled that of the god of light and fertility. 'There are a few characters which have stood the closest scrutiny and the severest tests, which have been tried in the furnace and have proved pure, which have been declared sterling by the general consent of mankind, and which are visibly stamped with the image and superscription of the Most High. Of these was Milton.' To descend a little to particulars. Milton's temper was especially admirable. 'The gloom of Dante's character discolours all the passions of men and all the face of nature, and tinges with its own livid hue the flowers of Paradise and the glories of the eternal throne.' But in our countryman, although 'if ever despondency and asperity could be excused in any man, they might have been excused in Milton,' nothing 'had power to disturb his sedate and majestic patience.' All this is just what an ardent admirer of the Puritan cause and of Milton would most wish to hear, and when he hears it he is in ecstasies.

But a disinterested reader, whose object is not to hear Puritanism and Milton glorified, but to get at the truth about them, will surely be dissatisfied. With what a heavy brush, he will say to himself, does this man lay on his colours! The Puritans Oromasdes, and the Royalists Arimanes? What a different strain from Chillingworth's, in his sermon at Oxford at the beginning of the Civil War! 'Publicans and sinners on the one side,' said Chillingworth, 'scribes and Pharisees on the other.' Not at all a conflict between Oromasdes and Arimanes, but a good deal of Arimanes on both sides. And as human affairs go, Chillingworth's version of the matter is likely to be nearer the truth than Macaulay's. Indeed, for any-one who reads thoughtfully and without bias, Macaulay himself, with the inconsistency of a born rhetorician, presently confutes his own thesis. He says of the Royalists: 'They had far more both of profound and of polite learning than the Puritans. Their manners were more engaging, their tempers more amiable, their tastes more elegant, and their households more cheerful.' Is being more kindly affectioned such an insignificant superiority? The Royalists too, then, in spite of their being insufficiently jealous for civil and ecclesiastical liberty, had in them something of Oromasdes, the principle of light.

And Milton's temper! His 'sedate and majestic patience;' his freedom from 'asperity!' If there is a defect which, above all others, is signal in Milton, which injures him even intellectually, which limits him as a poet, it is the defect common to him with the whole Puritan party to which he belonged,—the fatal defect of *temper*. He and they may have a thousand merits, but they are *unamiable*. Excuse them how one will, Milton's asperity and acerbity, his want of sweetness of temper, of the Shakspearian largeness and indulgence, are undeniable. Lord Macaulay in his Essay regrets that the prose writings of Milton should not be more read. They abound,' he says in his rhetorical way, 'with passages, compared with which the finest declamations of Burke sink into insignificance.' At any rate, they enable us to judge of Milton's temper, of his freedom from asperity. Let us open the *Doctrine and Discipline of Divorce* and see how Milton treats an opponent. 'How should he, a serving-man both by nature and function, an idiot by breeding, and a solicitor by presumption, ever come to know or feel within himself what the meaning is of *gentle*?' What a gracious temper! 'At last, and in good hour, we come to his farewell, which is to be a concluding taste of his jabberment in law, the flashiest and the fustiest that ever corrupted in such an unswilled hogshead.' How 'sedate and majestic!'

Human progress consists in a continual increase in the number of those, who, ceasing to live by the animal life alone and to feel the pleasures of sense only, come to participate in the intellectual life also, and to find enjoyment in the things of the mind. The enjoyment is not at first very discriminating. Rhetoric, brilliant writing, gives to such persons pleasure for its own sake; but it gives them pleasure, still more, when it is employed in commendation of a view of life which is on the whole theirs, and of men and causes with which they are naturally in sympathy. The immense popularity of Macaulay is due to his being pre-eminently fitted to give pleasure to all who are beginning to feel enjoyment in the things of the mind. It is said that the traveller in Australia, visiting one settler's hut after another, finds again and again that the settler's third book, after the Bible and Shakspeare, is some work by Macaulay. Nothing can be more natural. The Bible and Shakspeare may be said to be imposed upon an Englishman as objects of his admiration; but as soon as the common Englishman, desiring culture, begins to choose for himself, he chooses Macaulay. Macaulay's view of things is, on the whole, the view of them which he feels to be his own also; the persons and causes praised are those which he himself is disposed to admire; the persons and causes blamed are those with which he himself is out of sympathy; and the rhetoric employed to praise or to blame them is animating and excellent. Macaulay is thus a great civiliser. In hundreds of men he hits their nascent taste for the things of the mind, possesses himself of it and stimulates it, draws it powerfully forth and confirms it.

But with the increasing number of those who awake to the intellectual life, the number of those also increases, who, having awoke to it, go on with it, follow where it leads them. And it leads them to see that it is their business to learn the real truth about the important men, and things, and books, which interest the human mind. For thus is gradually to be acquired a stock of sound ideas, in which the mind will habitually move, and which alone can give to our judgments security and solidity. To be satisfied with fine writing about the object of one's study, with having it praised or blamed in accordance with one's own likes or dislikes, with any conventional treatment of it whatever, is at this stage of growth seen to be futile. At this stage, rhetoric, even when it is so good as Macaulay's, dissatisfies. And the number of people who have reached this stage of mental growth is constantly, as things now are, increasing; increasing by the very same law of progress which plants the beginnings of mental life in more and more persons who, until now, have never known mental life at all. So that while the number of those who are delighted with rhetoric such as

Macaulay's is always increasing, the number of those who are dissatisfied with it is always increasing too.

And not only rhetoric dissatisfies people at this stage, but conventionality of any kind. This is the fault of Addison's Miltonic criticism, once so celebrated; it rests almost entirely upon convention. Here is *Paradise Lost*, 'a work which does an honour to the English nation,' a work claiming to be one of the great poems of the world, to be of the highest moment to us. 'The *Paradise Lost*,' says Addison, 'is looked upon by the best judges as the greatest production, or at least the noblest work of genius, in our language, and therefore deserves to be set before an English reader in its full beauty.' The right thing, surely, is for such a work to prove its own virtue by powerfully and delightfully affecting us as we read it, and by remaining a constant source of elevation and happiness to us for ever. But the *Paradise Lost* has not this effect certainly and universally; therefore Addison proposes to 'set before an English reader, in its full beauty,' the great poem. To this end he has 'taken a general view of it under these four heads: the fable, the characters, the sentiments, and the language.' He has, moreover, endeavoured not only to prove that the poem is beautiful in general, but to point out its particular beauties and to determine wherein they consist. I have endeavoured to show how some passages are beautified by being sublime, others by being soft, others by being natural; which of them are recommended by the passion, which by the moral, which by the sentiment, and which by the expression. I have likewise endeavoured to show how the genius of the poet shines by a happy invention, or distant allusion, or a judicious imitation; how he has copied or improved Homer or Virgil, and raises his own imagination by the use which he has made of several poetical passages in Scripture. I might have inserted also several passages in Tasso which our author has imitated; but as I do not look upon Tasso to be a sufficient voucher, I would not perplex my reader with such quotations as might do more honour to the Italian than the English poet.

This is the sort of criticism which held our grandfathers and great-grandfathers spell-bound in solemn reverence. But it is all based upon convention, and on the positivism of the modern reader it is thrown away. Does the work which you praise, he asks, affect me with high pleasure and do me good, when I try it as fairly as I can? The critic who helps such a questioner is one who has sincerely asked himself, also, this same question; who has answered it in a way which agrees, in the main, with what the questioner finds to be his own honest experience in the matter, and who shows the reasons for this common experience. Where is the use of telling a man, who finds himself tired rather than delighted by

Paradise Lost, that the incidents in that poem 'have in them all the beauties of novelty, at the same time that they have all the graces of nature:' that 'though they are natural, they are not obvious, which is the true character of all fine writing'? Where is the use of telling him that 'Adam and Eve are drawn with such sentiments as do not only interest the reader in their afflictions, but raise in him the most melting passions of humanity and commiseration'? His own experience, on the other hand, is that the incidents in *Paradise Lost* are such as awaken in him but the most languid interest; and that the afflictions and sentiments of Adam and Eve never melt or move him passionately at all. How is he advanced by hearing that 'it is not sufficient that the language of an epic poem be perspicuous, unless it be also sublime;' and that Milton's language is both? What avails it to assure him that 'the first thing to be considered in an epic poem is the fable, which is perfect or imperfect, according as the action which it relates is more or less so;' that 'this action should have three qualifications, should be but one action, an entire action, and a great action;' and that if we 'consider the action of the *Iliad*, *Æneid*, and *Paradise Lost*, in these three several lights, we shall find that Milton's poem does not fall short in the beauties which are essential to that kind of writing'? The patient whom

Addison thus doctors will reply, that he does not care two straws whether the action of *Paradise Lost* satisfies the proposed test or no, if the poem does not give him pleasure. The truth is, Addison's criticism rests on certain conventions: namely, that incidents of a certain class *must* awaken keen interest; that sentiments of a certain kind *must* raise melting passions; that language of a certain strain, and an action with certain qualifications, *must* render a poem attractive and effective. Disregard the convention; ask solely whether the incidents *do* interest, whether the sentiments *do* move, whether the poem *is* attractive and effective, and Addison's criticism collapses.

Sometimes the convention is one which in theory ought, a man may perhaps admit, to be something more than a convention; but which yet practically is not. Milton's poem is of surpassing interest to us, says Addison, because in it 'the principal actors are not only our progenitors but our representatives. We have an actual interest in everything they do, and no less than our utmost happiness is concerned, and lies at stake, in all their behaviour.' Of ten readers who may even admit that in theory this is so, barely one can be found whose practical experience tells him that Adam and Eve do really, as his representatives, excite his interest in this vivid manner. It is by a mere convention, then, that Addison supposes them to do so, and claims an advantage for Milton's poem from the supposition.

The theological speeches in the third book of *Paradise Lost* are not, in themselves, attractive poetry. But, says Addison :—

> The passions which they are designed to raise are a divine love and religious fear. The particular beauty of the speeches in the third book consists in that shortness and perspicuity of style in which the poet has couched the greatest mysteries of Christianity. . . . He has represented all the abstruse doctrines of predestination, free-will, and grace, as also the great points of incarnation and redemption (which naturally grow up in a poem that treats of the fall of man) with great energy of expression, and in a clearer and stronger light than I ever met with in any other writer.

But nine readers out of ten feel that, as a matter of fact, their religious sentiments of 'divine love and religious fear' are wholly ineffectual even to reconcile them to the poetical tiresomeness of the speeches in question ; far less can they render them interesting. It is by a mere convention, then, that Addison pretends that they do.

The great merit of Johnson's criticism on Milton is that from rhetoric and convention it is free. Mr. Trevelyan says that the enthusiasm of Macaulay's *Essay on Milton* is, at any rate, 'a relief from the perverted ability of that elaborate libel on our great epic poet, which goes by the name of Dr. Johnson's *Life of Milton*.' This is too much in Lord Macaulay's own style. In Johnson's *Life of Milton* we have the straightforward remarks, on Milton and his works, of a very acute and robust mind. Often they are thoroughly sound. 'What we know of Milton's character in domestic relations is that he was severe and arbitrary. His family consisted of women; and there appears in his books something like a Turkish contempt of females as subordinate and inferior beings.' Mr. Trevelyan will forgive our saying that the truth is here much better hit, than in Lord Macaulay's sentence telling us how Milton's 'conception of love unites all the voluptuousness of the Oriental haram, and all the gallantry of the chivalric tournament, with all the pure and quiet affection of an English fireside.' But Johnson's mind, acute and robust as it was, was at many points bounded, at many points warped. He was neither sufficiently disinterested, nor sufficiently flexible, nor sufficiently receptive, to be a satisfying critic of a poet like Milton. 'Surely no man could have fancied that he read Lycidas with pleasure, had he not known the author!' Terrible sentence for revealing the deficiencies of the critic who utters it.

A completely disinterested judgment about a man like Milton is easier to a foreign critic than to an Englishman. From conventional obligation to admire 'our great epic poet' a foreigner is free. Nor has he any bias for or against Milton because he was a Puritan,--in his political and ecclesiastical doctrines to one of our great English parties a delight, to the other a bugbear. But a critic must have the requisite knowledge of the man and the works he is to judge; and from a foreigner,—particularly, perhaps, from a Frenchman,—one hardly expects such knowledge. M. Edmond Scherer, however, whose essay on Milton lies before me, is an exceptional Frenchman. He is a senator of France and one of the directors of the *Temps* newspaper. But he was trained at Geneva, that home of large instruction and lucid intelligence. He was in youth the friend and hearer of Alexandre Vinet,—one of the most salutary influences a man in our times can have experienced, whether he continue to think quite with Vinet or not. He knows thoroughly the language and literature of England, Italy, Germany, as well as of France. Well-informed, intelligent, disinterested, open-minded, sympathetic, M. Scherer has much in common with the admirable critic whom France has lost,—Sainte-Beuve. What he has not, as a critic, is Sainte-Beuve's elasticity and cheerfulness. He has not that gaiety, that radiancy, as of a man discharging with delight the very office for which he was born, which, in the *Causeries*, make Sainte-Beuve's touch so felicitous, his sentences so crisp, his effect so charming. But M. Scherer has the same open-mindedness as Sainte-Beuve, the same firmness and sureness of judgment; and having a much more solid acquaintance with foreign languages than Sainte-Beuve, he can much better appreciate a work like *Paradise Lost* in the only form in which it can be appreciated properly,—in the original.

We will commence, however, by disagreeing with M. Scherer. He sees very clearly how vain is Lord Macaulay's sheer laudation of Milton, or Voltaire's sheer disparagement of him. Such judgments, M. Scherer truly says, are not judgments at all. They merely express a personal sensation of like or dislike. And M. Scherer goes on to recommend, in the place of such 'personal sensations,' the method of historical criticism,—that great and famous power in the present day. He sings the praises of 'this method at once more conclusive and more equitable, which sets itself to understand things rather than to class them, to explain rather than to judge them; which seeks to account for a work from the genius of its author, and for the turn which this genius has taken from the circumstances amidst which it was developed;'—

the old story of 'the man and the *milieu*,' in short. 'For thus,' M. Scherer continues, 'out of these two things, the analysis of the writer's character and the study of his age, there spontaneously issues the right understanding of his work. In place of an appreciation thrown off by some chance comer, we have the work passing judgment, so to speak, upon itself, and assuming the rank which belongs to it among the productions of the human mind.'

The advice to study the character of an author and the circumstances in which he has lived, in order to account to oneself for his work, is excellent. But it is a perilous doctrine, that from such a study the right understanding of his work will 'spontaneously issue.' In a mind qualified in a certain manner it will, not in all minds. And it will be that mind's 'personal sensation.' It cannot be said that Macaulay had not studied the character of Milton, and the history of the times in which he lived. But a right understanding of Milton did not 'spontaneously issue' therefrom in the mind of Macaulay, because Macaulay's mind was that of a rhetorician, not of a disinterested critic. Let us not confound the method with the result intended by the method,—right judgments. The critic who rightly appreciates a great man or a great work, and who can tell us faithfully, life being short and art long and false information very plentiful, what we may expect from their study and what they can do for us, he is the critic we want, by whatever methods, intuitive or historical, he may have managed to get his knowledge.

M. Scherer begins with Milton's prose works, from which he translates many passages. Milton's sentences can hardly know themselves again in clear modern French, and with all their inversions and redundancies gone. M. Scherer does full justice to the glow and mighty eloquence with which Milton's prose, in its good moments, is instinct and alive; to the 'magnificences of his style,' as he calls them:—

> The expression is not too strong. There are moments when, shaking from him the dust of his arguments, the poet bursts suddenly forth, and bears us away in a torrent of incomparable eloquence. We get, not the phrase of the orator, but the glow of the poet, a flood of images poured around his arid theme, a rushing flight carrying us above his paltry controversies. The polemical writings of Milton are filled with such beauties. The prayer which concludes the treatise on Reformation in England, the praise of zeal in the Apology for Smectymnus, the portrait of Cromwell in the Second Defence of the English People, and, finally, the whole tract on the Liberty of Unlicensed Printing from beginning to end, are some of the most memorable pages in English literature, and some of the most characteristic products of the genius of Milton.

Maçaulay himself could hardly praise the eloquence

of Milton's prose writings more warmly. But it is a very inadequate criticism which leaves the reader, as Macaulay's rhetoric would leave him, with the belief that the total impression to be got from Milton's prose writings is one of enjoyment and admiration. It is not; we are misled, and our time is wasted, if we are sent to Milton's prose works in the expectation of finding it so. Grand thoughts and beautiful language do not form the staple of Milton's controversial treatises, though they occur in them not unfrequently. But the total impression from those treatises is rightly given by M. Scherer:—

In all of them the manner is the same. The author brings into play the treasures of his learning, heaping together testimonies from Scripture, passages from the Fathers, quotations from the poets; laying all antiquity, sacred and profane, under contribution; entering into subtle discussions on the sense of this or that Greek or Hebrew word. But not only by his undigested erudition and by his absorption in religious controversy does Milton belong to his age; he belongs to it, too, by the personal tone of his polemics. Morus and Salmasius had attacked his morals, laughed at his low stature, made unfeeling allusions to his loss of sight: Milton replies by reproaching them with the wages they have taken and with the servant-girls they have debauched. All this mixed with coarse witticisms, with terms of the lowest abuse. Luther and Calvin, those virtuosos of insult, had not gone farther.

No doubt there is, as M. Scherer says, 'something indescribably heroical and magnificent which overflows from Milton, even when he is engaged in the most miserable discussions.' Still, for the mass of his prose treatises, 'miserable discussions' is the final and right word. Nor, when Milton passed to his great epic, did he altogether leave the old man of these 'miserable discussions' behind him.

In his soul he is a polemist and theologian; a Protestant Schoolman. He takes delight in the favourite dogmas of Puritanism: original sin, predestination, free-will. Not that even here he does not display somewhat of that independence which was in his nature. But his theology is, nevertheless, that of his epoch, tied and bound to the letter of Holy Writ, without grandeur, without horizons, without philosophy. He never frees himself from the bondage of the letter. He settles the most important questions by the authority of an obscure text, or a text isolated from its context. In a word, Milton is a great poet with a Salmasius or a Grotius bound up along with him; a genius nourished on the marrow of lions, of Homer, Isaiah, Virgil, Dante, but also, like the serpent of Eden, eating dust, the dust of dismal polemics. He is a doctor, a preacher, a man of didactics; and when the day shall arrive when he can at last realise the dreams of his youth and bestow on his country an epic poem, he will compose it of two elements, gold and clay, sublimity and scholasticism, and will bequeath to us a poem which is at once the most wonderful and the most insupportable poem in existence.

From the first, two conflicting forces, two sources of inspiration, had contended with one another, says M. Scherer, for the possession of Milton,—the Renascence and Puritanism. Milton felt the power of both :—

Elegant poet and passionate disputant, accomplished humanist and narrow sectary, admirer of Petrarch, of Shakspeare, and hair-splitting interpreter of Bible-texts, smitten with pagan antiquity and smitten with the Hebrew genius; and all this at once, without effort, naturally ;—an historical problem, a literary enigma !

Milton's early poems, such as the *Allegro*, the *Penseroso*, are poems produced while a sort of equilibrium still prevailed in the poet's nature ; hence their charm, and that of their youthful author :—

Nothing morose or repellent, purity without excess of rigour, gravity without fanaticism. Something wholesome and virginal, gracious and yet strong. A son of the North who has passed the way of Italy ; a last fruit of the Renascence, but a fruit filled with a savour new and strange !

But Milton's days proceeded, and he arrived at the latter years of his life, a life which in its outward fortunes darkened more and more, *alla s'assombrissant de plus en plus*, towards its close. He arrived at the time when 'his friends had disappeared, his dreams had vanished, his eyesight was quenched, the hand of old age was upon him.' It was then that, 'isolated by the very force of his genius,' but full of faith and fervour, he 'turned his eyes towards the celestial light' and produced *Paradise Lost.* In its form, M. Scherer observes, in its plan and distribution, the poem follows Greek and Roman models, particularly the *Æneid.* 'All in this respect is regular and classical; in this fidelity to the established models we recognise the literary superstitions of the Renascence.' So far as its form is concerned, *Paradise Lost* is, says M. Scherer, 'the copy of a copy, a tertiary formation. It is to the Latin epics what these are to Homer.'

The most important matter, however, is the contents of the poem, not the form. The contents are given by Puritanism. But let M. Scherer speak for himself:—

Paradise Lost is an epic, but a theological epic; and the theology of the poem is made up of the favourite dogmas of the Puritans,—the Fall, justification, God's sovereign decrees. Milton, for that matter, avows openly that he has a thesis to maintain; his object is, he tells us at the outset, to 'assert Eternal Providence and justify the ways of God to man.' *Paradise Lost*, then, is two distinct things in one,—an epic and a theodicy. Unfortunately, these two elements, which correspond to the two men of whom Milton was composed and to the two tendencies which ruled his century, these two elements have not managed to get amalgamated. Far from doing so, they clash with one another, and from their juxtaposition there results a suppressed contradiction which extends to the whole work, impairs its solidity, and compromises its value.

M. Scherer gives his reasons for thinking that the Christian theology is unmanageable in an epic poem, although the gods may come in very well in the *Iliad* and *Æneid.* Few will differ from him here, so we pass on. A theological poem is a mistake, says M. Scherer; but to call *Paradise Lost* a theological poem is to call it by too large a name. It is really a commentary on a biblical text,—the first two or three chapters of Genesis. Its subject, therefore, is a story, taken literally, which many of even the most religious people nowadays hesitate to take literally; while yet, upon our being able to take it literally, the whole real interest of the poem for us depends. Merely as matter of poetry, the story of the Fall has no special force or effectiveness; its effectiveness for us comes, and can only come, from our taking it all as the literal narrative of what positively happened.

Milton, M. Scherer thinks, was not strong in invention. The famous allegory of Sin and Death may be taken as a specimen of what he could do in this line, and the allegory of Sin and Death is uncouth and unpleasing.

But invention is dangerous when one is dealing with a subject so grave, so strictly formulated by theology, as the subject of Milton's choice. Our poet felt this, and allowed little scope to free poetical invention. He adhered in general to data furnished by Scripture, and supplemented somewhat by Jewish legend. But this judicious self-limitation had, again, its drawbacks:—

If Milton has avoided factitious inventions, he has done so at the price of another disadvantage; the bareness of his story, the epic poverty of his poem. It is not merely that the reader is carried up into the sphere of religious abstractions, where man loses power to see or breathe. Independently of this, everything is here too simple, both actors and actions. Strictly speaking, there is but one personage before us, God the Father; inasmuch as God cannot appear without effacing everyone else, nor speak without the accomplishment of his will. The Son is but the Father's double. The angels and archangels are but his messengers, nay, they are less; they are but his decrees personified, the supernumeraries of a drama which would be transacted quite as well without them.

Milton has struggled against these conditions of the subject which he had chosen. He has tried to escape from them, and has only made the drawback more visible. The long speeches with which he fills up the gaps of the action are sermons, and serve but to reveal the absence of action. Then, as, after all, some action, some struggle, was necessary, the poet had recourse to the revolt of the angels. Unfortunately, such is the fundamental vice of the subject, that the poet's instrument has, one may say, turned against him. What his action has gained from it in movement it has lost in probability. We see a battle, indeed, but who can take either the combat or the combatants seriously? Belial shows his sense of this, when in the infernal council he rejects the idea of engaging in any conflict whatever, open or secret, with Him who is Allseeing and Almighty; and really one cannot comprehend how his mates should have failed to acquiesce in a consideration so evident. But, I repeat, the poem was not possible save at the price of this impossibility. Milton, therefore, has courageously made the best of it. He has gone with it all lengths, he has accepted in all its extreme consequences the most inadmissible of fictions. He has exhibited to us Jehovah apprehensive for his omnipotence, in fear of seeing his position turned, his residence surprised, his throne usurped. He has drawn the angels hurling mountains at one another's heads, and firing cannon at one another. He has shown us the victory doubtful until the Son appears armed with lightnings, and standing on a car horsed by four Cherubim.

The fault of Milton's poem is not, says M. Scherer, that, with his Calvinism of the seventeenth century, Milton was a man holding other beliefs than ours. Homer, Dante, held other beliefs than ours:—

But Milton's position is not the same as theirs. Milton has something he wants to prove, he supports a thesis. It was his intention, in his poem, to do duty as theologian as well as poet; at any rate, whether he meant it or not, *Paradise Lost* is a didactic work, and the form of it, therefore, cannot be separated from the substance. Now, it turns out that the idea of the poem will not bear examination; that its solution for the problem of evil is almost burlesque; that the character of its heroes, Jehovah and Satan, has no coherence; that what happens to Adam interests us but little; finally, that the action takes place in regions where the interests and passions of our common humanity can have no scope. I have already insisted on this contradiction in Milton's epic; the story on which it turns can have meaning and value only so long as it preserves its dogmatic weight, and, at the same time, it cannot preserve this without falling into theology,—that is to say, into a domain foreign to that of art. The subject of the poem is nothing if it is not real, and if it does not touch us as the turning-point of our destinies; and the more the poet seeks to grasp this reality, the more it escapes from him.

In short, the whole poem of *Paradise Lost* is vitiated, says M. Scherer, 'by a kind of antinomy, by the conjoint necessity and impossibility of taking its contents literally.'

M. Scherer then proceeds to sum up. And in ending, after having once more marked his objections and accentuated them, he at last finds again that note of praise, which the reader will imagine him to have quite lost:—

To sum up: *Paradise Lost* is a false poem, a grotesque poem, a tiresome poem; there is not one reader out of a hundred who can read the ninth and tenth books without smiling, or the eleventh and twelfth without yawning. The whole thing is without solidity; it is a pyramid resting on its apex, the most solemn of problems resolved by the most puerile of means. And, notwithstanding, *Paradise Lost* is immortal. It lives by a certain number of episodes which are for ever famous. Unlike Dante, who must be read as a whole if we want really to seize his beauties, Milton ought to be read only by passages. But these passages form part of the poetical patrimony of the human race.

And not only in things like the address to light, or the speeches of Satan, is Milton admirable, but in single lines and images everywhere :—

Paradise Lost is studded with incomparable lines. Milton's poetry is, as it were, the very essence of poetry. The author seems to think always in images, and these images are grand and proud like his soul, a wonderful mixture of the sublime and the picturesque. For rendering things he has the unique word, the word which is a discovery. Everyone knows his *darkness visible.*

M. Scherer cites other famous expressions and lines, so familiar that we need not quote them here. Expressions of the kind, he says, not only beautiful, but always, in addition to their beauty, striking one as the absolutely right thing (*toujours justes dans leur beauté*), are in *Paradise Lost* innumerable. And he concludes :—

Moreover, we have not said all when we have cited particular lines of Milton. He has not only the image and the word, he has the period also, the large musical phrase, somewhat long, somewhat laden with ornaments and intricate with inversions, but bearing all along with it in its superb undulation. Lastly, and above all, he has a something indescribably serene and victorious, an unfailing level of style, power indomitable. He seems to wrap us in a fold of his robe, and to carry us away with him into the eternal regions where is his home.

With this fine image M. Scherer takes leave of Milton. Yet the simple description of the man in Johnson's life of him touches us more than any image; the description of the old poet 'seen in a small house, neatly enough dressed in black clothes, sitting in a room hung with rusty green, pale but not cadaverous, with chalk stones in his hands. He said that, if it were not for the gout his blindness would be tolerable.'

But in his last sentences M. Scherer comes upon what is undoubtedly Milton's true distinction as a poet, his 'unfailing level of style.' Milton has always the sure, strong touch of the master. His power both of diction and of rhythm is unsurpassable, and it is characterised by being always present—not depending on an access of emotion, not intermittent, but, like the grace of Raphael, working in its possessor as a constant gift of nature.

Milton's style, moreover, has the same propriety and soundness in presenting plain matters, as in the comparatively smooth task for a poet of presenting grand ones. His rhythm is as admirable where, as in the line

> And Tiresias and Phineus, prophets old——

it is unusual, as in such lines as—

> With dreadful faces throng'd and fiery arms——

where it is simplest. And what high praise this is, we may best appreciate by considering the ever-recurring failure, both in rhythm and in diction, which we find in the so-called Miltonic blank verse of Thomson, Cowper, Wordsworth. What leagues of lumbering movement! what desperate endeavours, as in Wordsworth's

> And at the 'Hoop' alighted, famous inn,

to render a platitude endurable by making it pompous! Shakspeare himself, divine as are his gifts, has not, of the marks of the master, this one: perfect sureness of hand in his style. Alone of English poets, alone in English art, Milton has it; he is our great artist in style, our one first-rate master in the grand style. He is as truly a master in this style as the great Greeks are, or Virgil, or Dante. The number of such masters is so limited that a man acquires a world-rank in poetry and art, instead of a mere local rank, by being counted among them. But Milton's importance to us Englishmen, by virtue of this distinction of his, is incalculable. The charm of a master's unfailing touch in diction and in rhythm, no one, after all, can feel so intimately, so profoundly, as his own countrymen. Invention, plan, wit, pathos, thought, all of them are in great measure capable of being detached from the original work itself, and of being exported for admiration abroad. Diction and rhythm are not. Even when a foreigner can read the work in its own language, they are not, perhaps, easily appreciable by him. It shows M. Scherer's thorough knowledge of English, and his critical sagacity also, that he has felt the force of them in Milton. We natives must naturally feel it yet more powerfully. Be it remembered, too, that English literature, full of vigour and genius as it is, is peculiarly impaired by gropings and inadequacies in form. And the same with English art. Therefore for the English artist in any line, if he is a true artist, the study of Milton may well have an indescribable attraction. It gives him lessons which nowhere else from an Englishman's work can he obtain, and feeds a sense which English work, in general, seems bent on disappointing and baffling. And this sense is yet so deep-seated in human nature,—this sense of style,—that probably not for artists alone, but for all intelligent

Englishmen who read him, its gratification by Milton's poetry is a large though often not fully recognised part of his charm, and a very wholesome and fruitful one.

As a man, too, not less than as a poet, Milton has a side of unsurpassable grandeur. A master's touch is the gift of nature. Moral qualities, it is commonly thought, are in our own power. Perhaps the germs of such qualities are in their greater or less strength as much a part of our natural constitution as the sense for style. The range open to our own will and power, however, in developing and establishing them, is evidently much larger. Certain high moral dispositions Milton had from nature, and he sedulously trained and developed them until they became habits of great power.

Some moral qualities seem to be connected in a man with his power of style. Milton's power of style, for instance, has for its great character *elevation*; and Milton's elevation clearly comes, in the main, from a moral quality in him,—his pureness. 'By pureness, by kindness!' says St. Paul. These two, pureness and kindness, are, in very truth, the two signal Christian virtues, the two mighty wings of Christianity, with which it winnowed and renewed, and still winnows and renews, the world. In kindness, and in all which that word conveys or suggests, Milton does not shine. He had the temper of his Puritan party.

We often hear the boast, on behalf of the Puritans, that they produced 'our great epic poet.' Alas ! one might not unjustly retort that they spoiled him. However, let Milton bear his own burden ; in his temper he had natural affinities with the Puritans. He has paid for it by limitations as a poet. But, on the other hand, how high, clear, and splendid is his pureness ; and how intimately does its might enter into the voice of his poetry ! We have quoted some ill-conditioned passages from his prose; let us quote from it a passage of another stamp :—

And long it was not after, when I was confirmed in this opinion, that he, who would not be frustrate of his hope to write well hereafter in laudable things, ought himself to be a true poem ; that is, a composition and pattern of the best and honourablest things ; not presuming to sing high praises of heroic men, or famous cities, unless he have in himself the experience and the practice of all that which is praiseworthy. These reasonings, together with a certain niceness of nature, an honest haughtiness and self-esteem, either of what I was or what I might be (which let envy call pride), and lastly that modesty whereof here I may be excused to make some beseeming profession ; all these uniting the supply of their natural aid together kept me still above low descents of mind. Next (for hear me out now, readers), that I may tell you whither my younger feet wandered ; I betook me among those lofty fables and romances which recount in solemn cantos the deeds of knighthood founded by our victorious kings, and from hence had in renown over all Christendom. There I read it in the oath of every knight, that he should defend to the expense of his best blood, or of his life if it so befell him, the honour and chastity of virgin or matron; from whence even then I learnt what a noble virtue chastity sure must be, to the defence of which so many worthies by such a dear adventure of themselves had sworn. Only this my mind gave me, that every free and gentle spirit, without that oath, ought to be born a knight, nor needed to expect the gilt spur, or the laying of a sword upon his shoulder, to stir him up both by his counsel and his arm to secure and protect the weakness of any attempted chastity.

Mere fine professions are in this department of morals more common and more worthless than in any other. What gives to Milton's professions such a stamp of their own is their accent of absolute sincerity. In this elevated strain of moral pureness his life was really pitched; its strong, immortal beauty passed into the diction and rhythm of his poetry.

But I did not propose to write a criticism of my own upon Milton. I proposed to recite and compare the criticisms on him by others. Only one is tempted, after our many extracts from M. Scherer, in whose criticism of Milton the note of blame fills so much more place than the note of praise, to accentuate this note of praise, which

M. Scherer touches indeed with justness, but hardly perhaps draws out fully enough or presses firmly enough. As a poet and as a man, Milton has a side of grandeur so high and rare, as to give him rank along with the half-dozen greatest poets who have ever lived, although to their masterpieces his *Paradise Lost* is, in the fulfilment of the complete range of conditions which a great poem ought to satisfy, indubitably inferior.

Nothing is gained by huddling on 'our great epic poet,' in a promiscuous heap, every sort of praise. Sooner or later the question: How does Milton's masterpiece really stand to us moderns, what are we to think of it, what can we get from it? must inevitably be asked and answered. We have marked that side of the answer which is and will always remain favourable to Milton. The unfavourable side of the answer is supplied by M. Scherer. '*Paradise Lost* lives; but none the less is it true that its fundamental conceptions have become foreign to us, and that if the work subsists it is in spite of the subject treated by it.'

The verdict seems just, and it is supported by M. Scherer with considerations natural, lucid, and forcible. He, too, has his conventions when he comes to speak of Racine and Lamartine. But his judgments on foreign poets, on Shakspeare, Byron, Goethe, as well as on Milton, seem to me to be singularly uninfluenced by the conventional estimates of these poets, and singularly rational. Leaning to the side of severity, as is natural when one has been wearied by choruses of ecstatic and exaggerated praise, he yet well and fairly reports, I think, the real impression made by these great men and their works on a modern mind disinterested, intelligent, and sincere. The English reader, I hope, may have been interested in seeing how Milton and his *Paradise Lost* stand such a survey. And those who are dissatisfied with what has been thus given them may always revenge themselves by falling back upon their Addison, and by observing sarcastically that 'a few general rules extracted out of the French authors, with a certain cant of words, has sometimes set up an illiterate heavy writer for a most judicious and formidable critic.'

A FRENCH CRITIC ON GOETHE.

It takes a long time to ascertain the true rank of a famous writer. A young friend of Joseph de Maistre, a M. de Syon, writing in praise of the literature of the nineteenth century as compared with that of the eighteenth, said of Chateaubriand, that 'the Eternal created Chateaubriand to be a guide to the universe.' Upon which judgment Joseph de Maistre comments thus: 'Clear it is, my good young man, that you are only eighteen; let us hear what you have to say at forty.' '*On voit bien, excellent jeune homme, que vous avez dix-huit ans; je vous attends à quarante.*'

The same Joseph de Maistre has given an amusing history of the rise of our own Milton's reputation:—

> No one had any suspicion of Milton's merits, when one day Addison took the speaking-trumpet of Great Britain (the instrument of loudest sound in the universe), and called from the top of the Tower of London: 'Roman and Greek authors, give place!'

He did well to take this tone. If he had spoken modestly, if he had simply said that there were great beauties in *Paradise Lost*, he would not have produced the slightest impression. But this trenchant sentence, dethroning Homer and Virgil, struck the English exceedingly. They said one to the other: 'What, we possessed the finest epic poem in the world, and no one suspected it! What a thing is inattention! But now, at any rate, we have had our eyes opened.' In fact, the reputation of Milton has become a national property, a portion of the Establishment, a Fortieth Article; and the English would as soon think of giving up Jamaica as of giving up the pre-eminence of their great poet.

Joseph de Maistre goes on to quote a passage from a then recent English commentator on Milton,—Bishop Newton. Bishop Newton, it seems, declared that 'every man of taste and genius must admit *Paradise Lost* to be the most excellent of modern productions, as the Bible is the most perfect of the productions of antiquity.' In a note M. de Maistre adds: 'This judgment of the good bishop appears unspeakably ridiculous.'

Ridiculous, indeed! but a page or two later we shall find the clear-sighted critic himself almost as far astray as his 'good bishop' or as his 'good young man':—

The strange thing is that the English, who are thorough Greek scholars, are willing enough to admit the superiority of the Greek tragedians over Shakspeare; but when they come to Racine, *who is in reality simply a Greek speaking*

French, their standard of beauty all of a sudden changes, and Racine, who is at least the equal of the Greeks, has to take rank far below Shakspeare, who is inferior to them. This theorem in *trigonometry* presents no difficulties to the people of soundest understanding in Europe.

So dense is the cloud of error here that the lover of truth and daylight will hardly even essay to dissipate it; he does not know where to begin. It is as when M. Victor Hugo gives his list of the sovereigns on the world's roll of creators and poets: 'Homer, Æschylus, Sophocles, Lucretius, Virgil, Horace, Dante, Shakspeare, *Rabelais, Molière, Corneille, Voltaire.*' His French audience rise and cry enthusiastically: '*And Victor Hugo!*' And really that is perhaps the best criticism on what he has been saying to them.

Goethe, the great poet of Germany, has been placed by his own countrymen now low, now high; and his right poetical rank they have certainly not yet succeeded in finding. Tieck, in his introduction to the collected writings of Lenz, noticing Goethe's remark on Byron's *Manfred*,—that Byron had 'assimilated *Faust*, and sucked out of it the strangest nutriment to his hypochondria,'—says tartly that Byron, when he himself talked about his obligations to Goethe, was merely using the language of compliment, and would have been highly offended if anyone else had professed to discover them. And Tieck proceeds :—

> Everything which in the Englishman's poems might remind one of *Faust*, is in my opinion far above *Faust*; and the Englishman's feeling, and his incomparably more beautiful diction, are so entirely his own, that I cannot possibly believe him to have had *Faust* for his model.

But then there comes a scion of the excellent stock of the Grimms, a Professor Hermann Grimm, and lectures on Goethe at Berlin, now that the Germans have conquered the French, and are the first military power in the world, and have become a great nation, and require a national poet to match ; and Professor Grimm says of *Faust*, of which Tieck had spoken so coldly : 'The career of this, the greatest work of the greatest poet of all times and of all peoples, has but just begun, and we have been making only the first attempts at drawing forth its contents.'

If this is but the first letting out of the waters, the coming times may, indeed, expect a deluge.

Many and diverse must be the judgments passed upon every great poet, upon every considerable writer. There is the judgment of enthusiasm and admiration, which proceeds from ardent youth, easily fired, eager to find a hero and to worship him. There is the judgment of gratitude and sympathy, which proceeds from those who find in an author what helps them, what they want, and who rate him at a very high value accordingly. There is the judgment of ignorance, the judgment of incompatibility, the judgment of envy and jealousy. Finally, there is the systematic judgment, and this judgment is the most worthless of all. The sharp scrutiny of envy and jealousy may bring real faults to light. The judgments of incompatibility and ignorance are instructive, whether they reveal necessary clefts of separation between the experiences of different sorts of people, or reveal simply the narrowness and bounded view of those who judge. But the systematic judgment is altogether unprofitable. Its author has not really his eye upon the professed object of his criticism at all, but upon something else which he wants to prove by means of that object. He neither really tells us, therefore, anything about the object, nor anything about his own ignorance of the object. He never fairly looks at it, he is looking at something else. Perhaps if he looked at it straight and full, looked at it simply, he might be able to pass a good judgment on it. As it is, all he tells us is that he is no genuine critic, but a man with a system, an advocate.

Here is the fault of Professor Hermann Grimm, and of his Berlin lectures on Goethe. The professor is a man with a system; the lectures are a piece of advocacy. Professor Grimm is not looking straight at 'the greatest poet of all times and of all peoples;' he is looking at the necessities, as to literary glory, of the new German empire.

But the definitive judgment on this great Goethe, the judgment of mature reason, the judgment which shall come 'at forty years of age,' who may give it to us? Yet how desirable to have it! It is a mistake to think that the judgment of mature reason on our favourite author, even if it abates considerably our high-raised estimate of him, is not a gain to us. Admiration is positive, say some people, disparagement is negative; from what is negative we can get nothing. But is it no advantage, then, to the youthful enthusiast for Chateaubriand, to come to know that 'the Eternal did *not* create Chateaubriand to be a guide to the universe'? It is a very great advantage, because these over-charged admirations are always exclusive, and prevent us from giving heed to other things which deserve admiration. Admiration is salutary and formative, true; but things admirable are sown wide, and are to be gathered here and gathered there, not all in one place; and until we have gathered them wherever they are to be found, we have not known the true salutariness and formativeness of admiration. The quest is large ; and occupation with the unsound or half-sound, delight in the not good or less good, is a sore let and hindrance to us. Release from such occupation and delight sets us free for ranging farther, and for perfecting our sense of beauty. He is the happy man, who, encumbering himself with the love of nothing which is not beautiful, is able to embrace the greatest number of things beautiful in his love.

I have already spoken of the judgment of a French critic, M. Scherer, upon Milton. I propose now to draw attention to the judgment of the same critic upon Goethe. To set to work to discuss Goethe thoroughly, so as to arrive at the true definitive judgment respecting him, seems to me a most formidable enterprise. Certainly one should not think of attempting it within the limits of a single review-article. M. Scherer has devoted to Goethe not one article, but a series of articles. I do not say that the adequate, definitive judgment on Goethe is to be found in these articles of M. Scherer. But I think they afford a valuable contribution towards it. M. Scherer is well-informed, clear-sighted, impartial. He is not warped by injustice and ill-will towards Germany, although the war has undoubtedly left him with a feeling of soreness. He is candid and cool, perhaps a little cold. Certainly he will not tell us that 'the Eternal created Goethe to be a guide to the universe.' He is free from all heat of youthful enthusiasm, from the absorption of a discoverer in his new discovery, from the subjugation of a disciple by the master who has helped and guided him. He is not a man with a system. And his point of view is in many respects that of an Englishman. We mean that he has the same instinctive sense rebelling against what is verbose, ponderous, roundabout, inane,—in one word, *niais* or silly,—in German literature, just as a plain Englishman has.

This ground of sympathy between Englishmen and Frenchmen has not been enough remarked, but it is a very real one. They owe it to their having alike had a long-continued national life, a long-continued literary activity, such as no other modern nation has had. This course of practical experience does of itself beget a turn for directness and clearness of speech, a dislike for futility and fumbling, such as without it we shall rarely find general. Dr. Wiese, in his recent useful work on English schools, expresses surprise that the French language and literature should find more favour in Teutonic England than the German. But community of practice is more telling than community of origin. While English and French are printed alike, and while an English and a French sentence each of them says what it has to say in the same plain fashion, a German newspaper is still printed in black letter, and a German sentence is framed in the style of this which we quote from Dr. Wiese himself: 'Die Engländer einer grossen, in allen Erdtheilen eine Achtung gebietende Stellung einnehmenden Nation angehören!' The Italians are a Latin race, with a clear-cut language; but much of their modern prose has all the circuitousness and slowness of the German, and from the same cause: the want of the pressure of a great national life, with its practical discipline, its ever-active traditions; its literature, for centuries past, powerful and incessant. England has these in common with France.

M. Scherer's point of view, then, in judging the productions of German literature, will naturally, I repeat, coincide in several important respects with that of an Englishman. His mind will make many of the same instinctive demands as ours, will feel many of the same instinctive repugnances. We shall gladly follow him, therefore, through his criticism of Goethe's works. As far as possible he shall be allowed to speak for himself, as he was when we were dealing with his criticism on Milton. But as then, too, I shall occasionally compare M. Scherer's criticism on his author with the criticism of others. And I shall by no means attempt, on the present opportunity, a substantive criticism of my own, although

I may from time to time allow myself to comment, in passing, upon the judgments of M. Scherer.

We need not follow M. Scherer in his sketch of Goethe's life. It is enough to remember that the main dates in Goethe's life are, his birth in 1749; his going to Weimar with the Grand Duke, Carl-August, in 1775; his stay in Italy from September 1786 to June 1788; his return in 1788 to Weimar; a severe and nearly fatal illness in 1801; the loss of Schiller in 1805, of Carl-August in 1828; his own death in 1832. With these dates fixed in our minds, we may come at once to the consideration of Goethe's works.

The long list begins, as we all know, with *Götz von Berlichingen* and *Werther*. We all remember how Mr. Carlyle, 'the old man eloquent,' who in his younger days, fifty years ago, betook himself to Goethe for light and help, and found what he sought, and declared his gratitude so powerfully and well, and did so much to make Goethe's name a name of might for other Englishmen also, a strong tower into which the doubter and the despairer might run and be safe,—we all remember how Mr. Carlyle has taught us to see in *Götz* and in *Werther* the double source from which have flowed those two mighty streams,—the literature of feudalism and romance, represented for us by Scott, and the literature of emotion and passion, represented for us by Byron.

M. Scherer's tone throughout is, we have said, not that of the ardent and grateful admirer, but of the cool, somewhat cold critic. He by no manner of means resembles Mr. Carlyle. Already the cold tone appears in M. Scherer's way of dealing with Goethe's earliest productions. M. Scherer seems to me to rate the force and interest of *Götz* too low. But his remarks on the derivedness of this supposed *source* are just. The Germans, he says, were bent, in their 'Sturm und Drang' period, on throwing off literary conventions, imitation of all sorts, and on being original. What they really did, was to fall from one sort of imitation, the imitation of the so-called classical French literature of the seventeenth century, into another.

Götz von Berlichingen is a study composed after the dramatised chronicles of Shakspeare, and *Werther* is a product yet more direct of the sensibility and declamation brought into fashion by Jean Jacques Rousseau. All in these works is infantine, both the aim at being original, and the way of setting about it. It is exactly as it was with us, about 1830. One imagines one is conducting an insurrection, making oneself independent; what one really does is to cook up out of season an old thing. Shakspeare had put the history of his nation upon the stage; Goethe goes for a subject to German history. Shakspeare, who was not fettered by the scenic conditions of the modern theatre, changed the place at every scene ; *Götz* is cut up in the same fashion. I say nothing of the substance of the piece, of the absence of characters, of the nullity of the hero, of the commonplace of Weislingen 'the inevitable traitor,' of the melodramatic machinery of the secret tribunal. The style is no better. The astonishment is not that Goethe at twenty-five should have been equal to writing this piece ; the astonishment is that after so poor a start he should have subsequently gone so far.

M. Scherer seems to me quite unjust, I repeat, to this first dramatic work of Goethe. Mr. Hutton pronounces it 'far the most noble as well as the most powerful of Goethe's dramas.' And the merit which Mr. Hutton finds in *Götz* is a real one ; it is the work where Goethe, young and ardent, has most forgotten *himself* in his characters. 'There was something,' says Mr. Hutton (and here he and M. Scherer are entirely in accord), 'which prevented Goethe, we think, from ever becoming a great dramatist. He could never lose himself sufficiently in his creations.' It is in *Götz* that he loses himself in them the most. *Götz* is full of faults, but there is a life and a power in it, and it is not dull. This is what distinguishes it from Schiller's *Robbers*. The *Robbers* is at once violent and tiresome. *Götz* is violent, but it is not tiresome.

Werther, which appeared a year later than *Götz*, finds more favour at M. Scherer's hands. *Werther* is superior to *Götz*, he says, 'inasmuch as it is more modern, and is consequently alive, or, at any rate, has been alive lately. It has sincerity, passion, eloquence. One can still read it, and with emotion.' But then come the objections :—

Nevertheless, and just by reason of its truth at one particular moment, *Werther* is gone by. It is with the book as with the blue coat and yellow breeches of the hero ; the reader finds it hard to admit the pathetic in such accoutrement. There is too much enthusiasm for Ossian, too much absorption in nature, too many exclamations and apostrophes to beings animate and inanimate, too many torrents of tears. Who can forbear smiling as he reads the scene of the storm, where Charlotte first casts her eyes on the fields, then on the sky, and finally, laying her hand on her lover's, utters this one word : *Klopstock!* And then the cabbage-passage! . . . . *Werther* is the poem of the German middle-class sentimentality of that day. It must be said that our sentimentality, even at the height of the *Héloïse* season, never reached the extravagance of that of our neighbours . . . . Mdlle. Flachsland, who married Herder, writes to her betrothed that one night in the depth of the woods she fell on her knees as she looked at the moon, and that having found some glowworms she put them into her hair, being careful to arrange them in couples that she might not disturb their loves.

One can imagine the pleasure of a victim of 'Kruppism and corporalism' in relating that story of Mdlle. Flachsland. There is an even better story of the return of a Dr. Zimmermann to his home in Hanover, after being treated for hernia at Berlin; but for this story I must send the reader to M. Scherer's own pages.

After the publication of *Werther* began Goethe's life at Weimar. For ten years he brought out nothing except occasional pieces for the Court theatre, and occasional poems. True, he carried the project of his *Faust* in his mind, he planned *Wilhelm Meister*, he made the first draft of *Egmont*, he wrote *Iphigeneia* and *Tasso* in prose. But he could not make the progress he wished. He felt the need, for his work, of some influence which Weimar could not give. He became dissatisfied with the place, with himself, with the people about him. In the autumn of 1786 he disappeared from Weimar, almost by a secret flight, and crossed the Alps into Italy. M. Scherer says truly that this was the great event of his life.

Italy, Rome above all, satisfied Goethe, filled him with a sense of strength and joy. 'At Rome,' he writes from that city, 'he who has eyes to see, and who uses them seriously, becomes solid. The spirit receives a stamp of vigour; it attains to a gravity in which there is nothing dry or harsh,—to calm, to joy. For my own part, at any rate, I feel that I have never before had the power to judge things so justly, and I congratulate myself on the happy result for my whole future life.' So he wrote while he was in Rome. And he told the Chancellor von Müller, twenty-five years later, that from the hour when he crossed the Ponte Molle on his return to Germany, he had never known a day's happiness. 'While he spoke thus,' adds the Chancellor, 'his features betrayed his deep emotion.'

The Italy, from which Goethe thus drew satisfaction and strength, was Græco-Roman Italy, pagan Italy. For mediæval and Christian Italy he had no heed, no sympathy. He would not even look at the famous church of St. Francis at Assisi. 'I passed it by,' he says, 'in disgust.' And he told a young Italian who asked him his opinion of Dante's great poem, that he thought the *Inferno* abominable, the *Purgatorio* dubious, and the *Paradiso* tiresome.

I have not space to quote what M. Scherer says of the influence on Goethe's genius of his stay in Rome. We are more especially concerned with the judgments of M. Scherer on the principal works of Goethe as these works succeed one another. At Rome, or under the influence of Rome, *Iphigeneia* and *Tasso* were recast in verse, *Egmont* was resumed and finished, the chief portion of the first part of *Faust* was written. Of the larger works of Goethe in poetry, these are the chief. Let us see what M. Scherer has to say of them.

Tasso and *Iphigeneia*, says M. Scherer very truly, mark a new phase in the literary career of Goethe :—

They are works of finished style and profound composition. There is no need to inquire whether the *Iphigeneia* keeps to the traditional data of the subject ; Goethe desired to make it Greek only by its sententious elevation and grave beauty. What he imitates are the conditions of art as the ancients understood them, but he does not scruple to introduce new thoughts into these mythological *motives*. He has given up the aim of rendering by poetry what is characteristic or individual ; his concern is henceforth with the ideal, that is to say, with the transformation of things through beauty. If I were to employ the terms in use amongst ourselves, I should say that from romantic Goethe had changed to being classic ; but, let me say again, he is classic only by the adoption of the elevated style, he imitates the ancients merely by borrowing their peculiar sentiment as to art, and within these bounds he moves with freedom and power. The two elements, that of immediate or passionate feeling, and that of well-considered combination of means, balance one another, and give birth to finished works. *Tasso* and *Iphigeneia* mark the apogee of Goethe's talent.

It is curiously interesting to turn from this praise of *Tasso* and *Iphigeneia* to that by the late Mr. Lewes, whose

Life of Goethe, a work in many respects of brilliant cleverness, will be in the memory of many of us. 'A marvellous dramatic poem!' Mr. Lewes calls *Iphigeneia*. 'Beautiful as the separate passages are, admirers seldom think of passages, they think of the wondrous whole.' Of *Tasso*, Mr. Lewes says: 'There is a calm, broad effulgence of light in it, very different from the concentrated *lights* of effect which we are accustomed to find in modern works. It has the clearness, unity, and matchless grace of a Raphael, not the lustrous warmth of a Titian, or the crowded gorgeousness of a Paul Veronese.'

Everyone will remark the difference of tone between this criticism and M. Scherer's. Yet M. Scherer's criticism conveyed praise, and, for him, warm praise. *Tasso* and *Iphigeneia* mark, in his eyes, the period, the too short period, during which the forces of inspiration and of reflexion, the poet in Goethe and the critic in him, the thinker and the artist, in whose conflict M. Scherer sees the history of our author's literary development, were in equilibrium.

Faust also, the first part of *Faust*, the only one which counts, belongs by its composition to this *Tasso* period. By common consent it is the best of Goethe's works. For while it had the benefit of his matured powers of thought, of his command over his materials, of his mastery in planning and expressing, it possesses by the nature of its subject an intrinsic richness, colour, and warmth. Moreover, from Goethe's long and early occupation with the subject, *Faust* has preserved many a stroke and flash out of the days of its author's fervid youth. To M. Scherer, therefore, as to the world in general, the first part of *Faust* seems Goethe's masterpiece. M. Scherer does not call *Faust* the greatest work of the greatest poet of all times and all peoples, but thus he speaks of it :—

Goethe had the good fortune early to come across a subject, which, while it did not lend itself to his faults, could not but call forth all the powers of his genius. I speak of *Faust*. Goethe had begun to occupy himself with it as early as 1774, the year in which *Werther* was published. Considerable portions of the First Part appeared in 1790 ; it was completed in 1808. We may congratulate ourselves that the work was already, at the time of his travels in Italy, so far advanced as it was ; else there might have been danger of the author's turning away from it as from a Gothic, perhaps unhealthy, production. What is certain is, that he could not put into *Faust* his preoccupation with the antique, or, at any rate, he was obliged to keep this for the Second Part. The first *Faust* remained, whether Goethe would or no, an old story made young again, to serve as the poem of thought, the poem of modern life. This kind of adaptation had evidently great difficulties. It was impossible to give the story a satisfactory ending ; the compact between the Doctor and the Devil could not be made good, consequently the original condition of the story was gone, and the drama was left without an issue. We must, therefore, take *Faust* as a work which is not finished, and which could not be finished. But, in compensation, the choice of this subject had all sorts of advan tages for Goethe. In place of the somewhat cold symbolism for which his mind had a turn, the subject of *Faust* compelled him to deal with popular beliefs. Instead of obliging him to produce a drama with beginning, middle and end, it allowed him to proceed by episodes and detached scenes. Finally, in a subject fantastic and diabolic there could hardly be found room for the imitation of models. Let me add, that in bringing face to face human aspiration represented by Faust and pitiless irony represented by Mephistopheles, Goethe found the natural scope for his keen observations on all things. It is unquestionable that *Faust* stands as one of the great works of poetry; and, perhaps, the most wonderful work of poetry in our century. The story, the subject, do not exist as a whole, but each episode by itself is perfect, and the execution is nowhere defective. *Faust* is a treasure of poetry, of pathos, of the highest wisdom, of a spirit inexhaustible and keen as steel. There is not, from the first verse to the last, a false tone or a weak line.

This praise is discriminating, and yet earnest, almost cordial. '*Faust* stands as one of the great works of poetry; and, perhaps, the most wonderful work of poetry in our century.' The *perhaps* might be away. But the praise is otherwise not coldly stinted, not limited ungraciously and unduly.

Goethe returned to 'the formless Germany,' to the

Germanic north with its 'cold wet summers,' of which he so mournfully complained. He returned to Weimar with its petty Court and petty town, its society which Carl-August himself, writing to Knebel, calls 'the most tiresome on the face of the earth,' and of which the ennui drove Goethe sometimes to 'a sort of internal despair.' He had his animating friendship with Schiller. He had also his connexion with Christiana Vulpius, whom he afterwards married. That connexion both the moralist and the man of the world may unite in condemning. M. Scherer calls it 'a degrading connexion with a girl of no education, whom Goethe established in his house to the great embarrassment of all his friends, whom he either could not or would not marry until eighteen years later, and who punished him as he deserved by taking a turn for drink,—a turn which their unfortunate son inherited.' In these circumstances was passed the second half of Goethe's life, after his return from Italy. The man of reflexion, always present in him, but balanced for a while by the man of inspiration, became now, M. Scherer thinks, predominant. There was a *refroidissement graduel*, a gradual cooling down, of the poet and artist.

The most famous works of Goethe which remain yet to be mentioned are *Egmont*, *Hermann and Dorothea*, *Wilhelm Meister*, the *Second Part of Faust*, and the

Gedichte, or short poems. Of *Egmont* M. Scherer says:—

This piece also belongs, by the date of its publication, to the period which followed Goethe's stay in Rome. But in vain did Goethe try to transform it, he could not succeed. The subject stood in his way. We need not be surprised, therefore, if *Egmont* remains a mediocre performance, Goethe having always been deficient in dramatic faculty, and not in this case redeeming his defect by qualities of execution, as in *Iphigeneia*. He is too much of a generaliser to create a character, too meditative to create an action. *Egmont* must be ranked by the side of *Götz*; it is a product of the same order. The hero is not a living being; one does not know what he wants; the object of the conspiracy is not brought out. The unfortunate Count does certainly exclaim, as he goes to the scaffold, that he is dying for liberty, but nobody had suspected it until that moment. It is the same with the popular movement; it is insufficiently rendered, without breadth, without power. I say nothing of Machiavel, who preaches toleration to the Princess Regent and tries to make her understand the uselessness of persecution; nor of Claire, a girl sprung from the people, who talks like an epigram of the Anthology: 'Neither soldiers nor lovers should have their arms tied.' *Egmont* is one of the weakest among Goethe's weak pieces for the stage.

But now, on the other hand, let us hear Mr. Lewes: 'When all is said, the reader thinks of Egmont and Clärchen, and flings criticism to the winds. These are the figures which remain in the memory ; bright, genial, glorious creations, comparable to any to be found in the long galleries of art !' What a different tone !

Aristotle says, with admirable common-sense, that the determination of how a thing really is, is *ὡς ἂν ὁ φρόνιμος ὁρίσειεν*, 'as the judicious would determine.' And would the judicious, after reading *Egmont*, determine with Mr. Lewes, or determine with M. Scherer? Let us for the present leave the judicious to try, and let us pass to M. Scherer's criticism of *Hermann and Dorothea*. 'Goethe's epic poem,' writes Schiller, 'you have read ; you will admit that it is the pinnacle of his and all our modern art.' In Professor Grimm's eyes, perhaps, this is but scant praise, but how much too strong is it for M. Scherer !

Criticism is considerably embarrassed in presence of a poem in many respects so highly finished as the antico-modern and heroico-middle-class idyll of Goethe. The ability which the author has spent upon it is beyond conception ; and, the kind of poem being once allowed, the indispensable concessions having been once made, it is certain that the pleasure is doubled by seeing, at each step, difficulty so marvellously overcome. But all this cannot make the effort to be effort well spent, nor the kind of poem a true, sound and worthy kind. *Hermann and Dorothea* remains a piece of elegant cleverness, a wager laid and won, but for all that, a feat of ingenuity and nothing more. It is not quite certain that our modern society will continue to have a poetry at all; but most undoubtedly, if it does have one, it will be on condition that this poetry belongs to its time by its language, as well as by its subject. Has any critic remarked how Goethe's manner of proceeding is at bottom that of parody, and how the turn of a straw would set the reader laughing at these farm-horses transformed into coursers, these village innkeepers and apothecaries who speak with the magniloquence of a Ulysses or a Nestor? Criticism should have the courage to declare that all this is not sincere poetry at all, but solely the product of an exquisite dilettantism, and,—to speak the definitive judgment upon it,—a factitious work.

Once again we will turn to Mr. Lewes for contrast:—

Do not let us discuss whether *Hermann and Dorothea* is or is not an epic. It is a poem. Let us accept it for what it is,—a poem full of life, character and beauty; of all idylls it is the most truly idyllic, of all poems describing country life and country people it is the most truthful. Shakspeare himself is not more dramatic in the presentation of character.

It is an excellent and wholesome discipline for a student of Goethe to be brought face to face with such opposite judgments concerning his chief productions. It compels us to rouse ourselves out of the passiveness with which we in general read a celebrated work, to open our eyes wide, to ask ourselves frankly how, according to our genuine feeling, the truth stands. We all recollect Mr.

Carlyle on *Wilhelm Meister*, 'the mature product of the first genius of our times':—

Anarchy has now become peace; the once gloomy and perturbed spirit is now serene, cheerfully vigorous, and rich in good fruits . . . The ideal has been built on the actual; no longer floats vaguely in darkness and regions of dreams, but rests in light, on the firm ground of human interest and business, as in its true scene, and on its true basis.

Schiller, too, said of *Wilhelm Meister*, that he 'accounted it the most fortunate incident in his existence to have lived to see the completion of this work.' And again: 'I cannot describe to you how deeply the truth, the beautiful vitality, the simple fulness of this work has affected me. The excitement into which it has thrown my mind will subside when I shall have thoroughly mastered it, and that will be an important crisis in my being.'

Now for the cold-water douche of our French critic:—

Goethe is extremely great, but he is extremely unequal. He is a genius of the first order, but with thicknesses, with spots, so to speak, which remain opaque and where the light does not pass. Goethe, to go farther, has not only genius, he has what we in France call *esprit*, he has it to any extent, and yet there are in him sides of commonplace and silliness. One cannot read his works without continually falling in with trivial admirations, solemn pieces of simplicity, reflexions which bear upon nothing. There are moments when Goethe turns upon society and upon art a ken of astonishing penetration; and there are other moments when he gravely beats in an open door, or a door which leads nowhere. In addition, he has all manner of hidden intentions, he loves byways of effect, seeks to insinuate lessons, and so becomes heavy and fatiguing. There are works of his which one cannot read without effort. I shall never forget the repeated acts of self-sacrifice which it cost me to finish *Wilhelm Meister* and the *Elective Affinities.* As Paul de Saint-Victor has put it: 'when Goethe goes in for being tiresome he succeeds with an astonishing perfection, he is the *Jupiter Pluvius* of ennui. The very height from which he pours it down, does but make its weight greater.' What an insipid invention is the pedagogic city! What a trivial world is that in which the Wilhelms and the Philinas, the Eduards and the Ottilias, have their being! Mignon has been elevated into a poetic creation; but Mignon has neither charm, nor mystery, nor veritable existence; nor any other poetry belonging to her,—let us say it right out,—except the half-dozen immortal stanzas put into her mouth.

And, as we brought Schiller to corroborate the praise of *Wilhelm Meister*, let us bring Niebuhr to corroborate the blame. Niebuhr calls *Wilhelm Meister* 'a menagerie of tame animals.'

After this the reader can perhaps imagine, without any specimens of it, the sort of tone in which M. Scherer passes judgment upon *Dichtung und Wahrheit*, and upon Goethe's prose in general. Even Mr. Lewes declares of

Goethe's prose: 'He has written with a perfection no German ever achieved before, and he has also written with a feebleness which it would be gratifying to think no German would ever emulate again.'

Let us return, then, to Goethe's poetry. There is the continuation of *Faust* still to be mentioned. First we will hear Mr. Carlyle. In *Helena* 'the design is,' says Mr. Carlyle, 'that the story of *Faust* may fade away at its termination into a phantasmagoric region, where symbol and thing signified are no longer clearly distinguished,' and that thus 'the final result may be curiously and significantly indicated rather than directly exhibited.' *Helena* is 'not a type of one thing, but a vague, fluctuating fitful adumbration of many.' It is, properly speaking, 'what the Germans call a *Mährchen*, a species of fiction they have particularly excelled in.' As to its composition, 'we cannot but perceive it to be deeply studied, appropriate and successful.'

The 'adumbrative' style here praised, in which 'the final result is curiously and significantly indicated rather than directly exhibited,' is what M. Scherer calls Goethe's 'last manner.'

It was to be feared that, as Goethe grew older and colder, the balance between those two elements of art, science and temperament, would not be preserved. This is just what happened, and hence arose Goethe's last manner. He had passed from representing characters to representing the ideal, he is now to pass from the ideal to the symbol. And this is quite intelligible; reflexion, as it develops, leads to abstraction, and from the moment when the artist begins to prefer ideas to sensation he falls inevitably into allegory, since allegory is his only means for directly expressing ideas. Goethe's third epoch is characterised by three things: an ever-increasing devotion to the antique as to the supreme revelation of the beautiful, a disposition to take delight in æsthetic theories, and, finally, an irresistible desire for giving didactic intentions to art. This last tendency is evident in the continuation of *Wilhelm Meister*, and in the second *Faust*. We may say that these two works are dead of a hypertrophy of reflexion. They are a mere mass of symbols, hieroglyphics, sometimes even mystifications. There is something extraordinarily painful in seeing a genius so vigorous and a science so consummate thus mistaking the elementary conditions of poetry. The fault, we may add, is the fault of German art in general. The Germans have more ideas than their plasticity of temperament, evidently below par, knows how to deal with. They are wanting in the vigorous sensuousness, the concrete and immediate impression of things, which makes the artist, and which distinguishes him from the thinker.

So much for Goethe's 'last manner' in general, and to serve as introduction to what M. Scherer has to say of the second *Faust* more particularly:—

The two parts of *Faust* are disparate. They do not proceed from one and the same conception. Goethe was like Defoe, like Milton, like so many others, who after producing a masterpiece have been bent on giving it a successor. Unhappily, while the first *Faust* is of Goethe's fairest time, of his most vigorous manhood, the second is the last fruit of his old age. Science, in the one, has not chilled poetic genius; in the other, reflexion bears sway and produces all kind of symbols and abstractions. The beauty of the first comes in some sort from its very imperfection; I mean, from the incessant tendency of the sentiment of reality, the creative power, the poetry of passion and nature, to prevail over the philosophic intention and to make us forget it. Where is the student of poetry who, as he reads the monologues of Faust or the sarcasms of Mephistopheles, as he witnesses the fall and the remorse of Margaret, the most poignant history ever traced by pen, any longer thinks of the *Prologue in Heaven* or of the terms of the compact struck between Faust and the Tempter? In the second part it is just the contrary. The idea is everything. Allegory reigns there. The poetry is devoid of that simple and natural realism without which art cannot exist. One feels oneself in a sheer region of didactics. And this is true even of the finest parts,—of the third act, for example,—as well as of the weakest. What can be more burlesque than this Euphorion, son of Faust and Helen, who is found at the critical moment under a cabbage-leaf!—no, I am wrong, who descends from the sky 'for all the world like a Phœbus,' with a little cloak and a little harp, and ends by breaking his neck as he falls at the feet of his parents? And all this to represent Lord Byron, and, in his person, modern poetry, which is the offspring of romantic art! What decadence, good heavens! and what a melancholy thing is old age, since it can make the most plastic of modern poets sink down to these fantasticalities worthy of Alexandria!

In spite of the high praise which he has accorded to *Tasso* and *Iphigeneia*, M. Scherer concludes, then, his review of Goethe's productions thus:—

Goethe is truly original and thoroughly superior only in his lyrical poems (the *Gedichte*), and in the first part of *Faust*. They are immortal works, and why? Because they issue from a personal feeling, and the spirit of system has not petrified them. And yet even his lyrical poems Goethe has tried to spoil. He went on correcting them incessantly; and, in bringing them to that degree of perfection in which we now find them, he has taken out of them their warmth.

The worshipper of Goethe will ask with wrath and bitterness of soul whether M. Scherer has yet done. Not quite. We have still to hear some acute remarks on the pomposity of diction in our poet's stage pieces. The English reader will best understand, perhaps, the kind of fault meant, if we quote from the *Natural Daughter* a couple of lines not quoted, as it happens, by M. Scherer. The heroine has a fall from her horse, and the Court physician comes to attend her. The Court physician is addressed thus:—

> Erfahrner Mann, dem unseres König's Leben,
> Das unschätzbare Gut, vertraut ist . . .

'Experienced man, to whom the life of our sovereign, that inestimable treasure, is given in charge.' Shakspeare would have said *Doctor*. The German drama is full of this sort of roundabout, pompous language. 'Everyone has laughed,' says M. Scherer, 'at the pomposity and periphrasis of French tragedy.' The heroic King of Pontus, in French tragedy, gives up the ghost with these words:—

> Dans cet embrassement dont la douceur me flatte,
> Venez, et recevez l'âme de Mithridate.

'What has not been said,' continues M. Scherer, 'and justly said, against the artificial character of French tragedy?' Nevertheless, 'people do not enough remember that, convention being universally admitted in the seventeenth century, sincerity and even a relative simplicity remained possible' with an artificial diction; whereas Goethe did not find his artificial diction imposed upon him by conditions from without,—he made it himself, and of set purpose.

It is a curious thing; this style of Goethe's has its cause just in that very same study which has been made such a matter of reproach against our tragedy-writers,—the study to maintain a pitch of general nobleness in all the language uttered. Everything with Goethe must be grave, solemn, sculptural. We see the influence of Winckelmann, and of his views on Greek art.

Of Goethe's character, too, as well as of his talent, M. Scherer has something to say. English readers will be familiar enough with complaints of Goethe's 'artistic egotism,' of his tendency to set up his own intellectual culture as the rule of his life. The freshness of M. Scherer's repetition of these old complaints consists in his connecting them, as we have seen, with the criticism of Goethe's literary development. But M. Scherer has some direct blame of defects in his author's character which is worth quoting :—

It must fairly be confessed, the respect of Goethe for the mighty of this earth was carried to excesses which make one uncomfortable for him. One is confounded by these earnestnesses of servility. The King of Bavaria pays him a visit ; the dear poet feels his head go round. The story should be read in the journal of the Chancellor von Müller. 'Goethe after dinner became more and more animated and cordial. "It was no light matter," he said, "to work out the powerful impression produced by the King's presence, to assimilate it internally. It is difficult, in such circumstances, to keep one's balance and not to lose one's head. And yet the important matter is to extract from this apparition its real significance, to obtain a clear and distinct image of it."'

Another time he got a letter from the same sovereign ; he

talks of it to Eckermann with the same devout emotion—he 'thanks Heaven for it as for a quite special favour.' And when one thinks that the king in question was no other than that poor Louis of Bavaria, the ridiculous dilettante of whom Heine has made such fun! Evidently Goethe had a strong dose of what the English call 'snobbishness.' The blemish is the more startling in him, because Goethe is, in other respects, a simple and manly character. Neither in his person nor in his manner of writing was he at all affected; he has no self-conceit; he does not pose. There is in this particular all the difference in the world between him and the majority of our own French authors, who seem always busy arranging their draperies, and asking themselves how they appear to the world and what the gallery thinks of them.

Goethe himself had in like manner called the French 'the women of Europe.' But let us remark that it was not 'snobbishness' in Goethe, which made him take so seriously the potentate who loved Lola Montes; it was simply his German 'corporalism.' A disciplinable and much-disciplined people, with little humour, and without the experience of a great national life, regards its official authorities in this devout and awe-struck way. To a German it seems profane and licentious to smile at his Dogberry. He takes Dogberry seriously and solemnly, takes him at his own valuation.

We are all familiar with the general style of the critic who, as the phrase is, 'cuts up' his author. Such a critic finds very few merits and a great many faults, and he ends either with a phrase of condemnation, or with a phrase of compassion, or with a sneer. We saw, however, in the case of Milton, that one must not reckon on M. Scherer's ending in this fashion. After a course of severe criticism he wound up with earnest, almost reverential, praise. The same thing happens again in his treatment of Goethe. No admirer of Goethe will be satisfied with the treatment which hitherto we have seen Goethe receive at M. Scherer's hands. And the summing-up begins in a strain which will not please the admirer much better :—

To sum up, Goethe is a poet full of ideas and of observation, full of sense and taste, full even of feeling no less than of acumen, and all this united with an incomparable gift of versification. But Goethe has no artlessness, no fire, no invention ; he is wanting in the dramatic fibre and cannot create ; reflexion, in Goethe, has been too much for emotion, the *savant* in him for poetry, the philosophy of art for the artist.

And yet the final conclusion is this :—

Nevertheless, Goethe remains one of the exceeding great among the sons of men. 'After all,' said he to one of his friends, 'there are honest people up and down the world who have got light from my books ; and whoever reads them, and gives himself the trouble to understand me, will acknowledge that he has acquired thence a certain inward freedom.'

I should like to inscribe these words upon the pedestal of Goethe's statue. No juster praise could be found for him, and in very truth there cannot possibly be for any man a praise higher or more enviable.

And in an article on Shakspeare, after a prophecy that the hour will come for Goethe, as in Germany it has of late come for Shakspeare, when criticism will take the place of adoration, M. Scherer, after insisting on those defects in Goethe of which we have been hearing so fully, protests that there are yet few writers for whom he feels a greater admiration than for Goethe, few to whom he is indebted for enjoyments more deep and more durable; and declares that Goethe, although he has not Shakspeare's power, is a genius more vast, more universal, than Shakspeare. He adds, to be sure, that Shakspeare had an advantage over Goethe in not outliving himself.

After all, then, M. Scherer is not far from being willing to allow, if any youthful devotee wishes to urge it, that 'the Eternal created Goethe to be a guide to the universe.' Yet he deals with the literary production of Goethe as we have seen. He is very far indeed from thinking it the performance 'of the greatest poet of all times and of all peoples.' And this is why I have thought M. Scherer's criticisms worthy of so much attention;—

because a double judgment, somewhat of this kind, is the judgment about Goethe to which mature experience, the experience got 'by the time one is forty years old,' does really, I think, bring us.

I do not agree with all M. Scherer's criticisms on Goethe's literary work. I do not myself feel, in reading the *Gedichte*, the truth of what M. Scherer says,—that Goethe has corrected and retouched them till he has taken all the warmth out of them. I do not myself feel the irritation in reading Goethe's Memoirs, and his prose generally, which they provoke in M. Scherer. True, the prose has none of those positive qualities of style which give pleasure, it is not the prose of Voltaire or Swift; it is loose, ill-knit, diffuse; it bears the marks of having been, as it mostly was, dictated,—and dictating is a detestable habit. But it is absolutely free from affectation; it lets the real Goethe reach us.

In other respects I agree in the main with the judgments passed by M. Scherer upon Goethe's works. Nay, some of them, such as *Tasso* and *Iphigeneia*, I should hesitate to extol so highly as he does. In that peculiar world of thought and feeling, wherein *Tasso* and *Iphigeneia* have their existence, and into which the reader too must enter in order to understand them, there is something factitious; something devised and determined by the thinker, not given by the necessity of nature herself; something too artificial, therefore, too deliberately studied,—as the French say, *trop voulu.* They cannot have the power of works where we are in a world of thought and feeling not invented but natural,—of works like the *Agamemnon* or *Lear.* *Faust*, too, suffers by comparison with works like the *Agamemnon* or *Lear.* M. Scherer says, with perfect truth, that the first part of *Faust* has not a single false tone or weak line. But it is a work, as he himself observes, 'of episodes and detached scenes,' not a work where the whole material together has been fused in the author's mind by strong and deep feeling, and then poured out in a single jet. It can never produce the single, powerful total-impression of works which have thus arisen.

The first part of *Faust* is, however, undoubtedly Goethe's best work. And it is so for the plain reason that, except his *Gedichte*, it is his most straightforward work in poetry. Mr. Hayward's is the best of the translations of *Faust* for the same reason,—because it is the most straightforward. To be simple and straightforward is, as Milton saw and said, of the essence of first-rate poetry. All that M. Scherer says of the ruinousness, to a poet, of 'symbols, hieroglyphics, mystifications,' is just. When Mr. Carlyle praises the *Helena* for being 'not a type of one thing, but a vague, fluctuating, fitful adumbration of many,' he praises it for what is in truth its fatal defect. The *Mährchen*, again, on which Mr. Carlyle heaps such praise, calling it 'one of the notablest performances produced for the last thousand years,' a performance 'in such a style of grandeur and celestial brilliancy and life as the Western imagination has not elsewhere reached;' the *Mährchen*, woven throughout of 'symbol, hieroglyphic, mystification,' is by that very reason a piece of solemn inanity, on which a man of Goethe's powers could never have wasted his time, but for his lot having been cast in a nation which has never lived.

Mr. Carlyle has a sentence on Goethe which we may turn to excellent account for the criticism of such works as the *Mährchen* and *Helena*:—

> We should ask (he says) what the poet's aim really and truly was, and how far this aim accorded, not with us and our individual crotchets and the crotchets of our little senate where we give or take the law, but with human nature and the nature of things at large; with the universal principles of poetic beauty, not as they stand written in our text-books, but in the hearts and imaginations of all men.

To us it seems lost labour to inquire what a poet's *aim* may have been; but for aim let us read *work*, and we have here a sound and admirable rule of criticism.

Let us ask how a poet's work accords, not with any one's fancies and crotchets, but 'with human nature and the nature of things at large, with the universal principles of poetic beauty as they stand written in the hearts and imaginations of all men,' and we shall have the surest rejection of symbol, hieroglyphic, and mystification in poetry. We shall have the surest condemnation of works like the *Mährchen* and the second part of *Faust*.

It is by no means as the greatest of poets that Goethe deserves the pride and praise of his German countrymen. It is as the clearest, the largest, the most helpful thinker of modern times. It is not principally in his published works, it is in the immense Goethe-literature of letter, journal, and conversation, in the volumes of Riemer, Falk, Eckermann, the Chancellor von Müller, in the letters to Merck and Madame von Stein and many others, in the correspondence with Schiller, the correspondence with Zelter, that the elements for an impression of the truly great, the truly significant Goethe are to be found. Goethe is the greatest poet of modern times, not because he is one of the half-dozen human beings who in the history of our race have shown the most signal gift for poetry, but because, having a very considerable gift for poetry, he was at the same time, in the width, depth, and richness of his criticism of life, by far our greatest modern man. He may be precious and important to us on this account above men of other and more alien times, who as poets rank higher. Nay, his preciousness and importance as a clear and profound modern spirit, as a master-critic of modern life, must communicate a worth of their own to his poetry, and may well make it erroneously seem to have a positive value and perfectness as poetry, more than it has. It is most pardonable for a student of Goethe, and may even for a time be serviceable, to fall into this error. Nevertheless, poetical defects, where they are present, subsist, and are what they are. And the same with defects of character. Time and attention bring them to light; and when they are brought to light, it is not good for us, it is obstructing and retarding, to refuse to see them. Goethe himself would have warned us against doing so. We can imagine, indeed, that great and supreme critic reading Professor Grimm's laudation of his poetical work with lifted eyebrows, and M. Scherer's criticisms with acquiescence.

Shall we say, however, that M. Scherer's tone in no way jars upon us, or that his presentation of Goethe, just and acute as is the view of faults both in Goethe's poetry and in Goethe's character, satisfies us entirely? By no means. One could not say so of M. Scherer's presentation of

Milton; of the presentation of Goethe one can say so still less. Goethe's faults are shown by M. Scherer, and they exist. Praise is given, and the right praise. But there is yet some defect in the portraiture as a whole. Tone and perspective are somehow a little wrong; the distribution of colour, the proportions of light and shade, are not managed quite as they should be. One would like the picture to be painted over again by the same artist with the same talent, but a little differently. And meanwhile we instinctively, after M. Scherer's presentation, feel a desire for some last words of Goethe's own, something which may give a happier and more cordial turn to our thoughts, after they have been held so long to a frigid and censorious strain. And there rises to the mind this sentence: '*Die Gestalt dieser Welt vergeht;* und ich möchte mich nur mit dem beschäftigen, was bleibende Verhältnisse sind.' '*The fashion of this world passeth away;* and I would fain occupy myself only with the abiding.' There is the true Goethe, and with that Goethe we would end!

But let us be thankful for what M. Scherer brings, and let us acknowledge with gratitude his presentation of Goethe to be, not indeed the definitive picture of Goethe, but a contribution, and a very able contribution, to that definitive picture. We are told that since the war of

1870 Frenchmen are abandoning literature for science. Why do they not rather learn of this accomplished senator of theirs, with his Geneva training, to extend their old narrow literary range a little, and to know foreign literatures as M. Scherer knows them?

GEORGE SAND.

THE months go round, and anniversaries return; on the ninth of June [1] George Sand will have been dead just one year. She was born in 1804; she was almost seventy-two years old when she died. She came to Paris after the revolution of 1830, with her *Indiana* written, and began her life of independence, her life of authorship, her life as *George Sand.* She continued at work till she died. For forty-five years she was writing and publishing, and filled Europe with her name.

It seems to me but the other day that I saw her, yet it was in the August of 1846, more than thirty years ago. I saw her in her own Berry, at Nohant, where her childhood and youth were passed, where she returned to live after she became famous, where she died and has now her grave. There must be many who, after reading her books, have felt the same desire which in those days of my youth, in 1846, took me to Nohant,—the desire to

[1] 1877.

see the country and the places of which the books that so charmed us were full. Those old provinces of the centre of France, primitive and slumbering,—Berry, La Marche, Bourbonnais; those sites and streams in them, of name once so indifferent to us, but to which George Sand gave such a music for our ear,—La Châtre, Ste. Sévère, the *Vallée Noire*, the Indre, the Creuse; how many a reader of George Sand must have desired, as I did, after frequenting them so much in thought, fairly to set eyes upon them!

I had been reading *Jeanne*. I made up my mind to go and see Toulx Ste. Croix and Boussac, and the Druidical stones on Mont Barlot, the *Pierres Jaunâtres*. I remember looking out Toulx in Cassini's great map at the Bodleian Library. The railway through the centre of France went in those days no farther than Vierzon. From Vierzon to Châteauroux one travelled by an ordinary diligence, from Châteauroux to La Châtre by a humbler diligence, from La Châtre to Boussac by the humblest diligence of all. At Boussac diligence ended, and *patache* began. Between Châteauroux and La Châtre, a mile or two before reaching the latter place, the road passes by the village of Nohant. The Château of Nohant, in which Madame Sand lived, is a plain house by the road-side, with a walled garden. Down in the meadows, not far off, flows the Indre, bordered by trees. I passed Nohant without stopping, at La Châtre I dined and changed diligence, and went on by night up the valley of the Indre, the *Vallée Noire*, past Ste. Sévère to Boussac. At Ste. Sévère the Indre is quite a small stream. In the darkness we quitted its valley, and when day broke we were in the wilder and barer country of La Marche, with Boussac before us, and its high castle on a precipitous rock over the Little Creuse.

That day and the next I wandered through a silent country of heathy and ferny *landes*, a region of granite boulders, holly, and broom, of copsewood and great chestnut trees; a region of broad light, and fresh breezes, and wide horizons. I visited the *Pierres Jaunâtres*. I stood at sunset on the platform of Toulx Ste. Croix, by the scrawled and almost effaced stone lions,—a relic, it is said, of the English rule,—and gazed on the blue mountains of Auvergne filling the distance, and, south-eastward of them, in a still further and fainter distance, on what seemed to be the mountains over Le Puy and the high valley of the Loire.

From Boussac I addressed to Madame Sand the sort of letter of which she must in her lifetime have had scores, a letter conveying to her, in bad French, the homage of a youthful and enthusiastic foreigner who had read her works with delight. She received the infliction good-naturedly, for on my return to La Châtre I found a message left at the inn by a servant from Nohant that Madame Sand would be glad to see me if I called. The midday breakfast at Nohant was not yet over when I reached the house, and I found a large party assembled. I entered with some trepidation, as well I might, considering how I had got there; but the simplicity of Madame Sand's manner put me at ease in a moment. She named some of those present; amongst them were her son and daughter, the Maurice and Solange so familiar to us from her books, and Chopin with his wonderful eyes. There was at that time nothing astonishing in Madame Sand's appearance. She was not in man's clothes, she wore a sort of costume not impossible, I should think (although on these matters I speak with hesitation), to members of the fair sex at this hour amongst ourselves, as an out-door dress for the country or for Scotland. She made me sit by her and poured out for me the insipid and depressing beverage, *boisson fade et mélancolique*, as Balzac called it, for which English people are thought abroad to be always thirsting,—tea. She conversed of the country through which I had been wandering, of the Berry peasants and their mode of life, of Switzerland whither I was going; she touched politely, by a few questions and remarks, upon England and things and persons English,—upon Oxford and Cambridge, Byron, Bulwer. As she spoke, her eyes, head, bearing, were all of them striking; but the main impression she made was an impression of what I have already mentioned,—of *simplicity*, frank, cordial simplicity. After breakfast she led the way into the garden, asked me a few kind questions about myself and my plans, gathered a flower or two and gave them to me, shook hands heartily at the gate, and I saw her no more. In 1859 M. Michelet gave me a letter to her, which would have enabled me to present myself in more regular fashion. Madame Sand was then in Paris. But a day or two passed before I could call, and when I called, Madame Sand had left Paris and had gone back to Nohant. The impression of 1846 has remained my single impression of her.

Of her gaze, form, and speech, that one impression is enough; better perhaps than a mixed impression from seeing her at sundry times and after successive changes. But as the first anniversary of her death draws near, there arises again a desire which I felt when she died, the desire, not indeed to take a critical survey of her,—very far from it. I feel no inclination at all to go regularly through her productions, to classify and value them one by one, to pick out from them what the English public may most like, or to present to that public, for the most part ignorant of George Sand and for the most part indifferent to her, a full history and a judicial estimate of the woman and of her writings. But I desire to recall to my own mind, before the occasion offered by her death passes quite away,—to recall and collect the elements of that powerful total-impression which, as a writer, she made upon me; to recall and collect them, to bring them distinctly into view, to feel them in all their depth and power once more. What I here attempt is not for the benefit of the indifferent; it is for my own satisfaction, it is for myself. But perhaps those for whom George Sand has been a friend and a power will find an interest in following me.

Le sentiment de la vie idéale, qui n'est autre que la vie normale telle que nous sommes appelés à la connaître;—'the sentiment of the ideal life, which is none other than man's normal life as we shall some day know it,'—those words from one of her last publications give the ruling thought of George Sand, the ground-*motive*, as they say in music, of all her strain. It is as a personage inspired by this motive that she interests us.

The English public conceives of her as of a novel-writer who wrote stories more or less interesting; the earlier ones objectionable and dangerous, the later ones, some of them, unexceptionable and fit to be put into the hands of the youth of both sexes. With such a conception of George Sand, a story of hers like *Consuelo* comes to be elevated in England into quite an undue relative importance, and to pass with very many people for her typical work, displaying all that is really valuable and significant in the author. *Consuelo* is a charming story. But George Sand is something more than a maker of charming stories, and only a portion of her is shown in *Consuelo*. She is more, likewise, than a creator of characters. She has created, with admirable truth to nature, characters most attractive and attaching, such as Edmée, Geneviève, Germain. But she is not adequately expressed by them. We do not know her unless we feel the spirit which goes through her work as a whole.

In order to feel this spirit it is not, indeed, necessary to read all that she ever produced. Even three or four only out of her many books might suffice to show her to us, if they were well chosen; let us say, the *Lettres d'un Voyageur*, *Mauprat*, *François le Champi*, and a story which I was glad to see Mr. Myers, in his appreciative notice of Madame Sand, single out for praise,—*Valvèdre*. In these may be found all the principal elements of their author's strain: the cry of agony and revolt, the trust in nature and beauty, the aspiration towards a purged and renewed human society.

Of George Sand's strain, during forty years, these are the grand elements. Now it is one of them which appears most prominently, now it is another. The cry of agony and revolt is in her earlier work only, and passes away in her later. But in the evolution of these three elements,—the passion of agony and revolt, the consolation from nature and from beauty, the ideas of social renewal,—in the evolution of these is George Sand and George Sand's life and power. Through their evolution her constant motive declares and unfolds itself, that motive which we have set forth above: 'the sentiment of the ideal life, which is none other than man's normal life as we shall one day know it.' This is the motive, and through these elements is its evolution; an evolution pursued, moreover, with the most unfailing resolve, the most absolute sincerity.

The hour of agony and revolt passed away for George Sand, as it passed away for Goethe, as it passes away for their readers likewise. It passes away and does not return; yet those who, amid the agitations, more or less stormy, of their youth, betook themselves to the early works of George Sand, may in later life cease to read them, indeed, but they can no more forget them than they can forget *Werther*. George Sand speaks somewhere of her 'days of *Corinne*.' Days of *Valentine*, many of us may in like manner say,—days of *Valentine*, days of *Lélia*, days never to return! They are gone, we shall read the books no more, and yet how ineffaceable is their impression! How the sentences from George Sand's works of that period still linger in our memory and haunt the ear with their cadences! Grandiose and moving, they come, those cadences, like the sighing of the wind through the forest, like the breaking of the waves on the sea-shore. Lélia in her cell on the mountain of the Camaldoli—

Sibyl, Sibyl forsaken; spirit of the days of old, joined to a brain which rebels against the divine inspiration; broken lyre, mute instrument, whose tones the world of to-day, if it heard them, could not understand, but yet in whose depth the eternal harmony murmurs imprisoned; priestess of death, I, I who feel and know that before now I have been Pythia, have wept before now, before now have spoken, but who cannot recollect, alas, cannot utter the word of healing! Yes, yes! I remember the cavern of truth and the access of revelation; but the word of human destiny, I have forgotten it; but the talisman of deliverance, it is lost from my hand. And yet, indeed, much, much have I seen! and when suffering presses me sore, when indignation takes hold of me, when I feel Prometheus wake up in my heart and beat his puissant wings against the stone which confines him,—oh! then, in prey to a frenzy without a name, to a despair without bounds,

I invoke the unknown master and friend who might illumine my spirit and set free my tongue; but I grope in darkness, and my tired arms grasp nothing save delusive shadows. And for ten thousand years, as the sole answer to my cries, as the sole comfort in my agony, I hear astir, over this earth accurst, the despairing sob of impotent agony. For ten thousand years I have cried in infinite space: *Truth! Truth!* For ten thousand years infinite space keeps answering me: *Desire, Desire.* O Sybil forsaken! O mute Pythia! dash then thy head against the rocks of thy cavern, and mingle thy raging blood with the foam of the sea; for thou deemest thyself to have possessed the almighty Word, and these ten thousand years thou art seeking him in vain.

Or Sylvia's cry over Jacques by his glacier in the Tyrol—

When such a man as thou art is born into a world where he can do no true service; when, with the soul of an apostle and the courage of a martyr, he has simply to push his way among the heartless and aimless crowds which vegetate without living; the atmosphere suffocates him and he dies. Hated by sinners, the mock of fools, disliked by the envious, abandoned by the weak, what can he do but return to God, weary with having laboured in vain, in sorrow at having accomplished nothing? The world remains in all its vileness and in all its hatefulness; this is what men call, 'the triumph of good sense over enthusiasm.'

Or Jacques himself, and his doctrine—

Life is arid and terrible, repose is a dream, prudence is

useless; mere reason alone serves simply to dry up the heart; there is but one virtue, the eternal sacrifice of oneself.

Or George Sand speaking in her own person, in the *Lettres d'un Voyageur*—

Ah, no, I was not born to be a poet, I was born to love. It is the misfortune of my destiny, it is the enmity of others, which have made me a wanderer and an artist. What I wanted was to live a human life; I had a heart, it has been torn violently from my breast. All that has been left me is a head, a head full of noise and pain, of horrible memories, of images of woe, of scenes of outrage. And because in writing stories to earn my bread I could not help remembering my sorrows, because I had the audacity to say that in married life there were to be found miserable beings, by reason of the weakness which is enjoined upon the woman, by reason of the brutality which is permitted to the man, by reason of the turpitudes which society covers and protects with a veil, I am pronounced immoral, I am treated as if I were the enemy of the human race.

If only, alas, together with her honesty and her courage, she could feel within herself that she had also light and hope and power; that she was able to lead those whom she loved, and who looked to her for guidance! But no; her very own children, witnesses of her suffering, her uncertainty, her struggles, her evil report, may come to doubt her:—

My poor children, my own flesh and blood, will perhaps turn upon me and say : 'You are leading us wrong, you mean to ruin us as well as yourself. Are you not unhappy, reprobated, evil spoken of? What have you gained by these unequal struggles, by these much trumpeted duels of yours with custom and belief? Let us do as others do ; let us get what is to be got out of this easy and tolerant world.'

This is what they will say to me. Or at best, if, out of tenderness for me, or from their own natural disposition, they give ear to my words and believe me, whither shall I guide them? Into what abysses shall we go and plunge ourselves, we three?—for we shall be our own three upon earth, and not one soul with us. What shall I reply to them if they come and say to me : 'Yes, life is unbearable in a world like this. Let us die together. Show us the path of Bernica, or the lake of Sténio, or the glaciers of Jacques.'

Nevertheless the failure of the impassioned seekers of a new and better world proves nothing, George Sand maintains, for the world as it is. Ineffectual they may be, but the world is still more ineffectual, and it is the world's course which is doomed to ruin, not theirs. 'What has it done,' exclaims George Sand in her preface to Guérin's *Centaure*, 'what has it done for our moral education, and what is it doing for our children, this society shielded with such care?' Nothing. Those whom it calls vain complainers and rebels and madmen, may reply :—

Suffer us to bewail our martyrs, poets without a country

that we are, forlorn singers, well versed in the causes of their misery and of our own. You do not comprehend the malady which killed them; they themselves did not comprehend it. If one or two of us at the present day open our eyes to a new light, is it not by a strange and unaccountable good Providence; and have we not to seek our grain of faith in storm and darkness, combated by doubt, irony, the absence of all sympathy, all example, all brotherly aid, all protection and countenance in high places? Try yourselves to speak to your brethren heart to heart, conscience to conscience! Try it!—but you cannot, busied as you are with watching and patching up in all directions your dykes which the flood is invading. The material existence of this society of yours absorbs all your care, and requires more than all your efforts. Meanwhile the powers of human thought are growing into strength, and rise on all sides around you. Amongst these threatening apparitions, there are some which fade away and re-enter the darkness, because the hour of life has not yet struck, and the fiery spirit which quickened them could strive no longer with the horrors of this present chaos; but there are others that can wait, and you will find them confronting you, up and alive, to say: 'You have allowed the death of our brethren, and we, we do not mean to die.'

She did not, indeed. How should she faint and fail before her time, because of a world out of joint, because of the reign of stupidity, because of the passions of youth, because of the difficulties and disgusts of married life in the native seats of the *homme sensuel moyen*, the average sensual man, she who could feel so well the power of those eternal consolers, nature and beauty? From the very first they introduce a note of suavity in her strain of grief and passion. Who can forget the lanes and meadows of *Valentine*?

George Sand is one of the few French writers who keep us closely and truly intimate with rural nature. She gives us the wild-flowers by their actual names,—snowdrop, primrose, columbine, iris, scabious. Nowhere has she touched her native Berry and its little-known landscape, its *campagnes ignorées*, with a lovelier charm than in *Valentine*. The winding and deep lanes running out of the high road on either side, the fresh and calm spots they take us to, 'meadows of a tender green, plaintive brooks, clumps of alder and mountain ash, a whole world of suave and pastoral nature,'—how delicious it all is! The grave and silent peasant whose very dog will hardly deign to bark at you, the great white ox, 'the unfailing dean of these pastures,' staring solemnly at you from the thicket; the farmhouse 'with its avenue of maples, and the Indre, here hardly more than a bright rivulet, stealing along through rushes and yellow iris, in the field below,'—who, I say, can forget them? And that one lane in especial, the lane where Athénaïs puts her arm out of the side window of the rustic carriage and gathers May from the over-arching hedge,—that lane with its startled blackbirds, and humming insects, and limpid water, and swaying water-plants, and shelving gravel, and yellow wagtails hopping half-pert, half-frightened, on the sand,—that lane with its rushes, cresses, and mint below, its honeysuckle and traveller's-joy above,—how gladly might one give all that strangely English picture in English, if the charm of Madame Sand's language did not here defy translation! Let us try something less difficult, and yet something where we may still have her in this her beloved world of 'simplicity, and sky, and fields and trees, and peasant life,—peasant life looked at, by preference, on its good and sound side.' *Voyez donc la simplicité vous autres, voyez le ciel et les champs, et les arbres, et les paysans, surtout dans ce qu'ils ont de bon et de vrai.*

The introduction to *La Mare au Diable* will give us what we want. George Sand has been looking at an engraving of Holbein's *Labourer.* An old thick-set peasant, in rags, is driving his plough in the midst of a field. All around spreads a wild landscape, dotted with a few poor huts. The sun is setting behind a hill; the day of toil is nearly over. It has been a hard one; the ground is rugged and stony, the labourer s horses are but skin and bone, weak and exhausted. There is but one alert figure, the skeleton Death, who with a whip skips nimbly along at the horses' side and urges the team. Under the picture is a quotation in old French, to the effect that after the labourer's life of travail and service, in which he has to gain his bread by the sweat of his brow, here comes Death to fetch him away. And from so rude a life does Death take him, says George Sand, that Death is hardly unwelcome; and in another composition by Holbein, where men of almost every condition,—popes, sovereigns, lovers, gamblers, monks, soldiers,—are taunted with their fear of Death and do indeed see his approach with terror, Lazarus alone is easy and composed, and sitting on his dunghill at the rich man's door, tells Death that he does not dread him.

With her thoughts full of Holbein's mournful picture, George Sand goes out into the fields of her own Berry:—

My walk was by the border of a field which some peasants were getting ready for being sown presently. The space to be ploughed was wide, as in Holbein's picture. The landscape was vast also; the great lines of green which it contained were just touched with russet by the approach of autumn; on the rich brown soil recent rain had left, in a good many furrows, lines of water, which shone in the sun like silver threads. The day was clear and soft, and the earth gave out a light smoke where it had been freshly laid open by the plough-share. At the top of the field an old man, whose broad back and severe face were like those of the old peasant of Holbein, but whose clothes told no tale of poverty, was gravely driving his plough of an antique shape, drawn by two tranquil oxen, with coats of a pale buff, real patriarchs of the fallow, tall of make, somewhat thin, with long and backward-sloping horns, the kind of old workmen who by habit have got to be *brothers* to one another, as throughout our country-side they are called, and who, if one loses the other, refuse to work with a new comrade, and fret themselves to death. People unacquainted with the country will not believe in this affection of the ox for his yoke-fellow. They should come and see one of the poor beasts in a corner of his stable, thin, wasted, lashing with his restless tail his lean flanks, blowing uneasily and fastidiously on the provender offered to him, his eyes for ever turned towards the stable door, scratching with his foot the empty place left at his side, sniffing the yokes and bands which his companion has worn, and incessantly calling for him with piteous lowings. The ox-herd will tell you: There is a pair of oxen done for! his *brother* is dead, and this one will work no more. He ought to be fattened for killing; but we cannot get him to eat, and in a short time he will have starved himself to death.

How faithful and close it is, this contact of George Sand with country things, with the life of nature in its vast plenitude and pathos! And always in the end the human interest, as is right, emerges and predominates. What is the central figure in the fresh and calm rural world of George Sand? It is the peasant. And what is the peasant? He is France, life, the future. And this is the strength of George Sand, and of her second movement, after the first movement of energy and revolt was over, towards nature and beauty, towards the country, towards primitive life, the peasant. She regarded nature and beauty, not with the selfish and solitary joy of the artist who but seeks to appropriate them for his own purposes, she regarded them as a treasure of immense and hitherto unknown application, as a vast power of healing and delight for all, and for the peasant first and foremost. Yes, she cries, the simple life is the true one! but the peasant, the great organ of that life, 'the minister in that vast temple which only the sky is vast enough to embrace,' the peasant is not doomed to toil and moil in it for ever, overdone and unawakened, like Holbein's labourer, and to have for his best comfort the thought that death will set him free. *Non, nous n'avons plus affaire à la mort, mais à la vie.* 'Our business henceforth is not with death, but with life.'

Joy is the great lifter of men, the great unfolder. *Il faut que la vie soit bonne afin qu'elle soit féconde.* 'For life to be fruitful, life must be felt as a blessing':—

Nature is eternally young, beautiful, bountiful. She pours out beauty and poetry for all that live, she pours it out on all plants, and the plants are permitted to expand in it freely. She possesses the secret of happiness, and no man has been able to take it away from her. The happiest of men would be he who possessing the science of his labour and working with his hands, earning his comfort and his freedom by the exercise of his intelligent force, found time to live by the heart and by the brain, to understand his own work and to love the work of God. The artist has satisfactions of this kind in the contemplation and reproduction of nature's beauty; but when he sees the affliction of those who people this paradise of earth, the upright and human-hearted artist feels a trouble in the midst of his enjoyment. The happy day will be when mind, heart, and hands shall be alive together, shall work in concert; when there shall be a harmony between God's munificence and man's delight in it. Then, instead of the piteous and frightful figure of Death, skipping along whip in hand by the peasant's side in the field, the allegorical painter will place there a radiant angel, sowing with full hands the blessed grain in the smoking furrow

And the dream of a kindly, free, poetic, laborious, simple existence for the tiller of the field is not so hard to realise that it must be banished into the world of chimæras. Virgil's sweet and sad cry: 'O happy peasants, if they but knew their own blessings!' is a regret; but like all regrets, it is at the same time a prediction. The day will come when the labourer may be also an artist;—not in the sense of rendering nature's beauty, a matter which will be then of much less importance, but in the sense of feeling it. Does not this mysterious intuition of poetic beauty exist in him already in the form of instinct and of vague reverie?

It exists in him, too, adds Madame Sand, in the form

of that *nostalgia*, that home-sickness, which for ever pursues the genuine French peasant if you transplant him. The peasant has here, then, the elements of the poetic sense, and of its high and pure satisfactions.

But one part of the enjoyment which we possess is wanting to him, a pure and lofty pleasure which is surely his due, minister that he is in that vast temple which only the sky is vast enough to embrace. He has not the conscious knowledge of his sentiment. Those who have sentenced him to servitude from his mother's womb, not being able to debar him from reverie, have debarred him from reflexion.

Well, for all that, taking the peasant as he is, incomplete and seemingly condemned to an eternal childhood, I yet find him a more beautiful object than the man in whom his acquisition of knowledge has stifled sentiment. Do not rate yourselves so high above him, many of you who imagine that you have an imprescriptible right to his obedience; for you yourselves are the most incomplete and the least seeing of men. That simplicity of his soul is more to be loved than the false lights of yours.

In all this we are passing from the second element in George Sand to the third,—her aspiration for a social new-birth, a *renaissance sociale*. It is eminently the ideal of France; it was hers. Her religion connected itself with this ideal. In the convent where she was brought up, she had in youth had an awakening of fervent mystical piety in the Catholic form. That form she could not keep. Popular religion of all kinds, with its deep internal impossibilities, its 'heaven and hell serving .o cover the illogical manifestations of the Divinity's apparent designs respecting us,' its 'God made in our image, silly and malicious, vain and puerile, irritable or tender, after our fashion,' lost all sort of hold upon her :—

Communion with such a God is impossible to me, I confess it. He is wiped out from my memory : there is no corner where I can find him any more. Nor do I find such a God out of doors either ; he is not in the fields and waters, he is not in the starry sky. No, nor yet in the churches where men bow themselves ; it is an extinct message, a dead letter, a thought that has done its day. Nothing of this belief, nothing of this God, subsists in me any longer.

She refused to lament over the loss, to esteem it other than a benefit :—

It is an addition to our stock of light, this detachment from the idolatrous conception of religion. It is no loss of the religious sense, as the persisters in idolatry maintain. It is quite the contrary, it is a restitution of allegiance to the true Divinity. It is a step made in the direction of this Divinity, it is an abjuration of the dogmas which did him dishonour.

She does not attempt to give of this Divinity an account much more piecise than that which we have in

Wordsworth,—'*a presence that disturbs me with the joy of animating thoughts.*'

Everything is divine (she says), even matter; everything is superhuman, even man. God is everywhere; he is in me in a measure proportioned to the little that I am. My present life separates me from him just in the degree determined by the actual state of childhood of our race. Let me content myself, in all my seeking, to feel after him, and to possess of him as much as this imperfect soul can take in with the intellectual sense I have.

And she concludes:—

The day will come when we shall no longer talk about God idly, nay, when we shall talk about him as little as possible. We shall cease to set him forth dogmatically, to dispute about his nature. We shall put compulsion on no one to pray to him, we shall leave the whole business of worship within the sanctuary of each man's conscience. And this will happen when we are really religious.

Meanwhile the sense of this spirit or presence which animates us, the sense of the divine, is our stronghold and our consolation. A man may say of it: 'It comes not by my desert, but the atom of divine sense given to me nothing can rob me of.' *Divine sense*,—the phrase is a vague one; but it stands to Madame Sand for that to which are to be referred 'all the best thoughts and the best actions of life, suffering endured, duty achieved, whatever purifies our existence, whatever vivifies our love.'

Madame Sand is a Frenchwoman, and her religion is therefore, as we might expect, with peculiar fervency social. Always she has before her mind 'the natural law which *will have it* (the italics are her own) that the species *man* cannot subsist and prosper but by *association*.' Whatever else we may be in creation, we are, first and foremost, 'at the head of the species which are called by instinct, and led by necessity, to the life of *association*.' The word *love*—the great word, as she justly says, of the New Testament—acquires from her social enthusiasm a peculiar significance to her:—

The word is a great one, because it involves infinite consequences. To love means to help one another, to have joint aspirations to act in concert, to labour for the same end, to develop to its ideal consummation the fraternal instinct, thanks to which mankind have brought the earth under their dominion. Every time that he has been false to this instinct which is his law of life, his natural destiny, man has seen his temples crumble, his societies dissolve, his intellectual sense go wrong, his moral sense die out. The future is founded on love.

So long as love is thus spoken of in the general, the ordinary serious Englishman will have no difficulty in inclining himself with respect while Madame Sand speaks of it. But when he finds that love implies, with her, social equality, he will begin to be staggered. And in truth for almost every Englishman Madame Sand's strong language about equality, and about France as the chosen vessel for exhibiting it, will sound exaggerated. 'The human ideal,' she says, 'as well as the social ideal, is to achieve equality.' France, which has made equality its rallying cry, is therefore 'the nation which loves and is loved,' *la nation qui aime et qu'on aime.* The republic of equality is in her eyes 'an ideal, a philosophy, a religion.' She invokes the 'holy doctrine of social liberty and fraternal equality, ever reappearing as a ray of love and truth amidst the storm.' She calls it 'the goal of man and the law of the future.' She thinks it the secret of the civilisation of France, the most civilised of nations. Amid the disasters of the late war she cannot forbear a cry of astonishment at the neutral nations, *insensibles à l'égorgement d'une civilisation comme la nôtre*, 'looking on with insensibility while a civilisation such as ours has its throat cut.' Germany, with its stupid ideal of corporalism and *Kruppism,* is contrasted with France, full of social dreams, too civilised for war, incapable of planning and preparing war for twenty years, she is so incapable of hatred ;—*nous sommes si incapables de haïr !* We seem to be listening, not to George Sand, but to M. Victor Hugo, half genius, half charlatan; to M. Victor Hugo, or even to one of those French declaimers in whom we come down to no genius and all charlatan.

The form of such outbursts as we have quoted will always be distasteful to an Englishman. It is to be remembered that they came from Madame Sand under the pressure and anguish of the terrible calamities of 1870. But what we are most concerned with, and what Englishmen in general regard too little, is the degree of truth contained in these allegations that France is the most civilised of nations, and that she is so, above all, by her 'holy doctrine of equality.' How comes the idea to be so current; and to be passionately believed in, as we have seen, by such a woman as George Sand? It was so passionately believed in by her, that when one seeks, as I am now seeking, to recall her image, the image is incomplete if the passionate belief is kept from appearing.

I will not, with my scanty space, now discuss the belief; but I will seek to indicate how it must have commended itself, I think, to George Sand. I have somewhere called France 'the country of Europe where *the people* is most alive.' *The people* is what interested George Sand. And in France *the people* is, above all, the peasant. The workman in Paris or in other great towns of France may afford material for such pictures as those which M. Zola has lately given us in *L'Assommoir*—pictures of a kind long ago labelled by Madame Sand as 'the *literature of mysteries of iniquity*, which men of talent and imagination try to bring into fashion.' But the real *people* in France, the foundation of things there, both in George Sand's eyes and in reality, is the peasant. The peasant was the object of Madame Sand's fondest predilections in the present, and happiest hopes in the future. The Revolution and its doctrine of equality had made the French peasant. What wonder, then, if she saluted the doctrine as a holy and paramount one?

And the French peasant is really, so far as I can see, the largest and strongest element of soundness which the body social of any European nation possesses. To him is due that astonishing recovery which France has made since her defeat, and which George Sand predicted in the very hour of ruin. Yes, in 1870 she predicted *ce réveil général qui va suivre, à la grande surprise des autres nations, l'espèce d'agonie où elles nous voient tombés*, 'the general re-arising which, to the astonishment of other nations, is about to follow the sort of agony in which they now see us lying.' To the condition, character, and qualities of the French peasant this recovery is in the main due. His material well-being is known to all of us.

M. de Laveleye, the well-known economist, a Belgian and a Protestant, says that France, being the country of Europe where the soil is more divided than anywhere except in Switzerland and Norway, is at the same time the country where well-being is most widely spread, where wealth has of late years increased most, and where population is least outrunning the limits which, for the comfort and progress of the working classes themselves, seem necessary. George Sand could see, of course, the well-being of the French peasant, for we can all see it.

But there is more. George Sand was a woman, with a woman's ideal of gentleness, of 'the charm of good manners,' as essential to civilisation. She has somewhere spoken admirably of the variety and balance of forces which go to make up true civilisation ; 'certain forces of weakness, docility, attractiveness, suavity, are here just as real forces as forces of vigour, encroachment, violence, or brutality.' Yes, as real *forces*, although Prince Bismarck cannot see it ; because human nature requires them, and, often as they may be baffled, and slow as may be the process of their asserting themselves, mankind is not satisfied with its own civilisation, and keeps fidgeting at it and altering it again and again, until room is made for them. George Sand thought the French people,—meaning principally, again, by the

French people the *people* properly so called, the peasant, —she thought it 'the most kindly, the most amiable, of all peoples.' Nothing is more touching than to read in her *Journal*, written in 1870, while she was witnessing what seemed to be 'the agony of the Latin races,' and undergoing what seemed to be the process of 'dying in a general death of one's family, one's country, and one's nation,' how constant is her defence of the people, the peasant, against her Republican friends. Her Republican friends were furious with the peasant; accused him of stolidity, cowardice, want of patriotism; accused him of having given them the Empire, with all its vileness; wanted to take away from him the suffrage. Again and again does George Sand take up his defence, and warn her friends of the folly and danger of their false estimate of him. 'The contempt of the masses, there,' she cries, 'is the misfortune and crime of the present moment!' 'To execrate the people,' she exclaims again, 'is real blasphemy; the people is worth more than we are.'

If the peasant gave us the Empire, says Madame Sand, it was because he saw the parties of liberals disputing, gesticulating, and threatening to tear one another asunder and France too; he was told *the Empire is peace*, and he accepted the Empire. The peasant was deceived, he is uninstructed, he moves slowly; but he moves, he has admirable virtues, and in him, says George Sand, is our life:—

Poor Jacques Bonhomme! accuse thee and despise thee who will; for my part I pity thee, and in spite of thy faults I shall always love thee. Never will I forget how, a child, I was carried asleep on thy shoulders, how I was given over to thy care and followed thee everywhere, to the field, the stall, the cottage. They are all dead, those good old people who have borne me in their arms; but I remember them well, and I appreciate at this hour, to the minutest detail, the pureness, the kindness, the patience, the good humour, the poetry, which presided over that rustic education amidst disasters of like kind with those which we are undergoing now. Why should I quarrel with the peasant because on certain points he feels and thinks differently from what I do? There are other essential points on which we may feel eternally at one with him,—probity and charity.

Another generation of peasants had grown up since that first revolutionary generation of her youth, and equality, as its reign proceeded, had not deteriorated but improved them.

They have advanced greatly in self-respect and well-being, these peasants from twenty years old to forty: they never ask for anything. When one meets them they no longer take off their hat. If they know you they come up to you and hold out their hand. All foreigners who stay with us are struck with their good bearing, with their amenity, and the simple, friendly, and polite ease of their behaviour

In presence of people whom they esteem they are, like their fathers, models of tact and politeness; but they have more than that mere *sentiment* of equality which was all that their fathers had,—they have the *idea* of equality, and the determination to maintain it. This step upwards they owe to their having the franchise. Those who would fain treat them as creatures of a lower order dare not now show this disposition to their face; it would not be pleasant.

Mr. Hamerton's interesting book about French life has much, I think, to confirm this account of the French peasant. What I have seen of France myself (and I have seen something) is fully in agreement with it. Of a civilisation and an equality which makes the peasant thus *human*, gives to the bulk of the people well-being, probity, charity, self-respect, tact, and good manners, let us pardon Madame Sand if she feels and speaks enthusiastically. Some little variation on our own eternal trio of Barbarians, Philistines, Populace, or on the eternal solo of Philistinism among our brethren of the United States and the Colonies, is surely permissible.

Where one is more inclined to differ from Madame Sand is in her estimate of her Republican friends of the educated classes. They may stand, she says, for the genius and the soul of France; they represent its 'exalted imagination and profound sensibility,' while the peasant represents its humble, sound, indispensable body. Her *protégé*, the peasant, is much ruder with those eloquent gentlemen, and has his own name for one and all of them, *l'avocat*, by which he means to convey his belief that words are more to be looked for from that quarter than seriousness and profit. It seems to me by no means certain but that the peasant is in the right.

George Sand herself has said admirable things of these friends of hers; of their want of patience, temper, wisdom; of their 'vague and violent way of talking;' of their interminable flow of 'stimulating phrases, cold as death.' Her own place is of course with the party and propaganda of organic change. But George Sand felt the poetry of the past; she had no hatreds; the furies, the follies, the self-deceptions of secularist and revolutionist fanatics filled her with dismay. They are indeed the great danger of France, and it is amongst the educated and articulate classes of France that they prevail. If the educated and articulate classes in France were as sound in their way as the inarticulate peasant is in his, France would present a different spectacle. Not 'imagination and sensibility' are so much required from the educated classes of France, as simpler, more serious views of life; a knowledge how great a part *conduct* (if M. Challemel-Lacour will allow me to say so) fills in it; a better example. The few who see this, such as Madame Sand among the dead, and M. Renan among the living, perhaps awaken on that account, amongst quiet observers at a distance, all the more sympathy; but in France they are isolated.

All the later work of George Sand, however, all her hope of genuine social renovation, take the simple and serious ground so necessary. 'The cure for us is far more simple than we will believe. All the better natures amongst us see it and feel it. It is a good direction given by ourselves to our hearts and consciences;—*une bonne direction donnée par nous-mêmes à nos cœurs et à nos consciences.* These are among the last words of her *Journal* of 1870.

Whether or not the number of George Sand's works,—always fresh, always attractive, but poured out too lavishly and rapidly,—is likely to prove a hindrance to her fame, I do not care to consider. Posterity, alarmed at the way in which its literary baggage grows upon it, always seeks to leave behind it as much as it can, as much as it dares,—everything but masterpieces. But the immense vibration of George Sand's voice upon the ear of Europe will not soon die away. Her passions and her errors have been abundantly talked of. She left them behind her, and men's memory of her will leave them behind also. There will remain of her to mankind the sense of benefit and stimulus from the passage upon earth of that large and frank nature, of that large and pure utterance,—the *large utterance of the early gods.* There will remain an admiring and ever widening report of that great and ingenuous soul, simple, affectionate, without vanity, without pedantry, human, equitable, patient, kind. She believed herself, she said, 'to be in sympathy, across time and space, with a multitude of honest wills which interrogate their conscience and try to put themselves in accord with it.' This chain of sympathy will extend more and more.

It is silent, that eloquent voice! it is sunk, that noble, that speaking head! we sum up, as we best can, what she said to us, and we bid her adieu. From many hearts in many lands a troop of tender and grateful regrets converge towards her humble churchyard in Berry. Let them be joined by these words of sad homage from one of a nation which she esteemed, and which knew her very little and very ill. Her guiding thought, the guiding thought which she did her best to make ours too, 'the sentiment of the ideal life, which is none other than man's normal life as we shall one day know it,' is in harmony with words and promises familiar to that sacred place where she lies. *Exspectat resurrectionem mortuorum, et vitam venturi sæculi.*